THINK BIG!

To

From

I wish for you a life of wealth, health, and happiness; a life in which you give to yourself the gift of patience, the virtue of reason, the value of knowledge, and the influence of faith in your own ability to dream about and to achieve worthy rewards.

— Jim Rohn

THINK BIG!

Receive Special Bonuses When Buying the *Think Big!* Book

To access bonus gifts and to send us your testimonials and comments, please send an email to

gifts@LessonsFromThinkBig.com

Published by
Kyle Wilson International
KyleWilson.com

Distributed by
Kyle Wilson International
P.O. Box 2683
Keller, TX 76244
info@kylewilson.com

Think Big!
ISBN: 978-1-7357428-3-0

Printed in the United States of America

EXCERPTS FROM *THINK BIG!*

Everybody works for themselves. And each person creates value. You get a piece of the value that you create. So if you want to earn more money, create more value. Make a greater contribution. Do more.

— Brian Tracy, Iconic Speaker, Author & Trainer

I reinvented myself. I stopped labeling myself and I changed my habits. I stopped counting how many days I did not do the thing and instead counted the positive behaviors I was adding to my life. Every day I strive to be Powerful Eric.

— Eric Zuzack, Podcast Host, Speaker, Addiction Recovery Coach

In my life, I've had recurring themes and moments of people saying "I see you." These moments were possible because I wanted to be seen. I was able to move ahead because I made moves, identified my purpose, asked myself what the next level would look like, and put a demand on it. I've come to realize your purpose never changes, it only evolves.

— Rasheed Louis, Entrepreneur, Speaker, Business Strategist

God has a plan for everyone, and once you've discovered that plan, no one except you can stop it from coming to fruition. This has certainly been true in my life. I have personally experienced what it means to be victorious through Him who loves us. All of the things I've experienced have given me platforms to inspire others and share the love of God. By His grace, adversities made me stronger and helped me become the person I am today.

— Babette Brigitte Teno, Founder Sisters on Stages

My greatest honor is to be there for my friends on their worst days. They have been there for me, and I am always looking for ways I can be there for them. Friends are treasures! When you start to understand the Power of WHO and the magnitude of 2 Chairs, everything changes! Step out of the box and into your WHO. And then take a seat across from God, WHO always has something helpful to say, if you listen!

— Bob Beaudine, Sports Executive, Speaker & Author

Building a business or crafting a life takes lots of energy, and it is very easy to lose sight of why we are working so hard. Pushing the pause button and being intentional with carving out the necessary time to revisit why we are doing the things we do requires us to think BIGGER.

— Cheri Perry, Leadership Expert, Author & Speaker

When I was struggling with my career, always dreaming big helped me move forward and achieve my dreams. This is the process I have followed for years. First think big and then turn those big dreams into action and results. I know that you can do that too.

— Mark Livingston, Tax Strategist, Passive Investor

The humble "cuppa" is a symbol of connection. We need this warm connection with others at work and in our community. Throughout my career, my workplace friends and I have often shared conversations over a cuppa. These chats raised my confidence and strengthened our long-term connection. We would discuss our respective challenges at work and be there for each other.

— Angela Penteado, Executive Results Coach, Leader & Change Strategist

There is something about pursuing goals that requires me to grow, stretch, and become someone I have never been before. In my twenties, I had a sense, a stirring in my spirit, that there was much more to this life than I was conscious of.

— Andrew McWilliams, Real Estate Broker, Speaker & Mindset Coach

I have a principle. If you want to make your business big, make your focus small. My focus has been on serving the individual customer. When I'm speaking, when I'm doing a podcast, all I want to do is provide value. If people find value in what I share and want to find out what else I can offer them, I'm here to serve.

— Brian Buffini, Entrepreneur, Speaker, Real Estate Trainer

I was scared. This would be leaving the comfort of my job, although it was no longer serving my needs, to invest in my own business. My loving wife believed in me and urged me to do it. We had equity in our home and could take out a second mortgage. Still, I had serious doubts. Deep down, I was a failure still. What if this doesn't work? What if I fail? What would happen to the house? Our marriage? My reputation? I was torn.

— Craig Moody, Serial Entrepreneur, Biz Coach & Speaker

I believe anyone can experience major challenges. It is not a matter of coming out unscathed but a matter of coming out with elevated wisdom and understanding.

— Evette Rhoden, Didactic Poet, Writer, Thought Leader

It was not until I changed my question that I was able to see the light at the end of the tunnel. I switched from "Why me and why now?" to "Why not me and why not now?" Just one additional word—that is in its essence a negative word—made a defining difference.

— Saket Jain, Investor, Syndicator, Philanthropist

The loss of someone or something we hold dear is inevitable. How we process this loss differs from person to person. Our grief is intended to be used for a greater good. Grief isn't an obstacle to be overcome, but an opportunity to learn and grow to help others.

— Mark Hartley, Father, Chaplain, Teacher & Equipper

I spent four days in the ICU with only 10% lung capacity. Every minute of every hour of every day that I was laying in that bed, I prayed to God: Please do not let them intubate me! Please give me the strength to fight for my life, for my family, and for our future. Dear God, I'm not ready to go yet. I always seem to rise out of the ashes. COVID was my fourth brush with death.

— Michelle Kimbro, Investor, Entrepreneur, Efficiency Expert

There was no going back. I had just removed my safety net of a job and my dream of opening my own clinic. My head was spinning. What did I just do? I have a wife and three young boys at home. How do I go home and casually say, Hey I grabbed milk, and I quit my job...?

— *Thomas M. Barba, PT, Physical Therapist, Speaker & Entrepreneur*

As my business grew, so did my thinking processes. I saw that you can think big and set goals and that goals do work. I want to be like Sir Richard Branson, who surrounds himself with great teams and has many companies that help him make his money so he can give back to what matters to him. Ingrained thoughts and self-limiting beliefs don't change overnight, but surrounding myself with a great team and continued work go a long way. There is no limit to what I can do.

— *David Kafka, Broker, Syndicator, Investor & Belize Expert*

We had purpose. We had passion. We knew exactly the WHY, the WHAT, and the vision we were looking to create. But the HOW was still undefined. The Encompass team knew the impact we could make in the lives of children and families, but we had to think BIG by taking small action steps every day to see the future feeding therapy program come to fruition.

— *Dr. Ashley Blake, Entrepreneur, Leader, Behavior Analyst*

I have a dollar for every mistake I ever made. It's those mistakes and failures that led to the lessons that have led to the money! No one can expect that without failure you will ever get the winning formula. So, fail often, fail gloriously, and become a student of these lessons to become the winner you are designed to be.

— *Shannon Robnett, Second Generation Developer*

You may be looking at your life, saying, "Man, things are falling apart." The reality is that He's orchestrating things for your good. Even things that you think are bad, He has something great in mind that will come from it. I've had to remind myself of that over the last 18 years.

— *David Imonitie, Entrepreneur, Speaker & Author*

I realized I prefer being the owner over being a tenant. Arbitrage did not resonate with me anymore. I did not like the idea of paying down another landlord's mortgage while he was enjoying the tax benefits, principal pay down, appreciation, and other benefits that come with owning investment real estate.

— *Phillip Warrick, Creative Real Estate Investor, Coach, Author, Speaker*

I was so passionate about what I learned about investing that I couldn't wait to share it with the world. Investing changed my life and my family's lives for the better. I realized that if an immigrant like me could do it from scratch, everybody can do it. All they needed was access to the information that I had acquired over the years thanks to the great samaritans who crossed paths with me and helped me grow. It felt selfish to keep all that information to myself.

— *Lucelia Chou, Financial Literacy YouTuber & Educator*

Sometimes, in the middle of a storm, a multitude of small thoughts and small actions can compound into big thoughts and bigger actions. They were teaching me that to think big, I first needed to start small, in my own mind.

— Ben Andrews, Realtor, Speaker, US Track & Field Athlete

I realize, in a lifetime, I cannot do nearly as much charitable dentistry as a group of financially free dentists unleashed toward their own transformative purpose. To help them achieve their financial freedom as my massive transformative purpose is the best leverage strategy I could ever hope for.

— Dr. Eric N. Shelly, Tax Mitigation Expert, Fund Manager

I didn't know anything about the construction process, but my mission in Denmark had taught me how to meet, greet, and have a conversation with people. I was good at asking questions and figuring out what folks wanted. Within a few months, I was outperforming my boss. I listened to audiotapes whenever I had a free moment, and my truck became a traveling library.

— Glade Poulsen, Sales Trainer, Author & Entrepreneur

After finding myself in an unexpected financial situation, I chose to not let the experience define me. Rather, I chose to think big and create an exciting future through education and taking action.

— Nancy Lunter Yatzkan, Tax-Smart Investor, KOR Capital Fund

My coworkers and friends told me I was crazy! They said, "Don't liquidate your 401k and pay the tax. . . . You're smarter than that. Don't you know better?" Well, that's exactly what I did in 2012, and that was the second-best financial decision I've ever made. The best financial decision I've ever made was investing in my financial education to expand my mindset.

— Alan Stewart, Real Estate Investor, Leader, Entrepreneur

I came to understand that complex problems are best solved by bringing together people with different viewpoints to explore options and take decisive action. I also learned that successful leadership is not about power, authority, and influence, but about the ability to inspire.

— Jack Langenberg, Real Estate Investor, Wealth Building Mentor

Through the grace of God, with the help of many volunteers and staff, over time, we were able to get grants and materials. To date, we have repaired and rebuilt over 270 roofs, installed hundreds of doors and windows, repaired crumbling ceilings, installed kitchen cabinets and countertops, and fixed electrical systems. We have assisted 1,058 people in making their homes weathertight, providing support and hope to those who suffered the devastation of Maria. We helped over forty people appeal and overturn denials for help from FEMA.

— Vickie "Sunshine" Cortes, Founder Hope Builders, Coach, Mentor, Speaker

I've discovered that we all have infinite potential inside of us, and learning how to tap into that potential is key to designing a life of joy and happiness. I've learned through this process of personal development that the harder I work on myself through studying, networking, and skill development, the "luckier" I am. The best and most exciting part is that I'm in control of the outcome. The outcome will be based on my effort.

– Randy Wilson, Husband, Father, Leader, Coach, Author, Speaker

When you go out there, you could have prepared all day every day, but still, that first play, as you're waiting for the ball to be kicked off, you're kind of shaking. You're nervous. You're almost frozen for a minute, but then it all kicks in and it's just repetition. You know exactly what to say and what to do because you've practiced it. You have confidence because you put the work in.

– Chris Gronkowski, NFL Player, Shark Tank, Founder Ice Shaker

Self-absorption ruins the very thing it wants to promote. Ironically, raw, unfiltered, immature ego energy often creates the opposite of its desire. The wall or shell that raw ego manufactures slowly dissolves or destroys that which it intends to protect.

– Greg Zlevor, Author, Speaker, Global Leadership Expert

When God wishes to send you a gift in life, he often wraps it in a problem. In this case, my challenge was accepting the circumstances and finding the strength to care for my premature twins. I have learned that the good and bad in life tend to run on parallel tracks, and if you allow them to work together, they take you on a journey that results in achievement, pride, inspiration, and a new understanding of unconditional love.

– Imre Szenttornyay, Franchise Developer, CEO, Strategy Coach

I have tried to remain mindful and make love-based choices versus fear-based choices. Occasionally, this has involved my heart and ego duking it out for ten rounds in the boxing ring with a lot of sweat and tears until my heart won. One of my life's lessons has been to learn to follow my heart's wisdom. I play big by having the courage to take that first step in the direction of my true north.

– Laura Thompson, Social Impact Advisor, Leadership Coach & Author

Over time, we were not being challenged mentally and were not growing. The grit, determination, and our life purpose were not being satisfied, and there was an empty hole of fulfillment. I had minimal social impact in this world. I thought that if I were to die, I would not be remembered as I would like to be remembered. Something had to change.

– Dr. Jaime Gonzalez, Real Estate Syndicator, Entrepreneur & Biz Leader

As a result of running for congress, hundreds of conversations, and a 25-year entrepreneurial background, I have come to believe a major cause of our frustrations as a society is simply not asking the right questions.

– Ryan Chamberlin, Founder & CEO of TPN, Author & Speaker

Our wrinkles are signs of age, nothing to be hidden or erased. By erasing wrinkles or any sign of aging, aren't we erasing the evidence of the wisdom we've gained from the years we've lived? Those with the deepest wrinkles and the most lines often have the most wisdom to share.

– Phyllis Ayman, Author, Humanitarian, Eldercare Advocate

Thinking big has always been my driver. It all started unconsciously, when I did not even know the concept. THINK BIG is the vision that things can be better in the future than they are today. I started with me, when I was just a school kid who wanted to become more than I was. I wanted to be what every other child around me was, like everyone else. YOUR "think big" may not be doing something that will stun the world. NO, your "think big" is something that will stun you, that will make the whole difference to you and your life even if it looks ordinary to the world.

– Ravin S. Papiah, Top Leadership Speaker, Trainer & Coach

I say the bad is contagious, but the good is even more contagious. I always look at the bright side of things. I try not to look at the bad. I try not to poison myself, my house, my employees. I try to take the high road, not to bad mouth anybody, even if I've been caused harm. I try to be humble. I try to be happy, and it works.

– Wagner Nolasco, Real Estate Developer, Investor & Volunteer

Through patience, practice, and persistence, I learned to see others in a different way. There was always someone better off than me and someone worse off than me. I was on my own personal journey, as we all are. I had to be ME and that included what was considered "wrong" with me.

– Dan Armstrong, Author, Entertainer, Speaker & Storyteller

After my circumstances changed, I thought, Okay, I'm going to aim for what I really want to do, because I really have nothing to lose. I took a load of risks that I wouldn't have before losing everything. In the most real way, I got that if you're broke, if you have nothing to your name, all you need is resourcefulness, love, and belief.

– Erika De La Cruz, Bestselling Author, Speaker, Editor-in-Chief of The LA Girl

A daily reminder I tell myself is, "Today, I get to bring my gifts and serve somebody!" Daily, ask yourself this question: How can I bring my unique skills, gifts, experience, knowledge, relationships… to the marketplace and serve those that need it most and are a perfect fit?

– Kyle Wilson, Marketer, Strategist, Founder Jim Rohn International

TABLE OF CONTENTS

DISCLAIMER

The information in this book is not meant to replace the advice of a certified professional. Please consult a licensed advisor in matters relating to your personal and professional well-being including your mental, emotional and physical health, finances, business, legal matters, family planning, education, and spiritual practices. The views and opinions expressed throughout this book are those of the authors and do not necessarily reflect the views or opinions of all the authors or position of any other agency, organization, employer, publisher, or company.

Since we are critically-thinking human beings, the views of each of the authors are always subject to change or revision at any time. Please do not hold them or the publisher to them in perpetuity. Any references to past performance may not be indicative of future results. No warranties or guarantees are expressed or implied by the publisher's choice to include any of the content in this volume.

If you choose to attempt any of the methods mentioned in this book, the authors and publisher advise you to take full responsibility for your safety and know your limits. The authors and publisher are not liable for any damages or negative consequences from any treatment, action, application, or preparation to any person reading or following the information in this book.

This book is a collaboration between a number of authors and reflects their experiences, beliefs, opinions, and advice. The authors and publisher make no representations as to accuracy, completeness, correctness, suitability, or validity of any information in the book, and neither the publisher nor the individual authors shall be liable for any physical, psychological, emotional, financial, or commercial damages, including, but not limited to, special, incidental, consequential, or other damages to the readers of this book.

Dedication

To all the mentors and influences that have shaped the lives of each of our authors. To our families and loved ones who fan our flames and inspire us. To all those who read this book and are inspired to think big!

Acknowledgments

A big thank you—

To Takara Sights, our writing coach, editor, and project manager extraordinaire, for your endless hours of work and passion in this book! Despite the complexities involved with a project like this, you keep the process a pleasure and always provide first-class results. A thousand praises! You are a rockstar!

To Claudia Volkman, Joe Potter, and Anne-Sophie Gomez, who have put countless hours into designing this book. Technology and thoughtful design allow readers to receive the powerful wisdom of these authors. We are grateful!

To Adrian Shepherd, John Obenchain, Gary Pinkerton, Belinda Gravel, Aaron Nannini, Dan Armstrong, and Lynn Bodnar for being our second eyes and proofreading the manuscript. We so appreciate it!

And to Moe Rock, Simon T. Bailey, Olenka Cullinan, Russ Gray, Newy Scruggs, and ALL the amazing mentors and world-class thought leaders who took the time to read this book's manuscript and give us their endorsements—thank you!!

FOREWORD

by Robert Helms

Have you ever been totally excited and completely overwhelmed at the same time? If so, you've likely been face-to-face with an opportunity to think bigger.

Albert Einstein said, "A new type of thinking is essential if mankind is to survive and move toward higher levels." Your current level of thinking has brought you to exactly where you are right now. Everything in your life—your business, your income, your family life, your health, your fulfillment—is a result of the decisions you have made leading up to this moment.

If you want to have more, do more, and be more, then it's time to bring your thinking . . . and your decision-making . . . to a new level.

Your incredible brain is capable of so much more than you are currently using it for. And no matter how successful you are (or aren't), you really can achieve so much more. I know, because it has happened for me. And I'm convinced it can happen for you.

Thinking big led me on the path from young Cub Scout to Eagle Scout . . . a rank less than 5% of Scouts attain.

Thinking big took me from being an average real estate agent to the top 1% of agents in the largest real estate company in the world.

Thinking big helped me turn a part-time talk show on a local radio station into a nationally syndicated show and a podcast heard in more than 190 countries.

Thinking big transformed our modest resort project in Belize into the largest hotel by room count in the country.

Thinking big can catapult you to a higher level in whatever you are pursuing.

So what exactly does it mean to think big? While the answer is different for everyone, I believe it's a question best answered by example.

In this amazing book, you'll meet lots of interesting and successful folks who will give you real life examples of how learning to think bigger has led to incredible success. And you'll be privy to lots of empowering lessons they've learned along the way.

So, get ready to dive into these inspiring stories of challenge, frustration, opportunity, soul searching, and wealth building that will challenge you to think big.

To Your Amazing Future,
Robert Helms

 Robert Helms is co-author of *Equity Happens*. Robert's annual Create Your Future goals retreat provides a blueprint for achievement in life. Listen to *The Real Estate Guys™ Radio Show* at www.RealEstateGuysRadio.com. To learn about The Real Estate Guys™ programs, email SuccessHabits@realestateguysradio.com.

"So many of our dreams at first seem impossible, then they seem improbable, and then, when we summon the will, they soon become inevitable."

— Christopher Reeves

KYLE WILSON

Stretching the Rubber Band of Your Thinking

Kyle Wilson is an entrepreneur, business and marketing strategist, publisher, seminar promoter, and speaker. He is the founder of KyleWilson.com, Jim Rohn International, and LessonsFromExperts.com. Kyle hosts the Success Habits podcast and the Kyle Wilson Inner Circle Mastermind and has published dozens of #1 bestselling books.

The Plastics Guy

In the early '90s, shortly after going to work for a seminar company, I attended a personal development event.

Before lunch, we were asked to introduce ourselves to people around us and say what we did. The guy I had been sitting next to said he was a huge Tony Robbins and Jim Rohn fan. When he found out I was promoting seminars, he asked me to lunch.

Fortunately, he volunteered for us to go in his car. Having a new job in a new industry, I was just scraping by financially. As we walked to his car, I saw it was a new Jaguar convertible. Up until then, he had been asking me all the questions. Now, it was time to turn the table.

He said he had been in sales and done different entrepreneurial things, and he had been working as hard as he possibly could, but he could never make more than $50k-70k a year. So, he made the decision to take a step back and look for opportunities that could have a bigger payoff but with the same amount of time and effort. He soon found a niche in plastics (this was the '90s) and started his own company. He said he went from $70k a year to $70k a month and eventually $100k a month. Yet, he wasn't working longer or harder. He just found the right vehicle and learned how to scale it.

His profound words were, "It takes the same effort and time to make $70k a year as it does to make $70k a month. The difference is the opportunity and your mindset."

Wow! I caught the pass! That was my biggest lesson from that day.

I was new in the seminar business and was working for a promoter. I was struggling to get 200-300 people in my seminar rooms and was barely making any money. But, after meeting him (I don't even remember his name), I started asking, "How can I get 2,000 people in a room?"

Going Out on My Own

That continuous THINK BIG question (*How can I get 2,000 people in a room?*), eventually led me to leave my job and go out on my own. Within two years, I had totally changed my model and was now getting 2,000–2,500 people in a room and bringing in Jim Rohn, Brian Tracy, and Og Mandino to speak at my events.

That then led to making a deal with Jim Rohn for exclusive marketing rights in 1993 and my launching Jim Rohn International. That first year, I was able to take Jim from 20 speaking dates a year to over 110 dates while also tripling his fee. We also created dozens of new products over the coming years.

In 1995, I launched Your Success Store, which also allowed me and my team to start booking Brian Tracy, Les Brown, Mark Victor Hansen, Denis Waitley, and others to speak and to sell their books and training programs.

Over the next 14 years, I would put on hundreds of events, create over one hundred products (books, CDs, and DVD courses), plus publish multiple online newsletters with over 1,000,000 subscribers.

Looking back now, that one idea and tweak in perspective after lunch with the plastics guy helped me create success in a way I had never before come close to experiencing.

Five Keys to Thinking Big

1. What Do I Want to Be Known for in 3-5 Years?

An exercise I often do (and take coaching clients and Inner Circle members through) is a very powerful centering question:

"Who do I want to be in three years and what do I want to be known and/or famous for?"

I truly believe everyone has unique gifts and the potential to be world-class in specific areas of their lives. But it requires clarity, focus, and commitment.

When you are clear on what you should and should not do, it will impact everything from your daily to-do list, to the books and seminars you decide to invest in, to the people and mentors you choose to get around.

2. Take What Is Working and Innovate

Brian Tracy told me early on in the seminar business to follow other proven models of success but then innovate 10-20% to make the model fit my skills and secret sauce.

Over the years as an event promoter, agent, product creator, publisher, and mastermind and podcast host, I can say that I have tried to follow that advice to take what is working but then innovate and make it my own. And when you make it your own, that is when you can then start thinking how to grow it bigger.

3. Think Big, Start Small

Thinking Big often will open up new doors of creativity and opportunity. But, you must also take sustained action over a long period of time to get the results you desire.

My mentor Jim Rohn would say success is predictable. If you plant a tomato seed in the right soil and climate and provide it with water and sunshine, the odds are in your favor to eventually be able to harvest tomatoes.

Success is similar. It is principle-based and requires the right actions over a sustained period of time.

4. Get Around Big Thinkers

I met Mark Victor Hansen in 1994. He and his co-author Jack Canfield had just completed *Chicken Soup for the Soul* and were working on the second edition. Mark and I really hit it off, and I ended up adding Mark as a featured morning speaker on day two of our Jim Rohn Weekend events. Granted, Mark and Jim were totally different, but Mark brought an energy that was interesting to me; I called it "stretching the rubber band." Mark challenged people's current thinking and expectations.

Within a year of meeting Mark, we agreed that I would co-author *Chicken Soup for the Entrepreneurial Soul.* Throughout that two–three year period, we became good friends and dabbled in a number of projects together, and still do to this day.

Back then, I remember Mark made the bold statement that he and Jack would sell over 100 million books together! I smiled and thought, *There he goes again, exaggerating and over-hyping.* He and Jack no doubt had a major hit on their hands, but I couldn't imagine them doing more than 20-30 titles and maybe 10 million books—at best! **And that would have been a huge success—10 million books!**

Well, was I WRONG! They eventually blew past 100 million books sold and have **now well over 600 million books sold**, not to mention all kinds of other brand related products, even TV shows.

3

My mentor and 18-year business partner Jim Rohn would say, who you spend time with matters! Spending time with Mark and many other Big Thinkers over the years has stretched my rubber band of possibilities, allowed me to think outside the box, and instill my belief and faith in others to help them believe bigger too.

5. A Simple Mantra

A daily reminder I tell myself is, "Today, I get to bring my gifts and serve somebody!"

Daily, ask yourself this question: How can I bring my unique skills, gifts, experience, knowledge, relationships . . . to the marketplace and serve those that need it most and are a perfect fit?

When you approach business with a mindset of bringing your gifts and serving those that can best benefit, it's amazing how the right people show up.

Also, the right ideas begin to show up for you!

Reinventing Myself

I eventually sold all my companies, lists, and intellectual properties in 2007 to the same company that would go on to buy *Success Magazine*. I retired for seven years.

After my kids graduated from high school, I decided to come back to the industry I love and now host my Inner Circle Mastermind and the *Success Habits* podcast, and I love helping create and publish books like this one.

I wonder what would have happened had I not met the plastics guy? Would it have worked out the same? I don't know. What I do know is often we get stuck in our own world of what is possible.

I met this game-changing person at an event. And I have formed so many other amazing relationships and connections over the years through attending seminars and masterminds.

My challenge to you, and to myself, is to keep showing up where people and ideas are flowing and ceilings and expectations are raised. Say yes to opportunities. Say yes to invitations. Step out of your comfort zone. Occasionally do what scares you.

Here's to you having a 10x revenue idea and stretching the rubber band of your thinking!

To learn more about Kyle's Inner Circle Mastermind, #1 Bestseller Book Program, and Marketing VIP Coaching go to KyleWilson.com or email info@kylewilson.com.

To receive over a dozen interviews by Kyle with Darren Hardy, Les Brown, Brian Tracy, and more, email access@kylewilson.com with interviews in the subject. Follow Kyle on IG @kylewilsonjimrohn.

Tweetable: Daily, ask yourself this question: How can I bring my unique skills, gifts, experience, knowledge, relationships . . . to the marketplace and serve those that need it most and are a perfect fit?

ERIKA DE LA CRUZ

Beliefs Matter More Than Circumstances

Erika De La Cruz is editor-in-chief of The LA Girl, *a media publication reaching over three million women in Los Angeles and beyond. Erika is also the author of the bestselling book* Passionistas. *She has dedicated her life mission to helping people reach their full potential through vulnerable conversation.*

From the Crash Came Confidence

After the severe financial climate of 2009, my parents' business of 30 years closed. During this time, I was away at college as a freshman across the state in San Diego. At home, the gorgeous home where I grew up was slowly changing. The lawn was getting brown and the pool was getting green, and I remember thinking, *What are my parents going to do?*

They did everything they could to save the house while I was away, including getting the mayor involved. There was a strong sense of denial that the home my mom designed herself could be lost, but that was the reality. My mother was the hardest working person I knew, and that year she took several jobs waitressing to keep the house, but in the end, we'd have one day to pack up 18 years of family belongings.

This day was shortly after I arrived home to visit for the summer after freshman year. Pulling up to my home, I noticed there were chains across the windows and doors. My parents hadn't told me yet that it was being foreclosed. We didn't live there anymore.

Packing up a lifetime in a day was traumatic. It felt violent. They were drilling up the marble and taking out the palm trees from the backyard to sell. I put the stuff from my room in my '93 Honda Accord, and the rest went to storage units.

I stayed with a friend and, at the end of the summer, went back to school. I started a job at Jamba Juice, and the hard work my mother put in for tuition and financial aid paid off. After a few months back at school, I was told the stuff we had in storage was being sold to the state because our bill had gone unpaid. So, I let it go.

It felt oddly freeing. I had no "stuff" and, honestly, no cash, except for what Jamba Juice provided. My stuff was sold for the next four years. I remember looking down at my phone to read a Facebook message from a friend one day: "I think your photos are for sale here at a swap meet." My mom retreated from materialism for a while and chose a path of voluntary homelessness, essentially disconnecting us for the next five years. This was a path that was perfect for her own personal journey, and present day, I welcome it into our family's narrative. Everything happens to grow you— at 19, I remember feeling I had *no family, no stuff, just a blank slate and a choice.* It was definitely a moment of fight or flight... and I discovered that for me, it was fight.

My Start in Entertainment and Media

After my circumstances changed, I thought, *Okay, I'm going to aim for what I really want to do, because I really have nothing to lose.*

I took a load of risks that I wouldn't have before losing everything. In the most real way, I got that if you're broke, if you have nothing to your name, all you need is resourcefulness, love, and belief.

My type-A personality showed up and I, ironically, worked my butt off to get extra scholarships so that I could get internships that paid nothing in the entertainment industry. This was an industry I knew I wanted to be in, so I had never been more proud or happy. I began interning in the radio industry with the belief that the better my feelings became, the more opportunities I'd attract. Then it happened. It was the #1 station for women 25 to 45 in San Diego, and I was asked to be on the morning show and simultaneously the marketing director at the station. At age 23, I was the youngest ever female marketing director there.

Passionista, #1 Bestseller

At the time our family lost everything, I remember opening up *Marie Claire* and seeing this word: "passionista." It rhymed with "fashionista," and I thought, *This is cute.* I could be passionate in the world and work doing what I love. So, I cut it out and put it on a vision board. A little over three years later, *Passionstas* became the name of my book.

At 24, I got into speaking for women's groups on business topics. One group asked to hear my story, which surprised me. But I shared on stage for the first time how my family lost our home four years back.

The next thing I knew, I met a business partner, personal development legend, Kyle Wilson. He saw my talk and had a vision to co-create a compilation book with amazing women, sharing the vulnerable stuff—like my story—the difficult stuff that wasn't what you'd see on social media. *Passionistas: Tips, Tales and Tweetables From Women Pursuing Their Dreams* thrived in the space and became an Amazon #1 bestseller.

The book was published right after I moved to Los Angeles for red carpet reporting. I worked with film festivals and event companies and I was hustling hard. On the red carpet, I was doing fashion partnerships that entailed me wearing different looks and charging the company for visibility, and from the book, my social platforms garnered an audience of badass women. It was then, I learned what it meant to relate to myself as a personal brand and media asset.

When the book hit #1, people read about the obstacles I experienced in my life. I shared about losing contact with my mom, feeling like a fake, and feeling lonely. The vulnerability I shared normalized obstacles for other women, and I began receiving messages asking, "How do I get past my own hurdles?" I felt I could help, so I coached. I created a program and shared beautiful, vulnerable moments with one amazing person at a time. But I thought, *This shouldn't be accessible for 10 or 20 people, it should be accessible to tons.* So, my team and I started hosting events called Passion to Paycheck.

Passion to Paycheck combined fashion, television, and personal development. (All the parts of my world at that point.) We had Keltie Knight from E!'s *LadyGang*, powerful Latina Liz Hernandez from *Access Hollywood*, and Shaun Robinson powerfully speaking to this beautiful community that came together around these events. I merged my TV world, which I was still doing, with fashion and in between shared content about reaching your full potential. Each event was transformational versus informational.

Fashion Is Manifestation

Fashion has been a part of my journey since I was a little girl. I remember, my mom had her most expensive dress packed under our guest room bed. I'd sneak in and pull out the sparkly gown, thinking, *Wow, I'd have to be someone to wear this.* It made me feel like I could be anything and anyone. That dress was my first "statement" piece, even though I didn't know it.

When I got into radio, I was the spokesperson for a lot of up-and-coming clothing brands. I realized that what I wore to speak on stage influenced how I felt and the "someone" that I would grow into next.

If I had listened to my circumstances, or my bank accounts at various times, who knows what I would have felt worthy of wearing. Instead, I chose outfits projecting me into my future self. Sophisticated, fun pieces I loved lent a hand in becoming the woman I wanted to grow into without the "wait time." Wearing them, I began to believe I could be this person.

After two years in LA, I was invited to the Emmys and found myself on the "Best Dressed" list. I was in a form-fitting, flowing, yellow gown. I remember someone saying to me, "You're not a nominee. Do you really want to stand out on the carpet?"

I thought to myself, *Someone would wear this dress, and I'm someone.* As it turns out, other "someones" named *Alison Brie* and *Regina King* wore yellow too. The universe conspired, and we were in the headlines of *Today, Vogue,* and *Glamour* that week.

Many more opportunities came after that. Not only business ones but also so many messages from my audience. That weekend was a mini moment for thousands of women watching, not just me. Manifestation and trust in the process are real.

The LA Girl

The LA Girl happened in the wildest way possible. The original creator of *The LA Girl,* a Los Angeles lifestyle blog, had a chapter in *Passionistas.* She and I worked together, even after the book, and developed a close friendship. She'd had the publication since 2014, and was ready to move on. She was building a coaching and tech empire, moving to Minnesota, and was going to shut down *The LA Girl.*

In 2019, she invited me to dinner. She told me, "*The LA Girl* is my baby, and I wouldn't trust anyone with it except you. Would you ever be interested in acquiring the publication?" We talked for a while and started a negotiation. She was making a real exit, and I—an acquisition—nobody teaches you how to do that. I felt really aligned with it though. We struck the perfect deal. After almost two years of transition, in May 2021, I had the official reins as editor-in-chief.

Looking Forward

Since we took on *The LA Girl,* our audience has grown by 20,000 new readers and now reaches more than three million. I'm in the throes of it every day. I'm excited to expand our global community that thrives in the

"LA girl" perspective—a full, inspired lifestyle—no matter where that is. (And not so different from the women who were reading *Passionistas*.)

You're not limited by your resources but by your resourcefulness. All you have to have is conviction. You're one conversation away from the life that you want. I know that first-hand. Don't just be the girl thinking, *Oh, something will happen for me.* Have the conviction to believe the universe will match your effort and intention.

Follow Erika De La Cruz on Instagram and TikTok @_erikadelacruz and @thelagirl. Learn about her upcoming events, interviews, and more at ErikaDeLaCruz.com.

Tweetable: You're one conversation away from the life that you want. Believe the universe will match your effort and intention.

DAN ARMSTRONG

Being Bullied and Mocked Led to Positively Impacting Others

Dan Armstrong is author of The Adventures of a Real-Life Cable Guy, *a memoir of a career, and* Smart Dust—The Dawn of Trans-Humanism, *a science fiction novel based on real technology. Dan has made 8 trips to Japan to perform street magic. He is a heart-centered speaker who challenges audiences to serve others in a hurting world.*

A Brutal Attack

I didn't hear them approaching. The soft grass was enough to muffle the steps of the small band of bullies until they hit the dirt a few feet behind me.

My little fingers were clasped around the metal chain-link fence behind home plate of the baseball diamond. The group of third-graders ripped me from the fence, threw me to the ground, and jumped on me. One of the boys sat on my stomach and pinned my hands to the dirt.

The ringleader began a torrent of mockery. "Say your name!"

Because of a speech impediment, consonants were difficult for me to pronounce without a burst of air following them. I had not learned the practice of slowing down and thinking, taking the time to carefully speak.

He yelled again, "Spell it. Spell it, moron!"

Slowly, I spelled my last name. "A R M S T R O N G." The "S" and the "T" were loaded with air, but the last "G" was the worst.

They burst into laughter. I was so frightened. The bully holding me down in the dirt took the cues from his gang. He repeated the demands two more times, screaming into my face, spitting on me, while the other boys cheered him on.

I discovered I was being held on an anthill as the ants began to escape their underground nest, crawling up my neck and down my shirt. Tears welled up in my eyes, and the face of my menace blurred. The attack continued as the ants began to bite my skin.

The voice of the teacher on playground duty broke through. "Break it up, boys." Finally, someone was coming to the rescue. The boys scattered.

Seeking safety and solace, I began running to the teacher's side, frantically brushing the ants off my body. Shaken and scared, I reached her only to hear, "What is wrong with you? Are you retarded?"

A Gift for Life

I was born with a cleft palate, and the result was years of learning how to overcome a speech impediment. Being mocked and bullied was a common life experience. Surgery could not fix the hole in the roof of my mouth. Because of that, a plastic prosthesis was molded for me to close the hole where the surgery had failed. Every six months, I would visit Dr. Mohammad Mazaheri of the Lancaster Cleft Palate Clinic. His Iranian accent became a voice of comfort, and he became a hero of mine. Each visit to the clinic, he would speak words of encouragement, edifying me as I progressed. It was difficult to believe him. But, I found solace in his words despite my low self-esteem.

In school, I had speech therapy. Being pulled out of regular classes was an embarrassment, but the time spent with the speech instructors was so valuable. The therapist taught me to enunciate by placing my tongue in certain places. As difficult as it was, I learned to slow down and listen to myself when I opened my mouth to speak. Consonants had to be observed and practiced. My friends never gave it a second thought as they talked, but I had to slow down and think as I placed the words from my brain to my lips. I was learning the arduous task of communicating with new confidence.

Back to the Playground

That day on the playground, the teacher's words penetrated my soul. "What's wrong with you?" She was an adult, not a child. Couldn't she see I was frightened? The initial physical assault was traumatic enough as a seven-year-old boy, but then to be chided by an adult with the intimation that I was different from everyone else was too much. I crumpled to the ground in a fetal position and cried until I couldn't breathe.

My mother was called. She came and got me, cradling my shoulders as we walked to the car. I couldn't even speak through the sobs. At home, she removed my shirt to see hundreds of red bites on my back and chest. She prepared an Epsom salt bath and sat with me until I calmed down enough to tell her the story. I was vulnerable, afraid, and lost in the world of my peers.

The words my mother spoke then would change my life. "Danny, you are special. God made you the way you are to help others. You will see. Someday, you will help others."

Her words were bigger than the moment. She saw a future for me I couldn't possibly imagine. I wept because I didn't believe it.

But I needed to keep going, and at that tender age, her belief in me was enough. With my mother's words ringing in my ears, I would borrow her belief to get me through each day for years.

The nasal quality of my speech was always on my mind as a child, and being on the blunt end of hurtful remarks kept me quiet and shy. I was an angry child, often sick, and fearful of meeting new people; especially if I had to speak. But gradually, this difference would become a pivotal part of who I was. I developed a belief in myself, a belief from within, and I would become strong because of who I was.

Pushed on Stage

My parents began a singing group called The Armstrong Family Singers. We recorded an album in 1976. The years that followed put me on the stages of churches, campgrounds, and fairgrounds as we sang gospel songs across the country. It wasn't that my parents ignored the way I spoke; rather, they put me in circumstances as though I was as skilled as the rest of the family. The trivial speech impediment was no match for the big dreams ahead.

I knew what I sounded like. I knew others tilted their heads in an attempt to understand what I was saying, but the belief I had borrowed was becoming internalized confidence. I started to ignore the snide remarks and the careless words of other people. I actually began to feel sorry for them; if they couldn't HEAR past my voice and SEE me, they were missing out.

Putting Myself on the Stage

At age thirteen, I tried out for a school play and got the lead role. My high school years put me on stage eight more times with roles in every autumn and spring production. I loved the thrill of performing, the applause, and the feeling of accomplishment.

My passion for speaking in public was growing. I had a message of hope for those who suffered from low self-esteem, for those who were made fun of for something they had no control over.

The borrowed belief from my mother was now my own. I believed I was bigger than a physical malady. The way I was born was a challenge for me to seek more of who I was to be.

A year after graduation, I was asked to be part of a band called Damascus. I was the lead singer for some of the songs and also the frontman keeping the audience entertained between numbers. We recorded an album in 1984, and the song I wrote, "Saturday Morning Cartoons," is still being played today.

At one concert, I looked over the crowd of six thousand people and thought to myself, *How did I get here? Am I nuts?* I had to remind myself of the belief my mother gave me, and at that moment, the belief became my own on a deeper level. The thought occurred to me, *Of course I am on this stage. I belong here! I am not a victim of a cleft palate, I am Dan.*

My mind shifted to what I could do with the talents God gave me regardless of the stage I was standing on. Each platform was a step on this successful journey. Pulling out deep reservoirs of creativity, I expanded into new arenas. To me, it was no longer about what I sounded like but rather what my mind could think and then say out loud.

I was in the band from 1982 to 1987. Four years later, I was asked to record one-minute words of wisdom on a local radio station. The manager of the station had seen me perform several times and remembered the humorous stories I would tell on stage, keeping the audience engaged with short parables pertaining to the messages of our songs.

The Wacky Words of Dan Armstrong began in 1992 on our local radio station at 8:20 PM every weeknight for six years. I wrote over one thousand spots. Along with my writing ability being developed, my communication skills were expanding. I was recording messages for the radio to be heard by thousands of people INTENTIONALLY!

You Are Special

The little boy who was once mocked and bullied had now spoken to hundreds of thousands of people in various formats—churches, college campuses, radio, speaking gigs at banquets, and Toastmasters clubs—telling my story of triumph, and all because of my mother's words. "Danny, you are special. God made you the way you are to help others. You will see. Someday, you will help others."

Through patience, practice, and persistence, I learned to see others in a different way. There was always someone better off than me and someone worse off than me. I was on my own personal journey, as we all are. I had to be ME and that included what was considered "wrong" with me.

I learned to perform magic and develop my humor. I learned basic Japanese so I could travel to Japan to perform. My future was bigger, brighter, and far more interesting than I ever could have imagined without the borrowed belief from my mother.

We all seem to harbor secret pain. The heart is broken, the mind is dark, or the body is deformed. But, we are bigger than the labels, brighter than the limitations, and better for rising above them.

To compete or compare has always created struggle. *Why was I the one who had to endure this lifelong imperfection? Why were people so mean to me? I didn't ask to be born this way.* My healing process took a lot of time, tears, and trials, but when I look back at my journey, being born with a cleft palate has been my greatest asset.

A New Stage—The Author and Speaker

My writing skills developed in 2015 as I authored and published a book entitled *The Adventures of a Real-Life Cable Guy.* I served seven cable companies over more than thirty years and in doing so met well over 120,000 people in their homes. Each person I met was a stranger, and each person was an opportunity to use my speech to communicate.

Almost every day, I would come home and tell my wife of the adventures—the threats from people when I was disconnecting them for non-payment, people who had just lost their spouses, and a man who was beaten up so badly and I was the one to stave off the bleeding until the paramedics arrived. There was the man I spent some extra time with who I was the last one to see before he passed. Later, his sister would visit the office and thank me for praying with him.

I was aware that my career was a vehicle for me to be in someone's life, if only for an hour, to encourage them to see the bigger picture—they were special. My wife believed in me and prompted me to write the book. Not six months after publication, I found myself sitting in front of live TV cameras on ABC27 *Good Day PA!* speaking without fear. When I left the station, I waited until I was in my van, rolled up the windows, and let it all out.

My mother passed away two years before my first book came out. She was never able to see the full extent of what her little boy had accomplished. Through sobs, I whispered, "Mom, I am special. I am helping others. Thank you, Mom, thank you."

You Can Overcome

Sometimes I go back in my memory and see the little boy who was bullied on that anthill. I want to tell him that he will become a public speaker, a singer, a performer, and an author. I want to wipe his tears, whisper belief into his ears, and give him a huge hug in front of that insensitive teacher. I want to tell him he's going to be okay.

I was given a gift at birth. Yes, I said a gift. It turned out to be one of the most beneficial gifts God has given me. To this day, I wear a steel plate to "fix" the problem that surgery could not. It is still a defect but certainly not a deficit. The obstacle of a speech impediment has been overcome.

The tragedy of a little boy's fear and trauma would become a triumph. The pain would become a promise, and the struggle would become strength. Just as the moth or butterfly struggles to leave the cocoon, strengthens its wings, and flies, I was flying into a whole new world.

Every audience I speak to mirrors back to me the pains we all experience. We all have challenges to overcome, don't we? No matter what has got you thinking that you are less than others, IT IS NOT TRUE! We all have something that is preventing us from truly expressing who we are. Remember this—you are not alone! You CAN overcome! You CAN beat back the bully with belief and become the brave.

You were created as you were for greater things to come, warts and all. If you need to, borrow someone else's belief in you until it becomes your own. There is no shame. If no one in your world can lend it to you, take my belief in you and know—You Are Special!

Dan Armstrong is married and father to four daughters. He is a Certified DreamBuilder Coach. Dan is available for speaking engagements on heart-centered transformation and how to make an impact in the lives of those around you. Dan has two new books on the horizon.

Contact Dan at DanArmstrongAuthor@gmail.com

Tweetable: We all have something that is preventing us from truly expressing who we are. Remember this—you are not alone! Beat back the bully with belief. You are the brave.

WAGNER NOLASCO

USA Best Country in the World
My Passion, My Opportunity, My Home

Wagner Nolasco is the founder of Build 2 Rent Direct, one of the largest developers in Florida, with $700 million in delivered inventory. Wagner has over 5,000 hours of volunteer service. As a volunteer for the US Coast Guard Auxiliary, he received the Lifetime Presidential Achievement Award (2017).

The Country Everyone Wants to Build

I grew up in Brazil in a middle-class family. My grandfather was a very humble guy, uneducated, but very successful in his business. In 1991, my father, a bank executive, was shot during a bank robbery. He survived, thank God, and my family decided it was time to leave the country.

We immigrated to the United States of America in 1993. I was 13 years old. That's when my journey really began. I was always an admirer of the amazing USA. When I came here, I realized why: it's the people, the heritage, the culture. This is a country where everybody comes to build. People come to bring opportunity and to make the country better. I fell in love with and adopted that philosophy and very proudly became a US citizen.

I have always been optimistic. I have always been a dreamer, and I have always been a doer. There's no conquering anything unless you take action. You can think big, but unless you take action, I don't think you're going to get anywhere.

When I was old enough, I worked as a parking valet. Then I cleaned restaurants. Before I was 18 years old, I got into the construction business. I started very small as a supplier. I gave my best, treated my employees with respect, and made sure they were well-compensated. At the same time, I started the business to earn profits. As we grew, we did very simple jobs, a lot of single-family homes, until my family's background in the stone business in Brazil provided an opportunity. We started supplying very large luxury projects internationally such as Four Seasons Great Exuma, Trump Towers, Hard Rock Hotel and Casino, and Boca Beach Club for Blackstone. Once we had a US presence, we grew to be very big.

As a supplier, you have very little power, so this wasn't the best position to be in. The industry is not well-regulated. On every contract, we held a retainer, usually 10%, until the project was completed. Unfortunately, on big projects, we often could only collect 90%. If 10% was the profit margin, we wouldn't make any money on the project. Sometimes there wasn't even enough to pay for materials and labor. Big construction companies, big developers, and big hotel chains really had a lot of power over small providers. With no profit margins, we could not grow as a business, and worse, it became a strain to take good care of our people. Seeing this as unfair and inhuman, I promised myself and my family that I would make a difference in the industry. I wanted to sit on the other side of the table. I would become a developer so I could hold the checkbook and treat all of my suppliers fairly by paying them on time and in full.

Over 20 years ago, I started in the construction business in Florida as a developer. We have since completed over 400 flips. In 2008, we bought distressed properties, fixed them, and sold them. As of 2022, we have participated in delivering over $700 million in real estate sales, construction, and development. Today, we have $750 million and counting in the new construction pipeline for the next five years. Since day one, we have been diligent about treating people fairly, paying them on time, making sure their families are well taken care of, and being very humble, resilient, and optimistic.

The Photo That Changed My Life

As the construction business grew, I was looking for success. I wanted to make my family proud. When I started my first business, I had this vision of making money. I thought success was a million dollars, $2 million, $10 million. When I had that financial success in construction, I realized that I felt empty. Money wasn't what I was searching for.

In 2013, I built a humble house in a poor neighborhood in Orlando called Pine Hills. I sold the house to a young couple and met them to sign the documents. This was their first house. At the closing table, the lady said, "Can we take a picture with you?"

I said, "Sure! But can I ask why?" I was intrigued.

She said, "Today is a big day for us. Buying my first home is a dream come true."

I didn't know that this property—concrete, tile, and materials—could represent so much to someone. When that family told me that they wanted to have a picture with me because I made their dream come true, I was blown away.

After that day, I had a new perspective. I built my properties with a lot more love and care. These were not simply products, these were homes. I upgraded the materials, aiming to deliver the best value I could to the buyers. That was the turning point, a major shift in my values from money to quality.

I changed my attitude toward my employees. I started appreciating them more and thanked them for showing up. I changed the way I did payroll. At the time, we were paying monthly or biweekly. Now, I pay everybody weekly, every Friday. I'm very proud to do that and make sure no employee or subcontractor has problems due to the gap between paydays, because many do live paycheck to paycheck.

Upon successful completion of a project, as a token of appreciation, I bring my grill, meat, and my family, and we do a big Brazilian barbecue for everybody on the job and their families. It's a meal, bonding time, and a way for me to stay in touch. Many of my employees wouldn't think a successful business guy and his family would take the time to serve them. It's absolutely amazing the change in attitude. This tradition has inspired many to think big and become a better person, for themselves, their families, and the community. I'm very appreciative of what God gives me, and I am grateful for each and every person that provides services for us.

I changed my whole perspective the day I took the photo with that couple. I went from being a workaholic in a suit to being more in touch with my family, friends, and colleagues. I started spending more time traveling on my motorcycle, becoming a bigger volunteer in my community and embracing jobs where the pay was actually zero. The change in my values after that day made a whole world of difference.

In a seminar, I heard The Real Estate Guys say, "Have you ever thought about how many families you were able to provide with a safe, quality rental home?" By building quality products with great finishes, we make a daily difference in quality of life for people. I see now that business is about more than making a profit. It is about how I can serve others in my community.

Our business has grown to be one of the largest build to rent developers in Florida. We build in the whole Central Florida area, primarily near hospitals and senior living facilities, and cater to people who provide essential services. Our goal is to build entry-level properties for our tenants that are of superior quality to what the market is offering. Today, we have 3,270 units in construction representing over $750 million worth of development. Hopefully, God will give me many more years of health so I can continue to do what I do in this amazing country.

Serving More, Philanthropic Vision

I have multiple purely philanthropic goals. I want to continue to volunteer for our US Armed Forces through the United States Coast Guard Auxiliary. This is how I pay my dues as an American and help my community, serve my country, and make a difference. For over fifteen years, I have volunteered thousands of hours, and in 2017, I was honored with a Lifetime Presidential Achievement Award by President Donald Trump. Every hour that we donate, the Coast Guard gets back into their budget, which is an amazing opportunity to maximize our impact.

I also want to enjoy life more. Part of that will be more motorcycle rides. If I'm going to an investing or education event, rather than fly, I'll ride my motorcycle to allow myself to enjoy the journey as well as the destination.

Success Philosophy: Grateful Optimism Mindset

In every situation, you may have two perspectives. If I just had a car accident, I could say, "How unfortunate. This is a bad day." Or I could say, "Thank God nobody got hurt."

My mom was always a very positive, high-energy person. I was very inspired by her. I have always felt that I identify with happiness. People tend to be attracted to positive people. I noticed that I had two options: I could be happy or I could be sad. You attract more bees with honey than with vinegar. Nobody wants to share your problems with you, but if you're a glass half full person and a helping hand, people tend to like you and want to be around you.

I say the bad is contagious, but the good is even more contagious. I always look at the bright side of things. I try not to look at the bad. I try not to poison myself, my house, my employees. I try to take the high road, not to bad mouth anybody, even if I've been caused harm. I try to be humble. I try to be happy, and it works.

I want to make a difference. If I am a bitter, ungrateful person, I won't be able to help anybody, including myself. I believe a positive, gratitude mindset is a gift, but it's also a choice.

The happier you are, the more positive you are, the more grateful you are, the more you share your finances, the more you share your time, the more you volunteer, the more you do philanthropy, the more you connect with your community, the more you get. Because the biggest gift is not for the one that receives, it's really for the one that gives. Understanding that can dramatically change your life.

I believe the more you have, the more you are obligated to share. I believe, because of that, God has been very good to me. He has blessed me with a great family and two beautiful girls. I am so grateful for everything God and this country gave me.

I am working to leave a legacy for my daughters. I tell them to set an example for their sisters and cousins. I want them to understand that nothing is free in life. You have to be honest. You have to work hard. You have to give 100% every day. It doesn't matter what you choose to do— photographer, writer, nurse, McDonald's cashier—whatever you do, do it with love. And do what you love. Set an example, live in alignment with your core values, work hard, treat people fairly, and love what you do, and you are going to be happy and be able to help other people. I would like my daughters to take philanthropy and serving into their hearts and carry that torch into the future. I really hope they become good human beings who help in their local community, their country, and society.

It is amazing how much love and opportunity this country has provided me. If I made it, coming from a different country with no English and no college degree, I believe the same can happen for anyone. Then, you've got to give back. I invest in myself, I invest in my family, and I invest in my community, and money is the consequence.

Wagner Nolasco is a developer, real estate investor and syndicator, and founder of Build 2 Rent Direct in Central Florida. Connect directly with Wagner Nolasco about real estate development, sales, and investment syndication.

Instagram: build2rentdirect
Instagram Personal: wagnernolasco
YouTube: Wagner Nolasco | Build 2 Rent Direct
Email: wagner@b2rdirect.com
Linkedin: Wagner Nolasco | Build 2 Rent Direct

Tweetable: In every situation, you may have two perspectives. If I just had a car accident, I could say, *How unfortunate. This is a bad day.* Or I could say, *Thank God nobody got hurt.* The bad is contagious, but the good is even more contagious. Always look at the bright side of things.

BEN ANDREWS

My Longest Run
My Family Crisis That Built the Family Business

Ben Andrews is a Realtor and speaker based in Portland, Oregon. Ben works in the family business started with nothing to lose amid a family catastrophe. Prior to his work as a Realtor, Ben was a professional athlete and trained for the US Olympic trials as one of America's fastest milers.

You Have the Right to Remain Silent

"You have the right to an attorney. If you cannot afford an attorney, one will be provided for you."

I was in the first month of a fifth year of high school, but now, in an instant, my dreams of running for the Oregon Ducks were vanishing like the sound of a Nike swoosh. My fate was in the hands of someone I didn't know, didn't like, and didn't trust: my court-appointed public defender. He suggested I plead to a lesser charge. "Forget about running in college," he said. "Sign this, do your time, and get on with your life."

After our meeting, my parents committed to two things: they would hire an attorney and would figure out a way to pay for it.

My dad, Ted, worked in a can manufacturing plant, long days and crummy working conditions making cans that housed fruit, tuna, and other foods. During the summer months, temperatures were above 100 inside the plant. In the winter, it was in the mid-30s.

However, this job provided a luxury many households didn't have—insurance for the family and the ability for my mom to work less and be available to us boys before and after school. In our family, that made his job a dream job.

My mom, Cindy, worked as a housecleaner and cleaned the homes of neighborhood families, including the homes of a few of my classmates.

A few years before, my mom did a short stint working as a Realtor. As an independent contractor with a big national firm, she was fired after she talked her only clients out of buying a home. They were newlyweds and their money was tight. Her advice was to enjoy their first year of marriage, save up some money, and test the market the following year. The office manager told her, "You're more suited for cleaning toilets, not selling the houses they are in." So, after just six weeks of listening to Calloway's *I Wanna Be Rich* as our family soundtrack, my mom was back to cleaning toilets.

You're Just a Number Now

After I'd been processed and served dinner in Portland's Multnomah County Jail, I was handcuffed and shackled to other inmates and led towards a bus which was waiting to transfer inmates to another jail.

"Sir, my mom was going to post bail," I said to the guard.

"Get on the bus and shut your damn mouth. You're a number now."

Shackled, I shuffled at the pace set by the person in front of me and the person in front of him. The result was that I was dragging the person behind me.

Who are these people directing my steps?

As I entered the bus, I was overcome with emotion. I cried on the inside, refusing to show it on the outside.

"Lord, I need you now. I need a miracle," I whispered.

With each step in my county-issued jellies, I could feel cold steel cut my skin and dig into my ankle bone. I envisioned myself post-race after getting spiked by another runner.

I took my seat with 65 other inmates—numbers. The noise was deafening. Steel dragging and everyone talking over one another. Some yelling threats, some greeting old friends. Others just talked to themselves.

Their eyes told a story. A few were hopeful. Others were dead. Some seemed dazed.

"What are you in for?" my seatmate asked. I ignored him.

"What are you in for?" he asked again. I made eye contact with a man who looked as though he had lived two lives. Defeat in his face. Defeat in his eyes.

"Bro, this isn't a great place to make friends, but if you're rude, it's going to be much harder." Fighting tears, I nodded. But I couldn't formulate words. He said, "I've watched you today. You seem alright. You look scared. You don't belong in here."

"Do you?" I managed.

"Nowadays, absolutely. But I was once a good kid, too."

"What happened?" I asked.

"I just began to believe the shit people said about me. And more importantly, I hung around with people who didn't care to see the better version of me."

As men continued to shuffle onto the bus, my seatmate explained his first arrest, his time in prison, and how his life spiraled. With each transgression, he talked about a "friend" he was doing criminal acts with.

"Had I had the guts to have better friends, they wouldn't have allowed me to rob, steal, and cheat."

As he continued, I took inventory of who was in my life. I wasn't guilty of what I'd been charged with, but I came up with a few people to steer clear of.

"Andrews," I heard a voice say. I looked up to see the guard who'd called me a number.

"Yes?" I said quietly.

"Guess what? Your mommy and daddy posted bail. You get to go home and snuggle your parents tonight."

Laughter erupted. My cheeks blazed as another guard disconnected me from the chain gang and put me into my own cuffs.

"You have a mom? And a dad?" my seatmate asked.

"I do."

"Do them proud. Find and stick with friends who want to see the best in you."

My mom and I held hands the entire drive home, and when we arrived, my dad and my brother Matthew greeted us. In our small living room, we held one another for several minutes in silence. My dad broke the silence with some of the best advice I would ever receive: "You don't always get what you pray for. But you pray for what you get. And you trust that God is there in the midst of it all. He is here now, more than ever. So hold onto that."

REAL ESTATE 2.0

Several years removed from being fired as a Realtor, my mom prepared to start again, this time armed with something new: a why.

My mom reached out to her clients—whose toilets she had cleaned for years—and asked a simple question. "Can you do me a favor? When you hear of anyone talking about buying or selling a home, can you please connect us?"

Those were her words, but her soul was screaming, "I need you! My son is at the mercy of a public defender! Unlike Ted and I, this public defender isn't concerned about what is possible for Ben one, five, or thirty years from now. I am begging you, when you hear of anyone talking about buying or selling a home, connect us, please."

My mom continued cleaning houses and asking for referrals. She brought up her real estate business in every conversation.

My dad was taking as much overtime as he could get and realizing how much he was liked and respected at work. Coworkers would approach my dad, sometimes standing in line as if seeing Don Corleone in *The Godfather*, to solicit real estate advice. My dad took notes on the 100-decibel factory floor, and after a call to my mom on the payphone during breaks, would have answers for his coworkers. While working on an assembly line, my dad had created his own assembly line of real estate business.

My brother beautifully kept me distracted from my uncertain future by seeing to it that I wasn't alone. Mentally or emotionally.

The phone began ringing with business. And ringing. After each call, my mom would write a thank you note and insert a packet of forget-me-not seeds. My parents, who together had never made more than $50,000 annually, made $125,000 in real estate commissions over the next five months.

The Test

The Oregon prosecutors asked that I undergo a test, a humiliating experience where I was forced to view recorded acts of abuse to prove I was not a menace to society. I feared going to sleep. The horrific scenes I was subjected to would meet me in my dreams. Over time, the confidence my family had worked hard to instill in me began to crumble.

In the mornings, my mom would sit on the edge of my bed. "Ben, a year from now, this will all be behind us. A year from now, you'll be waking up in your dorm room. A year from now, you'll be on the track team at the University of Oregon. Keep focused on where you're going."

In the evenings, as I fought against another night of nightmares, my dad would come sit on the edge of my bed. "Ben, I know who you are. People can say anything they want about you, but I know who you are. You're my son. I love you. I love who you are. Listen to the people who know you. Those are the only voices that matter. Keep focused on where you're going."

Each day, my brother was beside me as we walked the school hallways, shielding me from any would-be hecklers and constantly reminding me of what was on the other side of this storm. "I can't wait to see you run for Oregon," he would say.

They were showing me that sometimes, in the middle of a storm, a multitude of small thoughts and small actions can compound into big thoughts and bigger actions. They were teaching me that to think big, I first needed to start small, in my own mind.

A Setback Is a Setup for a Comeback

Thirty years later, I have lived a life unimaginable. And that is all because my parents took a chance on me—and, ultimately, themselves. The work they did and the risk they took spared me from a jail sentence for a crime I didn't commit.

I went on to run for the University of Oregon Ducks. On Wednesdays, I would take a scenic drive along the McKenzie River to Nike co-founder Bill Bowerman and his wife Barbara's home, have lunch, and then take my afternoon run around their property. I qualified for the NCAA Championship and became one of America's fastest milers.

After college, as my dreams of making the US Olympic Team were beginning to slip away, I heard God whisper, asking me if I wanted to continue towards my Olympic goal.

"Of course, but how?" I thought.

While working at a bank, I met a stranger who gave me $200,000 and said, "I want you to quit your job and train as hard and smart as you can for the 2004 Olympic Trials . . . with one catch."

"Wait, what? What's the catch?" I asked.

"I want you to find a creative way to pay it forward to others throughout your lifetime."

We talked each Tuesday at 10:00 AM, and in the process, he became my first mentor. He introduced me to others along the way and shared with me books and tapes by Jim Rohn, Brian Tracy, Les Brown, and others.

A year removed from the University of Oregon, my coach Bill Dellinger casually asked, "You've been through a lot and you've made it to the other side. What are you doing to help those who are still in their own storm?"

I went to mentor, coach, and run with members of the running club at Oregon State Penitentiary—the very institution I narrowly avoided. Through letters and countless collect phone calls, I was offering hope, an opportunity for the inmates to free themselves from their mental and emotional shackles, and a guide to run faster.

I created a non-profit foundation and an online coaching service, helping over 2,000 runners in 13 countries chase their own personal bests. I hosted hundreds of kids at summer running camps for families who couldn't afford it. I ran with Nike and was coached by my childhood idol, running legend Alberto Salazar.

I didn't qualify for the US Olympic Trials. Disappointed, I called and apologized to my mentor and sponsor who said, "Ben, I supported you because of what attempting the goal makes you."

My wife Heidi and I joined the family real estate business, and with the help of another mentor, Brian Buffini, we have become one of the most successful real estate teams in the United States. Through Brian Buffini, our network of real estate agents is responsible for selling one in every eight homes in the United States. We can confidently tell our friends and clients that we can help them throughout Oregon and connect them with professionals in all 50 states.

My parents who, in the infancy of their business, vacillated between buying three For Sale signs or pushing the budget to get the price break at five, believed their steps were ordered by a higher power. They grew their business on the shoulders of people whose toilets they cleaned and who they worked alongside in a can manufacturing plant. Nothing sexy, just the people who already knew, liked, and trusted them. Over the last 30 years, that little business my mom, dad, and brother started in one corner of a basement bedroom has sold more than 5,000 homes.

I like to joke and tell my family that they should thank me for the storm that got them back into the real estate game. But the truth is, I thank them daily for supporting me through the storm. I thank them for believing in me. I thank them for teaching me that it's okay to take a chance on the unknown and expect everything will work out for the best. I thank them for showing me that when you think big, you are allowing God to open your eyes and your heart to all that He has in store for you, which is always bigger than we can dream.

Legacy

Juggling business and marriage with Heidi has been a joy, and our crowning achievement has been being parents to our son Henry. My hope is that I can live out the wonderful example my parents display for me and my brother: when times get tough, and they always will, I will trust in the Lord with all my heart. I will THINK BIG and know that He will make my paths straight.

My dad may have said it best: "You don't always get what you pray for. But you pray for what you get. And you trust that God is there in the midst of it all. He is here now, more than ever. So hold on to that."

To connect with Ben and Heidi Andrews regarding real estate, learn more about Ben's book, *The Long Run: Principles to Run Your Best Race in Business and Life*, and to book Ben for speaking engagements, visit BenAndrews.com

Tweetable: You don't always get what you pray for. But you pray for what you get. And you trust that God is there in the midst of it all. He is here now, more than ever. So hold on to that. — Ted Andrews, Dad to Ben Andrews

PHYLLIS AYMAN

How Caregiving Led to Advocacy and My Life's Work

Phyllis Ayman is an advocate for elder care and aging life management with 45 years of experience working in nursing homes. Her podcast SeniorsSTRAIGHTTalk brings informative conversations to our senior years. Her big vision is bringing elder wisdom to film. Phyllis also advises on personalized longevity plans for aging gracefully and healthfully.

My Teenage Caregiving Experience

In 1967, I was attending high school in Brooklyn, New York. My grandmother, an immigrant from Poland, diagnosed with Parkinson's disease was recovering from a broken hip. I remember hearing my mother on telephone calls with "Grandma," constantly encouraging her to leave her apartment for some fresh air. The answer was always the same; she wouldn't leave because she was ashamed of being seen with the "walker" she needed to help walk safely.

My mother, a housewife who didn't drive, took the bus and train for the two-hour journey from Brooklyn to the Bronx several times per week to help Grandma with household chores and errands. After the valiant year-long effort, the long trip and Grandma's deteriorating condition took their toll on my mother and our entire family. There were decisions to be made.

Mom wanted Grandma to move into our small house. My father, who was supportive of my mother's efforts to care for Grandma, was opposed to the idea. First, the hospital bed Grandma needed would have taken up most of the living room space of our small house. Secondly, and probably more importantly, we would all be on call 24 hours a day.

The family made the decision no one wants to make. It was time to move Grandma into a nursing home. There was a small nursing home a few blocks from where we lived. For many years, I passed that place on my walk to school or to a friend's house, but never gave it much thought.

In mid-winter of 1968, Grandma moved into Ingersoll Nursing Home. First thing every morning, my mother walked the five or six blocks with the eggnog drink she made for Grandma. Every evening, she returned with clothes to wash for the following day.

This was the routine for several months. That year, on the occasion of my parents' 25th wedding anniversary, my sister and I took the money we saved to send them on a two-week vacation. Although Mom was initially reluctant, my sister and I assured her we would care for Grandma in her absence.

My sister, seven years my senior, was in college. Fortuitously, her class schedule complemented mine perfectly. She went to Grandma every morning with the eggnog drink in tow. I was scheduled for the afternoon and dinner shift after returning from school.

The first day left an indelible mark on my mind and heart, and I believe is the through-line that led me to my life's work.

I remember walking up to the nursing home entrance, opening the front door, and seeing my extremely proud grandmother, the woman I knew and adored, slumped in a wheelchair in the lobby in a rather unkempt manner. Today, at the age of 69, I can still visualize it like it was yesterday.

Then there was the odor, a stench that assaulted my nostrils followed by a gagging sensation that swelled up in my throat.

I turned around and ran out the front door before Grandma could see me. I walked the square block several times with tears streaming down my face until I mustered the courage to go back inside and attend to Grandma's needs. After all, that was what I was supposed to do, and that was more important than how I felt about it.

To this day, though I know I fulfilled my care responsibility for the two weeks my parents were on vacation, it is only that first day I remember.

The Valuable Lesson I Learned

While my parents were on vacation, my uncle—mother's brother—his wife, and their two children came to visit for Mother's Day.

I remember all of us standing on our sunbaked front porch when my aunt said she did not want to visit Grandma, and more, she also didn't want my cousins, ages 14 and 18, to visit her either. Her reason: "It is too depressing." She did not want to go to an "old age home to see what happens to old people."

I was appalled and vividly remember saying, "How will they know how to care for you when you are old if they don't get a chance to see their Grandma?" a pretty brazen statement to make to an adult back in 1968.

I told my aunt that every visit helped me understand what it was like to grow old and to know how to care for my mother in her later years.

Circumstances did not allow me the opportunity to care for my mother that way. Still, through the years, I'm proud to have helped care for many mothers and grandmothers, fathers and grandfathers, husbands and wives, aunts and uncles, sisters and brothers.

The Road to Nursing Homes and Advocacy

My first job in a nursing home started shortly after I received my master of science degree from the University of Wisconsin, Madison. At that time, I chose to work in a nursing home because, as a new graduate, it was the only job available that offered a decent salary. I worked in several, one in Milwaukee, the other in a small town called Monroe.

After a few years, I returned to Brooklyn, NY, where I landed a speech pathologist position at the prestigious Rusk Institute. After marriage and my daughter, my family moved to New Rochelle, NY. I worked in various settings, including a special education preschool, but there was something always tugging at me that I couldn't quite identify. When a position in a nursing home became available, I jumped at the opportunity.

That nursing home was sold shortly thereafter. The administrator who had moved to another a short distance away called me to work with him at a skilled nursing facility that had a unit with people who were ventilator dependent. I welcomed the challenge.

Shortly into that position, there was a situation that would impact my life's course as much as the nursing home experience with my grandmother. I was complaining to colleagues about the care being delivered to some of the patients. My exact words were, "They are going to kill someone here."

The director of the department overheard and blasted me with these words: "You have a decision to make. Either you are going to be part of the solution or part of the problem."

Ever since then, I've lived by those words and the words of John Lewis, "Never give in. Stand up. Speak up. When you see something that is not right, not fair, not just, you have a moral obligation to do something, to say something, and not be quiet."

I realized the early experience with my grandmother led me back to work in nursing homes. I felt pangs reminiscent of when I saw Grandma sitting in the nursing home lobby. The advocate that seemed to always be part of me began to speak out beyond my scope of practice.

There is a price to speaking up. People are uncomfortable with change;

they prefer to continue along the comfortable path. Whether or not they know things are not right, going along is a tacit agreement that everything is fine. When you speak up, you become labeled as a troublemaker and are often ostracized.

It's been a difficult journey, but I've embraced being a catalyst for change.

The Path to Becoming an Author

In 2016, the company that owned the nursing home where I was working made a budgetary decision which edged me out of my position. I was extremely disappointed and remember feeling heartbroken. I had put my heart and soul into developing the clinical program and made great strides in improving life for the residents in a variety of ways. This has always been a great source of personal and professional satisfaction. But, when one door closes, another opens. Leaving my position opened the door to looking outside the sheltered nursing home world I knew. What I found country-wide was an industry not living up to what older adults deserve.

That was the beginning of my journey to raise awareness and inspire a national dialogue on how we value, care for, and treat older adults as they continue to age. An especially important consideration since there will be 10,000 people turning 65 each day from now until 2034. Are baby boomers going to tolerate receiving the level of care our nation's nursing homes are providing? We need to stand up and speak out to ensure our loved ones, and we ourselves, receive quality care and continue to live a quality life.

My Lightbulb Moment

After writing my first two books, I thought a radio show would be an effective way to continue the dialogue and broadcast the message. In 2019, I launched Voices for Eldercare Advocacy and converted the radio show to the podcast *SeniorsSTRAIGHTTalk* in July 2020.

In the early months of the radio show, I interviewed a dear friend who, in retirement, cares for her grandchildren. She recalled a story that changed my thinking about how we present ourselves and how society sees older adults.

Her granddaughter asked, "Nana, why do you have so many wrinkles?"

Her response: "I've earned these wrinkles. These wrinkles say how much I've learned through my long life. These wrinkles help me teach you."

That was a lightbulb moment. I realized that our wrinkles are signs of age, nothing to be hidden or erased. By erasing wrinkles or any sign of aging, aren't we erasing the evidence of the wisdom we've gained from the years we've lived? The booming US anti-aging market would have us think otherwise.

My experience with the thousands of older adults I have met is that, like every other person, they offer tremendous value. I learned from my father a tried and true lesson: "Don't judge a book by its cover." I've learned a tremendous amount from the people I've cared for, ranging in age from sixty to a hundred years and more. Those with the deepest wrinkles and the most lines often had the most wisdom to share.

My first book, *Nursing Homes to Rehabilitation Centers: What Every Person Needs to Know*, was published in December of 2017. My second book, *OVERDUE Quality Care for Our Elder Citizens*, and my third, *Dignity & Respect: Are Our Aging Parents Getting What They Deserve?*, published in 2020, became international bestsellers.

Advocacy—How Do We View Older Adults?

Essentially, the present societal view is that people are valued wherever they are along the age spectrum until the benchmark of retirement age. Because they may no longer be productive members of the workforce, they have outlived their value, and with that goes their dignity, respect, and rights. Despite that fact, most people think fondly or lovingly about the elders in their family.

Society tremendously affects our view of ourselves. Today, print ads, commercials, and films depict older adults more realistically in various activities and venues. Yet, there is still the notion that cosmetic injections and hair dyes are the remedy for being identified as being "old," which is to be avoided at all costs. These stigmatizing societal attitudes become internalized long before we reach the senior years of our lives.

In other contexts, becoming a senior is considered an accomplishment—think high school senior or senior executive. If we reimagine reaching our senior years as an accomplishment, a continuation towards a zenith, it may help reshape attitudes towards older adults.

How can we empower young people to view older adults in a way that celebrates and values the achievement of reaching an advanced age? This is an important aspect of my vision—to have young people think of themselves as "evolving elders." Being an evolving elder is an active process. Attaining wisdom from a long life of a wealth of experiences is an accomplishment to be embraced, desired, and celebrated. This may help change how we value, care for, and treat older adults.

Since I authored my first book, my vision has been to bring this message to a national stage, to spark a conversation, and to hopefully move us to see the value we should afford older adults wherever they reside, along with quality care, and purposeful lives. This is what I expect to accomplish with a film about elder wisdom and wise leadership based on the books *In the Arms of Elders* and *Tribes of Eden*, by Dr. Bill Thomas.

Mindful Longevity & Elder Wisdom

"I am not here to merely make a living. I am here to enrich the world and to enable it to live with greater vision, hope and achievement. If I'm not doing so, I have not lived up to the errand." – Woodrow Wilson

These words, which I came upon recently, inspired me to reflect on my life's journey. I'm living up to the errand, and I also have embraced becoming an elder.

I always knew I made a large impact in the lives of the thousands of nursing home residents and families with whom I've worked. When I stepped out of the nursing world with my vision to inspire a national dialogue about eldercare, I had no idea how that would take shape. The journey has had twists and turns. I have followed the winding road and along with me it has grown. Growth is necessary to fully bloom. I believe on that winding road I've found my why, which has helped me find my way. In that journey, rooted in experiences from my youth, I believe I am fulfilling the errand.

Each of us has a unique fingerprint; therefore, we leave an imprint unlike any other person.

We never know how what we say, and what we do, small or large, impacts another.

In my present work environment, I'm surrounded by colleagues many years my junior. I've been sharing my philosophy about evolving elders and the importance of conscious choices and mindful longevity.

Experiences in the past few days have punctuated this point. A gal who just turned thirty shared with me that I inspired her to think differently about how she is approaching the choices she is making, especially eating choices. Another, age 45, told me that her ship has sailed on her ambition of becoming an artist. I shared my journey and my age. She told me I inspired her to take action and revisit her dream.

My big vision has been to impact society's overall thinking about older adults, the value they represent in our lives, in our communities, and in society as a whole, leading to positive changes in the quality of care they receive no matter where they reside.

But I also want to inspire and guide you to embrace the journey. Impart your wisdom as an act of kindness but also because wisdom is meant to be shared. Live up to the elder you have become. Embrace mindful longevity to live healthfully and gracefully so you can be the shining example of the beauty of elderhood.

Phyllis Ayman is available for speaking engagements and webinars. She offers family care strategy and mediation sessions and develops personalized longevity plans for people as they age.

phyllis@phyllisaymanassociates.com
www.phyllisaymanassociates.com

Follow SeniorsSTRAIGHTTalk: www.voiceamerica.com/show/3911/seniors-straight-talk

 Tweetable: We are all "evolving elders." Becoming an elder is to be celebrated for achieving wisdom from living a long life. Share your wisdom and be a shining example of the beauty of elderhood.

RYAN CHAMBERLIN

Could Entrepreneurism Be the Answer to America's Problems?

Ryan Chamberlin is the co-founder of TPN, a social media platform where all voices are heard. For 25 years he worked with thousands of entrepreneurs and leaders across the United States, assisting them in growing their influence and profitability. Ryan is also a congressional candidate (2020), bestselling author, and TEDx speaker who believes in principle over politics.

My First Lesson in Principle Over Politics

1980 was an important year for me. It was the first time I participated in a full-blown campaign and the first time I asked someone for their vote. This was my hometown, in Stockbridge, Georgia. Everyone was talking politics. Republican candidate Ronald Reagan was running for president, and the Democrat candidate for State House of Representative was my dad. Both won their races, and in this case, my dad, the Democrat, outspokenly supported the Republican. This was my first lesson in principles over politics. These were the only two political figures I remember from that era. I was six years old.

It Is All About the Questions

About fifteen years later, I married my high school sweetheart. We were just getting started with big goals when we realized we had no idea what we were going to do for business, or how we would become people of influence, or whether one or both of us should go back to school. Then it happened!

An entrepreneurial door opened. This opening provided me over the next five years outstanding mentorship, a powerful opportunity in business, and the direction needed to become a communicator, leader, and big thinker. This grounded me in applying and allowed me to teach what I now call, "5 questions for a great America."

These questions helped launch a massive business that impacted hundreds of thousands of entrepreneurs over an extraordinarily successful twenty-year period. They are also responsible for the recent launch of the social media platform TPN (True Patriot Network).

The questions are:

1. The Values Question: What are the values I'm not willing to compromise?
2. The Purpose Question: What is it that I'm passionate about and how will it affect others?
3. The Communication Question: How can I create a win-win solution without compromising my values?
4. The Momentum Question: What are the highest leverage activities I can do daily?
5. The Responsibility Question: Who do I need to become in order to succeed?

Faith Over Fear

In January of 2019, at 45 years of age, my wife and I celebrated our 25th wedding anniversary in Europe. We had four handsome sons of whom we could not be prouder, and we were in the first phase of becoming empty nesters. It also was a time when, through a series of events, we decided to exit the security of a business we had tasted success in over several decades. It was time for a new future but not without second thoughts. The decision to change sometimes comes with a lot of fear. It's during these times we lean on faith.

In December of 2019, a friend mentioned that our four-term congressman was not seeking re-election. A few people were wondering if I would consider running for the empty seat. Running for Congress was a fulfillment of a childhood dream. Having a leadership track record in business, the door was now opened to enter the political arena. This seemed the right time to serve my country and on February 5, 2020, we launched. Campaigning at the congressional level would prove to be a full-time effort.

I quickly realized that among my strengths were that I had never run for office (so I was not a political insider) and I had built businesses.

Unfortunately, I was the last of fourteen candidates to enter the race and soon after the COVID-19 pandemic was announced. There was no time to overthink things. It was time to win the voters over and win them fast! The only way I knew how to do this was through hundreds of conversations.

Through those conversations, here is what was learned.

America's Greatness Began with Its Values

My answers to voters' questions were based on commonsense and my core values. In business, common sense, driven by values, provides answers to questions. Great companies are known for their values. America's greatness originated with its values, specifically the Godly values of faith, family, and freedom. These values have been driven by an enterprising spirit of freedom for over 200 years. When we move away from them, there is conflict. When we embrace them, along with entrepreneurial principles, we uncover solutions to some of America's biggest challenges.

Our campaign had the best ground game out of all fourteen candidates. Unfortunately, the lessons learned in fundraising and traditional campaign marketing by post, radio, and TV were a little too late.

The campaign, started in February, ended in August of 2020. Just six short months.

After the campaign, people would ask two questions: 1. Will you run again? 2. What is the number one thing learned while campaigning?

The answer to question #1 to this day is, "I am keeping my options open." The answer to question #2 has a little more detail.

During the campaign, there were hundreds of conversations. There were real distinctions in how people processed his or her political frustrations. I noticed that those with strong entrepreneurial backgrounds processed everything differently than those without a similar background.

I also noticed the individuals that lived by the entrepreneurial principles in these five questions, whether they owned a business or not, viewed themselves as being part of the solution rather than viewing the problem as something someone else needed to fix.

If our educational curriculum focused on entrepreneurial development, would we have the same problems we are dealing with today? Unlikely.

If you and I asked the five questions, would our country show considerable improvement? Let us see.

1. What are the values I'm not willing to compromise? Am I values driven? Have I defined my top 10 values? Do my goals in business, and in life, reflect these values?

Have you ever wondered why you can't stay focused on your goals? The reality is, most people don't have a how-to problem. They have a focus problem. And they can't stay focused because without defining the values that drive their decisions, they lack clarity for their dreams and their goals. Big thinkers realize—the success of any worthwhile goal or dream will be defined by its core values.

2. What is it that I'm passionate about and how will it affect others?
Often the passion we have for a project is limited because we really don't know why we are doing it. We may like something and be able to temporarily focus on it, but if the reason we are doing it isn't big enough, we'll either quit or be miserable through the journey. Big thinkers often have big goals, but one question they always ask is, "How will the result I'm looking for impact others for good?" Big thinkers understand—the purpose for which you do something will always determine the level of passion in how you do it.

3. How can I create a win-win solution without compromising my values?
Do you communicate in a manner that inspires others to want to reach their potential? Do you know the values, dreams, and goals of the people closest to you? People of influence are respected because of what they have done for others. How can you help others win if you don't really know what they want? Big thinkers ask themselves—How do I create a win-win solution out of a complicated scenario without compromising my values?

4. What are the highest leverage activities I can do daily?
The most productive leaders in the world identify their top 3-5 HLAs (highest leverage activities) and invest the majority of their time in these areas. In contrast, most people that feel frustrated and unaccomplished spend most of their time on things that won't move them toward their goals. Life rewards action, not intention. In most cases, it does not really matter why something did not get done, it only matters whether we get it done. Big thinkers fill their calendars with HLAs and either build a team to help with the rest or drop it.

5. Who do I need to become in order to succeed? Am I spending time with people that are influencing me to be better? Do I take responsibility for where I am in life?
Do you own how you react when tough situations present themselves? When things go wrong in life, what course corrections must you take? What new skills will you develop as a result? How can you act more and blame others less? As long as why you didn't achieve a goal is someone else's fault, it will never be your fault. And, if it's never your fault, then you will not make the course corrections necessary to win. It is amazing how many problems go away when we focus on our areas of improvement rather than dwelling on

everyone else's. Big thinkers embrace the principle that challenges make us stronger, not weaker, but only if we take responsibility for our results.

The bottom line is, to launch and sustain any great movement, the above five questions must be answered over and over. America is no different.

America Was Founded by Entrepreneurs

Can you imagine George Washington, Thomas Jefferson, or Abraham Lincoln not asking the above five questions? Wasn't there a clearly defined set of values that drove their decisions? Weren't they purpose-driven with passion for creating a free society? Didn't they attach themselves to a greater cause and learn to communicate in a way that inspired others to want to win? As seasoned leaders, doesn't it make sense that all three spent their time working on the most productive things possible? As big thinkers, how much did they really blame others for their situations? Rather, were they not completely engaged in continual action and personal improvement?

In comparison to our current political environment, hasn't the elimination of a clearly defined set of values caused much of America to long for true leadership? How many short-term agendas are being pushed without legitimate purpose? When was the last time a compromise didn't go against your values and you could find a win-win for all parties involved? When was the last time you felt that those elected to serve were engaged in productive activities that help create solutions for our biggest issues? Lastly, if more leaders would take responsibility for their own actions, wouldn't it translate into more of society taking responsibility for theirs? I'm not trying to present utopia here. I realize there is not a quick fix. I do, however, believe that the further we get away from the principles in these five questions, the more chaotic our surroundings become.

As a result of running for congress, hundreds of conversations, and a 25-year entrepreneurial background, I have come to believe a major cause of our frustrations as a society is simply not asking the right questions. The pursuit of these five questions and others is the solution to these frustrations.

I firmly believe entrepreneurism is the answer to America's biggest problems. Not because it sounds good but because true success is built on principles, not politics. Entrepreneurism is a set of principles on which our country was founded.

So, to answer question #2, the greatest thing I learned during the campaign was actually a change in how I viewed myself. I now view myself as a constitutional entrepreneur—an individual who believes in the constitution and views entrepreneurial principles as solutions to some of the country's biggest problems.

The constitution was written by entrepreneurs. And those who view what is going on in our country through this mindset are equipped to fix problems differently than those who do not.

What would happen if many of the topics that occupy the news today were filtered through these five questions? Would they even be issues? The principles in these questions should not be party-line principles. They are, in fact, principles that when violated create conflict and cause America to be out of alignment.

An Entrepreneurial Solution to a Big Problem

Toward the end of my campaign, a fundamental attack on personal and entrepreneurial freedom became national. Big tech decided to shut down the free speech communication platform named Parlor. Twitter decided to cancel the president of the United States. Several of the biggest social media platforms openly and unforgivingly justified filtering opinions. The atmosphere was set for an entrepreneurial solution to a big problem. These muted voices of America need the True Patriot Network (TPN).

What people see and hear over and over they tend to eventually believe. If what people see and hear is controlled, beliefs can be controlled—no matter what the belief. If beliefs can be influenced, then the direction of society can be influenced. That is not how a free society operates.

Over 62% of adults now get their news on social media. On social media, election integrity, government spending, religious freedom, immigration, education, and health care are all discussed. If Facebook, Twitter, and Google are really the modern-day public square, and if they continue down the path they are going, everything our free society has fought for is at risk. The internet is truly the new battleground for beliefs.

The big challenge here is although many of us do not agree with the decisions of big tech or their collaboration with a specific political agenda, we do value free enterprise and an entrepreneurs' freedom to operate his or her business the way he or she sees fit.

So in 2021, TPN was born as a free-market solution, an entrepreneurial solution, and an answer to a big problem. It is built on the principles in the five questions and is described as the no judgment, uncensored social media app that operates under the values of faith, family, free enterprise, and free speech. Our platform allows people from all sides to share their true passions, feelings, and lives without fear of unnecessary censorship.

So how can entrepreneurism be the answer to America's problems?

First, a values-driven entrepreneur asks a different set of questions, including the five written in this chapter. Their decisions and behaviors are based on core values. They have a dream that is engineered with purpose and fueled by passion. The most successful people value helping others succeed while accomplishing their goals. They are the true opportunity creators. They value productivity over activity, and the discussion is no longer about who is at fault. The conversation is about solutions. This all is built on an extreme commitment to personal responsibility and personal growth.

Second, they are big thinkers and the only ones who build businesses, like TPN, that can perpetuate freedom.

Our country was founded on Godly values, driven by entrepreneurial principles and is inspired by big thinkers. Believing in the greatness of our country requires someone to accept these principles as the driving force behind what has made America dynamic.

For these reasons, I conclude that entrepreneurs who think big and ask the five questions are the answer to America's biggest problems.

Ryan Chamberlin is a constitutional entrepreneur, bestselling author, and CEO of the True Patriot Network (TPN). To find out more about the TPN APP and to get a FREE copy of one of Ryan's books, go to www.RyanChamberlin.com

Tweetable: Entrepreneurism is the answer to America's biggest problems. Not because it sounds good, but because true success is built on principles, not politics. – Ryan Chamberlin

DR. JAIME GONZALEZ

From Dumpster to Grit, Gratitude, and Financial Freedom

Dr. Jaime Gonzalez, originally from Juarez, Mexico, is a seasoned entrepreneur, business leader, eye doctor, and accredited real estate investor and syndicator. He has ownership in over $300M in real estate acquisitions and is invested in over 5,000 apartment units as of 2021, and he helps busy professionals attain financial freedom.

The Garbage

I started to smell the garbage burning as I sat at the kitchen table. I could overhear the people behind our house saying to pour more gasoline. I could almost taste the smoke as it spilled into our humble adobe house. I looked at my younger brother and saw the disappointment on his face. My mother did not allow us to go to the landfill behind our house when garbage was burning.

That was our backyard. It was a place to play, enjoy, experiment, and get away. We both climbed on top of our concrete fence to take a look, hoping the fire was only a small pile that would burn quickly. The pile of garbage was unfortunately extremely large and would burn for at least an hour. The white smoke was thick and started to fill the sky.

The day was Saturday. We sat back down, and I continued to eat my eggs and refried beans as I came up with plan B. Back in the 1980s, we could roam anywhere in our neighborhood we desired. We decided to go down the hills and see how close we could get to our grandparents' house without our parents worrying about us. We made it about one block down the hill before we started to worry about how far we were from our house. I was six years old at the time and my brother was four.

Life in Juarez, Chihuahua, Mexico was extremely difficult for our parents but was extremely enjoyable for me, my older sister, and my younger brother. Our family had all the necessities but we did not have any of the luxuries. We had a very small convenience store in one of our rooms, and the store supplemented the income for our family. Our home was small but held up really well.

Our car was old. Still, my father always appreciated how it did not have one visible chip of paint and shined like a beautiful new car. My father woke up every Saturday morning to wash and clean his car. After cleaning his car, he would irrigate our dirt road in front of our house to have a more appealing curbside. He always seemed extremely happy doing these tasks, and it seemed as if he appreciated and was proud of what he had. The feeling of being proud trickled down to me, and I felt proud of him and extremely excited going for a ride in his car.

One day, someone broke into our home and took most of the items from the convenience store. The 35mm camera with two years' worth of film was gone. To my parents, the memories captured on camera were erased and those moments were ripped away from their hearts. This pivotal moment caused my parents to decide this was not safe or a place to raise children. They started to search for another way of life in another country.

Dumpster Diving

Arriving in the United States as a six-year-old child was not difficult for me. Our family moved into my uncle's three-bedroom duplex in Irving, Texas. I now had a family of eight, which was extremely exciting. Our family struggled with the language barrier for the first year, but by the second year, my brother and sister had adapted very well. I assimilated pretty well with others, and for the most part, was a shy, quiet kid that only cared about playing outdoors. We moved out of my uncle's house after about a year, not yet knowing that the hospitality, love, and life teachings would propel us to a better life in the United States.

We moved around from apartment to apartment, house to house, for several years. My father retained a steady job in construction and my mother as a seamstress. They worked for minimum wage and barely made ends meet. On weekdays, my father would come home from work but then leave for several hours for his second job.

When I was twelve years old, I remember my father asking me if I would like to accompany him in the evening to work with him. My mother was hesitant about me joining him, but I wanted to help. I decided to get inside his green and white Ford pickup truck and headed to work.

Dad stopped at the grocery store in front of our apartment complex but parked in the back of the building and asked me to get down. I was a bit confused about where we were and what we were about to do. I could see the excitement in my father's face as he stated this was a great opportunity for us to get some cardboard boxes and then sell them at the recycling center. He directed me to climb inside the large dumpster and obtain as much cardboard as was inside. Kids were playing outside, people were passing by, a woman was looking at us, and embarrassment set upon me. I had not felt that feeling so deep inside me in my young life.

As I assessed the situation, I felt the warmth reach my face, and my forehead started to sweat. In a few seconds, I would be digging in the dumpster. I was now a dumpster diver.

Once I jumped inside, I somehow felt comfortable—maybe because of my younger days playing in our landfill, maybe because I wanted to help or was just curious. The first dumpster was a goldmine. We recovered plenty of cardboard boxes, and at the same time, I obtained a lot of candy that was thrown away due to expiration dates. At the end of the night, the recycling center handed my father fifteen dollars for a truckful of cardboard, and I kept the bag full of candy. I was ecstatic. I was going to be the most popular kid in our apartment complex for the next several days.

I accompanied my father on several other occasions to collect cardboard. I continued to feel embarrassed. The feeling would reach a little deeper each time. I would feel very self-conscious, that I was not enjoying myself, a bit sad about what we were doing, and only hopeful I would find another sweet candy goldmine.

I believe my father sensed those feelings inside of me. One day, as he was preparing to gather cardboard, he told me I could no longer accompany him. He stated that collecting cardboard was not where I needed to be. I needed to concentrate on obtaining excellent grades in school so I could not be jumping inside dumpsters.

My parents wanted me to take advantage of being in the United States and not take this opportunity lightly. I saw for the first time that I had to become someone, to think bigger, to outwork others, to have grit, to have character—just like my parents. At twelve years old, I knew this was a turning point in my life.

Clear Vision to Clear Roadmap

In elementary and middle school, when I would go to the school nurse for eye examinations, I would try to be the last person in line so I could memorize the bottom letters of the eye chart. I did not want to wear glasses.

In seventh grade, there was no one in front of me in line. It was the school nurse and me inside the room by ourselves. I could not memorize the letters, I could not squint, and I failed the eye test. I was sent down to an optometrist in our town, received my first pair of glasses, and did not believe what I was seeing. I remember staying up until midnight walking around our neighborhood and appreciating the leaves on the trees, how green the grass seemed, how clear the lights were. I could now see the stars. I could see how bright the moon was. I could see and feel the cars passing by. I was starting to appreciate the small things in life.

I was afraid this new vision would not look the same the following day. The next morning, I walked into the school library and checked out two books regarding the anatomy and physiology of the eye. These two books opened my eyes to a fascinating world and one of the most beautiful and complicated organs in the human body.

After completing these books, my path to my career was drawn. The more I learned about the eye, the more I did not understand. The more I learned, the more curious and excited I became. I realized that I was craving the ability to help others.

Ego Set In and Quickly Backfired

I graduated towards the top of my class in high school and college, competed in math and science competitions, and received many awards. I applied for optometry school in Houston, Texas, and was accepted, which had been my only goal since I was twelve years old.

As soon as I arrived at school, I thought I was invincible. I lost my laser-focused approach. I lost the passion. I was complacent, and I lost the grit I had for so many years. I had gained an ego and developed a party lifestyle.

Test week arrived, and I was completely unprepared. I failed most of my midterm exams and had my first panic attack after reviewing my scores. It was a reality check.

I struggled immensely to concentrate in the first year of optometry school, and my grades and my relationships with family and friends took a dive for the worse. I felt alone for the first time in my life. I would go home after class with racing thoughts. I was unable to sleep most nights and felt exhausted in the mornings.

By the end, I felt embarrassed and ashamed that I had not performed well. *How can I continue going to school like this? Why did this happen to me? Why is this feeling not going away? Why is concentrating and learning so difficult now when it came so easy to me just a few months ago? Why is God not helping me? Why am I letting my family down? Will they be ashamed of me too?*

The Gift of Poverty

I went home for the summer and attempted to work on myself. I took several days off and started to pray. I had not prayed since I was accepted into school the previous year.

The power of prayer, breathwork practice, and my parents' guidance saved me from dropping out of optometry school and placed me on my path to graduate as an optometrist four years later.

My last year of optometry school, I met my beautiful wife, Dr. Hoa Nguyen. She was my lab partner and before long became my partner for life. She became my rock.

Grit, meaningful relationships, gratitude, extreme clarity, belief in a higher power, a strong enough purpose, contribution, and a healthy lifestyle have made me successful in life and in my career. I am so blessed my parents instilled in me grit and determination. I will never forget what my parents have taught me and will never take their effort to come to this great country in vain.

One of my friends told me something I will never forget: He was given the gift of poverty. This gift was also given to me. That gift will always burn inside me, and I will never forget where I came from or how poverty made me feel. As I look back, a driving factor that I held inside myself was that I never wanted to go inside that dumpster again. I am so grateful for my experience of poverty because it has fueled my grit.

A New Mindset Sets In

My wife and I opened two multimillion-dollar optometry practices in the Dallas area and have been practicing optometrists since 2006. The first ten years, we had a wonderful, thriving income as eye doctors and worked inside our practice five days a week with a sixth day of administration. We also became parents to my energetic baby daughter Athena.

Over time, we were not being challenged mentally and were not growing. The grit, determination, and our life purpose were not being satisfied, and there was an empty hole of fulfillment. I had minimal social impact in this world. I thought that if I were to die, I would not be remembered as I would like to be remembered. Something had to change. There had to be more to life.

My wife and I were in search of a new mindset. We were thinking too small. We had all the resources, but in our eyes, our impact in this world was not fulfilling us. We started attending educational, inspirational, and motivational seminars.

These seminars and the relationships I formed were another turning point in my life and mindset.

What Have I Learned?

Hoa and I found a way to massively expand our impact. We formed an apartment complex investing company with which families can invest and receive purely passive, residual income on a monthly basis without the families performing any work. In a year and a half, our apartment investing company exploded, and at the end of 2021, with our partners, we owned over $300 million in assets while practicing once a week in our eye care practices.

I gained time freedom, financial freedom, and most of all, a completely different mindset—a mindset of giving, developing a consistent prayer practice, and expanding my vision. I started nurturing great relationships, practicing non-inflammatory eating, and creating a legacy for my community, staff, and family. Today, my days outside my eye care practice are spent in apartment investing opportunities, finding ways to give back to the community, and creating memories with my family. In the past two years, my quality of life has dramatically changed, my heart is more fulfilled, and I believe I am creating more of an impact by helping more people.

I owe everything to this great country. Being an immigrant, I never felt I was a victim. I always had a victor mentality. I owe my success to the wonderful people that gave me an opportunity and to my grit instilled in me when I was young. The rest I learned along the way.

The garbage goldmine of sweets might be where I started my life's journey, but where I am today is sweeter than I could have ever imagined. If all my wealth was lost or taken away, my wealth of knowledge would help me make it all back. The character, mindset, and values I have built along the way will forever keep me fulfilled and in gratitude for all that life has to offer. Poverty will always be my gift, and that gift will never be forgotten.

Dr. Jaime Gonzalez enjoys educating investors, business owners, and doctors regarding passive, residual income opportunities through apartment investing to reduce taxes and create even more financial freedom for families. Connect with his team today to help you with your financial freedom journey.

jaime@eyepiecesinvesting.com
www.PassiveWealth23.com

Tweetable: Grit, meaningful relationships, gratitude, extreme clarity, belief in a higher power, a strong enough purpose, contribution, and a healthy lifestyle have made me successful in life and in my career.

LAURA THOMPSON

A Global Citizen's Labyrinth of Life
The Journey That Led to
Compassionate Leadership

Laura Thompson is known as an award-winning author, a conscious leadership coach, a social impact advisor to CEOs of global companies, NGOs, and nonprofits, a board director, and a humanitarian. Through her coaching and advisory services, she co-strategizes with her clients' sustainable solutions.

Education, Travel, and Cultural Diversity

During my formative years, I lived in different states in the USA, mostly on the Eastern seaboard from Massachusetts to Florida. In middle school, reading Charles Dickens' *A Tale of Two Cities*, set in London and Paris around the French Revolution, ignited my inner revolutionary spirit with a desire to explore humanity. After Simmons University in Boston and a year abroad at the Sorbonne in Paris, my life began as an American expat traversing seven countries across three different continents. Living and working abroad educated me on cultural diversity and appreciation long before embracing diversity, equity, and inclusion in the workplace became prevalent.

After a divorce in Geneva, Switzerland, I worked globally in public relations, focusing on strategic communications for Fortune 500 companies. That new chapter in my life was transatlantic between my two favorite cities—Paris and New York—with a passionate lover before I eventually settled down in Manhattan as a single woman and became an executive coach. Or perhaps I haven't settled down and I will soon be off living between two cities again.

Evolution and Expansion

Ever since I was a child, my universe has been reorienting, causing me to continuously adapt to my new circumstances. Sometimes the circumstances were external disruptions beyond my control like the death of my father from leukemia when I was eight years old. Sometimes the circumstances were internal eruptions led by my soul's need for adventure and transformation. I must admit, when my daddy died, the first thought that traversed my young mind was, "Life is short. Enjoy it." And, I have pretty much lived my life taking the road less traveled. It has been a roller coaster ride with highs and lows, depending on whether I followed my heart's wisdom merged with my rational brain or made fear-based choices caused by the negative side of pride. My soul thinks big while my ego plays small—an eternal battle many of us fight.

Fear blocks us all from time to time. I created a mantra for an Egyptian friend from Alexandria overcoming thyroid cancer: "Focus on faith over fear." She was scared of the cancer metastasizing; this simple phrase gave her hope. I passed on the mantra to a colleague who had lost their job during the pandemic and was looking for a new position. I used it when I decided to reinvent myself rather than stay stuck in a rut. But more importantly, I have tried to remain mindful and make love-based choices versus fear-based choices. Occasionally, this has involved my heart and ego duking it out for ten rounds in the boxing ring with a lot of sweat and tears until my heart won. One of my life's lessons has been to learn to follow my heart's wisdom. I play big by having the courage to take that first step in the direction of my true north.

One morning, I was talking with a journalist friend of mine. I told her how a dear college friend and international businesswoman, Tracy Nickl once remarked, "Every time your family starts to understand you, you change." My journalist friend then wryly commented, "Did your family ever understand you?" Both conversations caused laughter to erupt in our bellies. People consistently comment on how they love the sound of my laughter which compels everyone around to laugh even more.

Having a sense of humor and a desire to have fun despite the curve balls thrown at you in life is a choice. Life is short. Enjoy it. Other ways to deal with harsh circumstances in life are exercise, entertainment, spicy food, love and blissful orgasms, changing one's environment, or even flying in a plane and looking up at the stars to gain a higher perspective. There are many strategies one can engage in to overcome change, uncertainty, and adversity while keeping the faith and daring to dream big.

Open to New Experiences and Exploration

I was single, married, and then divorced. I went from speaking one language to being multilingual. I went from living as an American citizen to being a global citizen. I dated a Christian, a Jew, and a Muslim consecutively. I aligned myself with Catholicism, Zen Buddhism, and world interfaith harmony. I progressed from follower to leader to advocate for humanitarian causes. Dare I add, I might have shifted from heterosexuality to bisexuality. My sexual identity remains a mystery and may be linked to my soul memory of past lives with a couple of individuals. It could also signify that I have achieved a balance of my inner divine feminine and inner divine masculine based on self-love, self-compassion, and self-acceptance. This new experience turned my world upside down, but I learned to accept this part of myself, and my compassion for the LGBTQIA+ community expanded.

We are all multi-faceted human beings. It would be nice to celebrate all the things that we are rather than practicing limited thinking and putting people in boxes. *It's time to embrace our whole selves, respect human dignity, lead with compassion, and improve unity in global diversity.*

My contrasting cycles and circles of existence have allowed me to relate to people from different walks of life all over the world with empathy and compassion. This has proved beneficial to building an enriching personal and professional global network. I have friendships around the world for which I am grateful.

For some, my self-portrait might be confusing. When my story comes up, I have often remained quiet or chosen to portray only one aspect of myself—which aspect, depending on the context. In the artist world, I'm the author and poet. In finance, I'm an angel investor. In the nonprofit space, I'm an advocate for human rights. In academia, some Columbia Business School alumni call me a Renaissance woman. On LinkedIn, the term is multi-hyphenate. Many people are multi-talented. Accepting our multidimensionality requires stepping into our magnificence, being bold, and no longer hiding in the background or playing small. The world needs all of our unique contributions. It takes a village to thrive. This is the beauty of mankind's interconnectivity.

Resilience

The COVID-19 pandemic affected the whole world. When it hit, the agility, resilience, and ability to manage chaos I had built up through my life and work experiences kicked in. We often don't know what we are capable of until tested. Apparently, I respond to high-stakes crises with leadership, effective communications, and Zen-like calmness.

I advised two organizations to pivot to digitization—a non-governmental organization in Europe and a nonprofit in Asia. They helped hundreds of thousands of people worldwide overcome challenges and thrive through education. Digitization is now embedded in their business model. Being part of causes larger than myself makes my life more purposeful and meaningful.

Since we were often in lockdown, it was a good time to write. I contributed a chapter on *The Future of Work: How to Prepare for It* with co-authors from Harvard, Stanford, MIT, and INSEAD for the Center for Asia Leadership (CAL) which became a great resource for employees. Later, with the same leadership institute, I co-founded the CAL Coaching Council which after one year has received excellent feedback from senior decision makers in Asia.

For me, 2020 turned out to be a productive year, characterized by work for these two educational nonprofits and CAL, pro bono due to their economic hardships. Overall, the pandemic was a crucible moment which tested us all, causing us to examine our values, draw strength from within, co-create strategies, and engage in critical thinking to make decisions and overcome uncertainty and adversity. It's a choice to transform crises into opportunities. It took courage for all of us to adapt to our new world.

Compassionate Leadership

From 2020 to 2021, a startup US nonprofit focused on saving lives and alleviating human suffering gained traction through the work of philanthropist, humanitarian, businesswoman, and founder Mitzi Perdue. I am fortunate to have established a friendship with Mitzi as we served two years together as board members. I was on the board as both treasurer and secretary.

In September 2021, my universe spun out of control. I was lying on my bed with the room rotating like I had a severe hangover but without having had anything to drink. It was diagnosed as positional vertigo and became something I've now had to manage long-term.

One Friday, my cell phone rang. When I answered, it was my eldest brother Bob. He said, "Mom had six strokes. Her left side is paralyzed. She has less than a week to live. Don't bother to come. They won't let you see her because of COVID, but WhatsApp, FaceTime, or Zoom works." Although he relayed this message in a matter-of-fact way, I could hear the tears in his voice. I wondered if my body's recent extreme dizziness and nausea were picking up on my mother's condition, as I'm highly empathic.

I received another call a bit later. It was Mitzi as the board chair of the aforementioned humanitarian organization, checking in to go over items on the agenda for Monday's board meeting. She asked, "How are you?"

I replied, "Do you really want to know?"

She said, "Yes."

Normally, I keep my private life separate from business, but this woman had demonstrated to me that you can lead with compassion. I value her as an amazing and enlightened human being, so I opened up and told her my mom had days left to live.

Mitzi turned out to be my Earth angel and helped me in numerous ways to prepare for the loss of a parent. She shared her own touching, personal experiences of loss. Monday's board meeting came, and she mentioned to the board the condition of my mom. Again, this was a first for me—a leader showing humanity. It was wonderful to witness compassionate leadership in action. I had been coaching leaders to lead with values, show respect for others' human dignity, and communicate mindfully. I share the ideals of conscious and compassionate leadership because I saw firsthand as a former corporate employee how often they were lacking.

After the board meeting, I called the chaplain to facilitate a Zoom call with my mom, but she preferred I remember my mom in her angelic state and would only let me speak through the mobile held up to mom's ear. I heard my mom's staccato breathing and knew this was a sign she was near death. I expressed how much I loved her and assured her I would be happy in whatever I chose to be or do in life.

I ended the call. Then, I wrote up the board minutes. As I proofread the document, I felt my mom's presence standing behind me, as though she were reading what I wrote. And then I heard her say, "You're doing interesting work."

Seconds later, that fateful day, I sent the minutes to the board chair for her review at the exact time my mother died. To me, this was Mom's message that confirmed life exists between worlds beyond our concept of time, space, and dimension. The labyrinth of life expanded from an Earthly existence to one of other worlds where life-after-life and life-between-lives exist.

Later, on Zoom with the chaplain and the two 24/7 nurses who cared for my mom during her decline, I mentioned my gratitude. They told me they were touched by my stories and my love for my mom. We all learned and grew together. We walked the talk, practicing loving kindness and compassion centering on Mom's human dignity until her final hours.

I learned some people are blessings in your life, like Mitzi, my brother Bob, and my brother Mark. They were there during some of my darkest hours. Others are there for you to learn lessons and practice forgiveness. Everyone plays a role in our lives, providing learning and growth opportunities so we evolve into higher states of awareness, consciousness, compassion, and love. Let's embrace becoming more conscious human beings, aware of ourselves, others, and our environment. Through this stratagem, we can be our best selves, creating a network of harmonious relationships.

Everyone's journey is unique. I have dared to consistently leave my comfort zone and step through countless thresholds spiraling upwards, downwards, and sideways. With great conviction, love-based choices were the true north on my compass, while my values of love, forgiveness, joy, and gratitude represented the north, east, south, and west positions. Curiosity, bravery, and open-mindedness nudged my progression onwards toward evolution and expansion.

I am grateful for all the people who have touched my life and caused me to continuously learn and grow, be my best self, vibrate at my highest, and live life with joyful energy. I appreciate all who have acted as catalysts for me to share my insightful messages through my writing, coaching, and strategic advising for nonprofit and for-profit organizations worldwide.

What are you going to do to spread your wings?

Connect with author, coach, and senior advisor Laura Thompson, MA, for her coaching and advisory services for individuals, groups, and companies. She specializes in conscious leadership development, strategic communications, creative foresight thinking, and social impact strategies.

IG: Laura.Thompson888 | LinkedIn: LauraThompson888 | laurathompson.world

Tweetable: It's time to embrace our whole selves, respect human dignity, lead with compassion, and improve unity in global diversity.

IMRE SZENTTORNYAY

You Had Me at Howdy!

Imre Szenttornyay is founder and former chief revenue officer of CieloIT, one of the fastest-growing private companies in the US, featured on the Inc 500 and MSP 500 lists 2018-2022. Imre pioneered the SmartFranchise™ system with partners, allowing multi-unit franchise owners to scale operations more profitably. Imre now scoops hope and happiness in every pint of amazing ice cream he serves as a multi-unit franchisee developer of Howdy Homemade Ice Cream.

Mister Softee! Run

When I close my eyes, I can still hear the Mister Softee ice cream truck jingle growing louder from around the corner of Vietor Avenue and Elmhurst Avenue in Queens, New York.

It's the summer of 1980, and I am just shy of turning eight years old. Between these six-story brownstone apartments, it feels like a brick oven with the heat of the day radiating off the buildings and the concrete jungle floor. I spot Mister Softee's iconic blue and white step van and start yelling as loud as possible up to my immigrant mother in apartment 4F, "Mom, Mom, Mama … throw me some money!"

I luck out this time. She hears my cries of youthful desperation. It's a timing issue because Mister Softee waits for no one. "Here, Hijo! Buy me an orange creamsicle," my immigrant mother from Nicaragua responds in her Latina accent as a couple of quarters wrapped in a dollar bill fall from the sky like manna from heaven. And so it begins, the chase! Mister Softee never ever stops in the middle of the street; instead, the driver seems to take sadistic pleasure from watching a gaggle of children pursuing his truck down the road.

So, I run. Fast.

Life. It's Complicated.

Never quit. If you want something bad enough, you chase it down the street for as long, and as fast as your little legs can take you.

My reward that early summer evening? A bomb pop. At that time, I thought this was as good as it was ever going to get for an only child born to a Hungarian father who grew up in Communist Hungary, surviving the Hungarian Revolution and Soviet Invasion of 1956, and a Nicaraguan mother whose father was from India and who barely knew the American language.

My father, Csaba Zsolt, passed away on October 17, 2017. He had two brothers and one sister. My mother, Norma Indrani, passed away on August 3, 1986, at age 49 after a 10-year battle with cancer. She was one of 14 children, so I have many cousins—more than I can count, have met, or will ever have the pleasure of meeting.

I have been blessed to be married for 25 years to Cindy Ann. And, I have had the delight of raising four exceptional children with her: our two youngest sons, Sebestyen and Ben, and our two oldest twins, both of whom have had special needs since being born severely premature at 24 weeks: Elek and Gyorgi, now 23-year-old adults living with intellectual and developmental disabilities.

In early 2022, I looked around my study, and I gazed upon the black and white photos of myself as a child with my father. One picture was of me at around two years old in a cardboard box. My dad was holding me and we both had a big smile on our faces. Another picture was of one-year-old me with Dad balancing me on his shoulders while wading in a pool, also with a big smile on both our faces. There was another picture of me at around six months old with him holding me in his arms close to his chest, with yet another big smile on his face and an even bigger smile on mine, feeling so safe and secure.

The simplicity of life and my childhood joy were captured in these moments. The proverbial innocence of youth. Could it be true that ignorance is bliss? I wondered when and why I had lost my smile along the way. Where did it go? Or is life just complicated?

The Paradox of Fatherhood

Fatherhood changes a man completely.

When life threw me some curveballs early in my thirties and things didn't go exactly the way I planned (i.e., unemployment, bankruptcy, twins born at 24 weeks, and a marriage on the rocks), I just wanted to hide in my closet in the fetal position. I would be lying if I didn't tell you that I had thoughts of suicide going through my tormented mind. For me, it seemed like the easy way out and selfish at the same time. I felt like an absolute failure with no way to dig myself out of a premature grave. Then,

God Himself coaxed me out of the closet when I heard my newborn baby crying.

I sat there holding and staring down at this little human being that was totally dependent on me for survival. I struggled to enjoy fatherhood as the joy was overshadowed by the responsibility of taking care of two special needs children. I felt robbed, hijacked even, by life dealing me a cruel hand. My firstborns were supposed to bring me joy. Instead, the stress was testing me and the mettle of my marriage. I grieved.

Then, all of a sudden, everything seemed okay. Fatherhood changed my heart when I saw that tiny smile of my newborn child, and I transformed from being selfish to selfless. When God wishes to send you a gift in life, he often wraps it in a problem. In this case, my challenge was accepting the circumstances and finding the strength to care for my premature twins. I have learned that the good and bad in life tend to run on parallel tracks, and if you allow them to work together, they take you on a journey that results in achievement, pride, inspiration, and a new understanding of unconditional love. When my twins came, I learned how to become a better person.

Learning from Regret

Tolerance teaches us to accept other people for who they are, differences and all, rather than who we wish them to be.

If I would have understood this earlier in life, it would have saved me some heartaches and regret.

I regret being embarrassed about my parents growing up. Culturally, my family was "different" from my friends in public school. As an adult, I realized that we were all immigrants in my old neighborhood in Queens. I distanced myself from my parents to "fit in" rather than embrace who we were and build a much deeper relationship with my mother and father.

I regret not learning more about my parents' history, their individual stories, and what shaped them. I regret not accepting them for who they were. I am disappointed I wasted so much time shaping them into parents I thought they needed to be. I didn't appreciate diversity back then. I felt enormous pressure from what I perceived as social norms, which in hindsight, were likely made up in my head and never existed in reality.

In the same way, I regret spending so much time trying to fix my children. I spent years needlessly working on my son Elek and my daughter Gyorgi.

The reality is, the way I saw them was broken. I had allowed my heart to become hardened and calloused and found myself routinely working on getting them to fit into my perceived social norms rather than allowing them to blossom in their own right.

Regret lives on the left side of the ledger of life. If you just focus on it, you will end up only seeing red. For life to be balanced, debits and credits must be equal. The lesson of regret is that it facilitated positive change in my life. I started to allow myself to witness my twin's true purpose in this world—to soften the hearts of judgmental people, like me—and appreciate them for who they were, not who I wished them to become. As my understanding grew, my relationship with all people began to change.

Discovering My Why
Your life has a purpose. Don't waste it!

God led me down a path of discovering my "ikigai." In the Japanese language, the concept of retirement doesn't really exist. Rather, the Japanese use the word ikigai to describe a way or purpose for living. Ikigai, your reason for being, is the intersection of: 1) what you love, 2) what you are good at, 3) what earns you money, and most importantly, 4) what the world needs. You can find your passion, profession, vocation, and mission in life at the crossroads of these four cornerstone tenants.

I spent the last 30 years in three of these four quadrants. I loved the technology industry, I was good at business development, and I founded a successful company that made the Inc 500 list four times in a row.

I was passionate about my career, and I enjoyed a great profession. I found a vocation that put my sons through private school and college, went on awesome family vacations, and paid for the best caregivers I could find for my special needs twins.

Even so, I simply wasn't happy. The world didn't need another IT company. Despite being able to contribute financially to society through nonprofits and political campaigns, I found myself struggling and seeking something I could do that would contribute more.

Then, I met founder Tom Landis from Howdy Homemade Ice Cream in his relentless pursuit to create more jobs for people with developmental disabilities using the power of their smiles and ice cream.

Howdy Homemade is all about amazing ice cream served by amazing people. Howdy Homemade is a franchise concept that is committed to providing job opportunities and empowering people with developmental disabilities because we are more alike than different. It's ice cream for dreamers and every pint matters!

Finally, when I heard about this mission, I felt a calling. This was an opportunity for personal growth and what the world needs more of! I found my purpose, a reason for being. My ikigai is to fight for a population that has been marginalized for far too long by creating jobs for them, starting with the 3.1 million Texans living with intellectual and developmental disabilities like my twins: Elek and Gyorgi. And the ice cream is damn good!

Always Get the Extra Scoop!

Time is nonrefundable. Always get the extra scoop!

My son Sebestyen and I have followed our hearts by investing in Howdy Homemade and have secured the franchise development rights for all of West Texas. As a recent founder of Howdy West Texas, LLC, I have never been more afraid and excited at the same time. But, if the last 30 years of my life have taught me anything, it is to do the right things, for the right reasons and God will pour out His abundance of love, grace, and support for you.

It has been said, luck is what happens when preparation meets opportunity. I guess luck is on my side, as I have spent the better part of my life as an entrepreneur waiting for an investment that would feed my soul and not just the bottom line.

God has always blessed our family with everything we need and has always challenged us to rely on Him with unrequited faith. Max Lucado said, "God loves you just the way you are, but He refuses to leave you that way." When I think back on all of the challenges which I thought God allowed to happen to me, I see they were opportunities for refinement.

Losing close friends and family members, early years in the neonatal intensive care unit, family health challenges such as my wife's battle with cancer, my heart attack and surviving COVID in the same month, overcoming poverty growing up, a failed startup in 2000, bankruptcy during the financial crisis of 2007—these were simply precursors to all the success and blessings of abundance that God had in store for me today! Without the difficult times, I would not and could not appreciate all that He has shared with me now.

Howdy West Texas!

Howdy Homemade is a small company with big plans. We see the opportunity to create jobs inside and outside of our industry for adults with intellectual and developmental disabilities. We are the change. At Howdy West Texas, we have plans to train over 100 ready adults to make ice cream and donate a percentage of ice cream sale proceeds back to High Point Village, a community for adults with intellectual and developmental disabilities that allows them to live, learn, work, and worship. I have witnessed firsthand how this population is overlooked and underserved, and feel that, as a whole, we need to retrain ourselves about how we perceive those with disabilities. They are not broken… our perception is.

We have to change the way we see each other as human beings. We need to experience what's possible with this population of God's children and what lessons they have to offer and teach us.

Now, when I tour our Howdy Homemade Ice Cream shops and look into the eyes of Coleman, Kalin, Lindsey, Brandt, Elek, Gyorgi, and the rest of our "heroes" who welcome everyone visiting the shop with a larger than life smile, and an emphatic "Howdy!", I pause to thank God for helping me find my purpose in this world. I am grateful that I never quit. I now have the privilege of scooping up hope and happiness in every pint we serve our patrons. And, I find myself smiling again. You had me at howdy!

To learn more about becoming an investor or franchise development partner of Howdy Homemade Ice Cream and to join a social revolution that is making amazing ice cream served by amazing people while creating jobs for individuals with IDDs, email Imre Szenttornyay at howdy@howdywesttexas.com.

Tweetable: Search for purpose to feed your soul and find your smile. #YouHadMeAtHowdy

ALAN STEWART

Earning a Seat at the Table
While Creating Legacy

Alan Stewart is a Christian, family man, business leader, and 20-year corporate consulting executive turned multifamily real estate syndicator and investor of over 3,400 units. Alan's mission is to help busy professionals and high net worth investors create their own legacies through strategic real estate investment.

Work Hard and Climb the Corporate Ladder

I'm a life-long learner and love to grow. I studied hard, was a very involved student leader, and graduated with engineering honors from Texas A&M University. I joined Accenture right out of school and learned from so many smart, driven colleagues and clients for almost a decade. I worked hard to deliver client value first as an entry-level analyst, and over time, took on additional responsibility and was promoted several times to solution architect and a project manager of large teams. I continued my consulting career at North Highland where I took on more responsibility for very large projects and became an executive.

I finished my 20-year corporate career as a managing partner at Gartner Consulting with responsibility for the Greater Texas portfolio of manufacturing, energy, and utilities industry verticals.

In a nutshell, I did what everyone told me to do: studied hard, got good grades, got a good job, and then worked hard every day, focused on solving problems, moving the ball forward, and climbing the corporate ladder.

"Alan, That's Crazy!"

My coworkers and friends told me I was crazy! They said, "Don't liquidate your 401k and pay the tax. . . . You're smarter than that. Don't you know better?"

Well, that's exactly what I did in 2012, and that was the second-best financial decision I've ever made. The best financial decision I've ever made was investing in my financial education to expand my mindset.

Turns out, I've been told I'm crazy several times now. I've come to embrace it. I've found that it tells me I'm on the right track of thinking bigger, growing, and achieving bigger goals in the process.

In 2001, three years into my consulting career, I saw Robert Kiyosaki, author of *Rich Dad Poor Dad*, speak at a conference in Dallas for the first time. Robert talked about the benefits of investing in rental real estate. He said instead of trading time working for money to pay bills, you need to buy income-producing assets that create cash flow to pay your bills for you. The light bulb went off for me.

This was the beginning of what I call my real financial education, the type of pragmatic financial education not typically taught in schools. I started thinking bigger. My mindset had changed forever. I began attending more investing conferences and searching for a way to get started.

Make a Decision and Take Action

I took a turn at single-family wholesaling for several years. I learned a lot, had some success, and made several mistakes, but I wasn't getting the leverage of time and money I was looking for—like Robert Kiyosaki described with rental real estate. Ultimately, I found a mentor in 2012 who introduced me to multifamily (apartments) syndicating and investing.

Through multifamily syndication, I finally found the vehicle for time and money leverage I was looking for.

This was another big light bulb that went off for me. I used to think some rich guy or a big corporation owned apartment buildings, but it turns out, many are owned by people like you and me that put deals together and make it happen. I made a decision to invest in my financial education and a mentor to leverage his experience to help me go faster with less risk.

Then the most important thing happened; I started taking action—consistent, small actions every day towards my goals.

It took me six years of early mornings, late nights, and weekends, but my team built a multifamily portfolio of over 3,300 units across 16 properties which I syndicated or invested in, and I retired from my 20-year corporate consulting career.

Don't A-Class Deals Have Lower Returns?

Part of thinking bigger often means being a contrarian. Common knowledge, or what the "masses" think, is not always correct. My first eight years in multifamily investing were focused on class B and C value-add apartment deals. Some had a lot of "hair" on them and were really difficult. But, we bought and operated them right, and they turned out to be great investment successes.

All along, my fellow multifamily investors were doing the same type of B and C-class deals. We'd all say (including me), "We don't buy A-class (newer and nicer) multifamily assets. . . . That's what big institutions buy, and the returns aren't as good, and they cost too much. We're the smarter people buying the older assets that have more value-add to them with higher returns." That's what I thought at the time.

Over the last several years, I have continued expanding my mindset and thinking bigger. As capitalization rates have compressed between asset classes, I've come to realize that A-class multifamily properties can actually have better risk-adjusted returns than B and C-class assets. I started learning more about investing in newer and nicer properties and started talking about the potential. Typically, the response I'd get was, "Oh, with class A deals can you get any good returns?" Or "Aren't they too expensive?"

As I expanded my thinking, I finally decided, *I'm going to stop just talking about it and start doing it.* In 2021, my partners and I bought my first true A-class, 2016-built, multifamily property located in Uptown Dallas.

It wasn't easy. When I was working on the deal, it was so much bigger, so much newer, so much nicer than anything I had done before. The brokers knew me as a B and C apartment buyer, not an A-class buyer.

Even so, my partners and I decided to go all in to make it happen. We told the brokers we were buying the property and that there was no need to waste time continuing to market it to other prospective buyers. At first, I think the brokers thought we were kidding. We were not kidding. We were 100% focused on what the sellers' needs were and how we were the solution. We told the broker we'd be straight with them and wanted the chance to prove we would be a great buyer and execute well.

Before we even made an offer on the property, the team was together for dinner in early May. I said, "Pull out your phones." I did some quick calculations on dates and said, "I think we'll have it closed on July 28. Let's put this date on the calendar and plan a dinner in celebration of successfully closing the deal."

We put it out there, and when it was all said and done, we ended up closing our A-class property within three days of July 28. On August 2, we closed and had our celebration dinner. It's amazing the power of thinking big and putting your intentions out there!

I'll Never Have Dinner with a Celebrity

I'm a big fan of Darren Hardy, his book *The Compound Effect*, and all of his training courses including *Insane Productivity*, *Business Masterclass*, and most recently *The Hero's Journey*. So, of course, I thought it would be an honor to meet Darren Hardy, but I never thought it would be possible. I simply put him in the bucket of people I thought weren't accessible to me.

Legendary executive recruiter Bob Beaudine shares an idea in his book *The Power of Who*. Bob describes that you already know everyone you need to know. Your friends know lots of people who know lots of other people. You just need to ask your good friends who they know and ask for an introduction.

My good friend and mentor Kyle Wilson (who is also the publisher of this book) has worked with lots of extraordinary people including bestselling author and speaker Denis Waitley. Kyle organized a three-day retreat to honor Denis Waitley at his home in San Diego for a small group of fellow Inner Circle mastermind members. When Kyle offered me a chance to attend, I said yes without hesitation.

I mean, wow! Of course I would say yes to an opportunity to spend three days with Denis and his family and soak up all of the wisdom from an 88-year-old, simply amazing person.

The first night at dinner, to my surprise, Kyle had invited Darren Hardy, Brian Tracy, John Assaraf, and their wives to join us to honor Denis. All I can say is, that experience was one of the richest in my life, and I learned so much from everyone at the table.

It never occurred to me that I could ever have dinner with Darren AND his wife Georgia, or Denis Waitley, or any other famous person. Yet, there I was. My mindset expanded through this experience. Now I have a sense of certainty that I can really meet and connect with pretty much anyone in the world. All I need to do is decide who I want to connect with and then start asking my friends who they know. If done the right way for the right reasons, over time, I can make the connection happen.

Connect the Dots

Once I retired from my corporate career, I initially started to get complacent. I had achieved the big goal of getting out of the rat race that I used to think was impossible.

I am thinking bigger now, much bigger. Whereas I used to never even think about being a multifamily real estate investor, and whereas more recently, I never thought about buying newer and nicer A-class apartment buildings, now I intend to continue growing my businesses and become an institutional player. My mindset is no longer, *Oh, that's something I could never do.* Now it's, *Why not just decide, sit down, and figure out how to connect the dots to make it happen.* Consistent daily actions compounded over time make it happen.

The time is now, I'm doubling down and I'm just getting started!

Creating Legacy

Our Catholic faith has always been a central part of our family life and has brought us so many blessings of friends, peace, love, and mercy, especially when we needed it most.

As of this writing, my wife and I have been married for over 26 years and have two adult children we love very much.

My family is very important to me, and my love for them drives me to learn, grow, and expand my mindset so I may be a good leader and an example of the reality that anything is possible with hard work, focus, and consistent action over time.

I view myself as a provider and want to create a great lifestyle for my family full of rich experiences. I would love to create generational family traditions much like Mitzi Perdue—widow of poultry magnate Frank Perdue, daughter of Sheraton Hotels cofounder Ernest Henderson, and business leader. I want to provide annual family trips that everyone looks forward to. I want to provide formal and practical education for my kids and eventually their kids.

I want to set an example that is worthy of my kids and others I influence. I have plenty of fears and challenges to overcome just like everyone else. At the same time, I feel like I need to step up, persevere, and show that big challenges can be overcome along the way to achieving big goals.

Be a Steward and Inspire Others

While I was in the middle of trying to find a way out of the corporate rat race, I used to jokingly (but always somewhat seriously) tell my wife that we could always move to Hawaii—I could work at Costco and we'd just live simply. Fast forward to today, I could always put the brakes on and live a life of ease, but I want to be a good steward of the time, talents, and treasure God has given me by inspiring and making a positive impact on others.

I want to give back by helping people expand their mindset to one of growth and abundance and by providing quality investment opportunities to maximize that growth financially. I love to continually learn and grow and have witnessed firsthand that proximity to big thinkers is powerful. You can't help but expand your mindset and think bigger when you are around successful people who have already accomplished more than you previously thought possible, especially when they continually challenge you to take it to the next level.

As Jim Rohn would say, it is who you become in the process. I intend to continue to earn my seat at the table and to positively impact my family and all those I influence by the person I'm becoming in the process.

I have my intentions set on continuing to build my businesses and my real estate investment portfolio to create a legacy for my family, and further, provide quality investment opportunities that create a path for busy professionals and high net worth investors to create their own family legacies.

To learn more about real-life multifamily investing, visit AlanStewart.com. To apply to be a part of upcoming passive income investment opportunities and start your journey to financial freedom, contact Alan at info@alanstewart.com or visit AlanStewart.com.

Tweetable: Expand your mindset, think big, decide, take action, and show that big challenges can be overcome along the way to achieving big goals.

CHRIS GRONKOWSKI

From the NFL to *Shark Tank* as the Founder of Ice Shaker

Chris Gronkowski played four years in the NFL along with his three brothers, Rob, Dan, and Glenn. Chris graduated from the University of Arizona and after leaving the NFL appeared on Shark Tank in 2017. He left the Tank with a deal with Alex Rodriguez and Mark Cuban for his company Ice Shaker. Chris is from Buffalo, NY, and now lives in Southlake, TX, with his wife Brittany and three kids.

Growing Up in Buffalo with Four Competitive Brothers

My parents raised five boys. Growing up, they said, "You're not gonna sit around playing video games and watching TV. Get outside and get rid of some energy."

In Buffalo, we lived in this awesome neighborhood. Every couple of houses there was another kid our age. We had that house where everyone comes over, and we would make up games in the backyard and play against each other. Every sport you can imagine, we competed in. I believe that bred competition among us brothers and the neighborhood kids.

As we got older, we started playing competitive sports in leagues, mostly hockey, baseball, and football.

My dad started a fitness equipment company from scratch and worked long hours. My mom was in charge of getting all five of us to school and sports events. Five boys. We all played multiple sports for multiple teams and were on travel teams. I still don't know how she got all of us to all our practices. She physically could not bring us all to every practice and game. Plus, we were going to church and other functions too. She had to bring in coaches, friends, and family in other neighborhoods. Thinking back on it, she did all that without a cell phone.

My mom cooked every meal and made all our school lunches. If we all behaved, she would reward us once a month with the $1.99 Out of Your Mind Grand Slam Breakfast at Denny's. There were multiple times when we were good for the whole month, and halfway to Denny's, we were all fighting in the back of the car, so she'd turn right back around and we'd have to eat at home!

I had my mom on my podcast for a Mother's Day episode, and I told her, "Wow, the more kids I have, the more impressed I am with you, Mom!"

Ivy League or Football Scholarship

My dad played college football, and at one point, he had a Bill's contract hanging on the wall at home. He was a good player but then got injured.

All five of us brothers grew up wanting to go to college and play pro sports, and all of us did.

I wanted to play college football but wanted to make sure I also got a good education so I could become a CPA and make good money if pro sports didn't work out.

I committed first to the University of Pennsylvania. My dad was excited. I would be the first Ivy League son in the family. We wouldn't just be the family of dumb jocks. And I was the one to prove it.

At the last minute, I ended up getting a full scholarship offer to the University of Maryland. I wanted to play at the highest level, but at the same time, I also didn't want to pay for college. At the University of Pennsylvania, I would probably graduate with $200,000 in debt. So, two weeks before the summer ended, I accepted a full D1 scholarship to Maryland.

That scholarship really came about because a bunch of their players were about to go on academic probation and some of the incoming players didn't make it because of grades. So they gave it to the guy who had good grades that could come in and bump up the GPA for the football team a little bit. I tell people all the time, I got the first athletic college scholarship by having good academics.

I ended up transferring to the University of Arizona where my younger but much bigger brother Rob had also decided to go play. He was a coveted 4-star recruit. I was just hoping to make the team. Since I was a transfer, I had to sit out a year. So, that first year, I played baseball, and after two years, I went full-time in football.

I never thought I'd make it to the pro level, but I got my chance.

NFL for Four Years

I was undrafted. I was fortunate to have an agent believe in me and sponsor me to train for several months in Miami for the NFL Combine. That led to an opportunity to try out for the Dallas Cowboys. My wife is from Buffalo, but her dad got transferred to Dallas-Fort Worth six years before I went to the Cowboys, and everyone fell in love with the area.

I made the team. I hoped I would be playing for the Cowboys forever. It lasted a season before I started bouncing around to other teams.

I made it four seasons in the NFL, which locked in some nice benefits. After I retired, we came back to the Dallas area. We love it here. It's a great business environment and having family around is really important.

Life After the NFL That Led to *Shark Tank*

I wasn't rich by any stretch, but I had a pension and a nice 401K built up (the NFL offers a nice double match). Plus, you get severance pay and healthcare benefits. So, I had a good chunk of money without debt. I had gone to school and only had to pay for the one semester. At age 26, I was leaving the NFL far ahead of everyone else my age.

I had this money that I could invest into whatever I wanted to. I first went into business with my wife. She had started a business and Etsy shop while I was playing with Denver so she could work from home.

She did really well. I helped her, and we ended up making more money than when I was playing in the NFL. It was a good transition for me.

But having grown up in fitness and having played football my whole life, making wedding gifts wasn't really me. After five years, I thought of the idea for Ice Shaker. I could go to the gym, and I could call it work by making product videos at the gym. It was awesome. I thought, *Let's go all in and see where it goes. Let's start this as a side hustle. Let's see if it gets to a place where we can make this a full-time thing.*

Lessons from the Tank

I remembered getting an email in 2012 when I was with the Broncos that said ABC's *Shark Tank* was looking for current or former NFL players to pitch them. Four and a half years later, I emailed back. That was the spark that got me to pitch the Sharks.

Being on *Shark Tank* was huge for us. I first reached out to them about three months into the company's life. We only had $20k in sales, but at least I had proof of concept. They asked me to submit a video. They liked it and said I had three months before we would film and I should get ready. My focus became to get as much revenue as I could so I could get the best valuation possible.

When I went on the show, we had around $80k in sales, and I was asking for $100k for 10% of the company.

After I did the initial pitch, I had all my brothers come on. They brought a lot of energy, and we had fun with the Sharks.

One of the big lessons is to just show up with confidence, have fun, and know what you're talking about!

I watched every episode. I wrote down every question they ever asked. I felt like I was best friends with every single Shark. So, when I walked out there, instead of being nervous, I could say, "Hey, I feel like I know you guys."

I ended up getting a deal with Mark Cuban and Alex Rodriguez. Later, my brother Rob bought Alex's position.

Right away, with their help, I was able to get Ice Shaker into Vitamin Shop, Lifetime Fitness, and GNC, as well as appear on *QVC*, *Good Morning America*, and many other outlets. Most recently, Ice Shaker went into 1,900 Walmarts.

Starting, Growing, and Scaling a Business

I love a shaker bottle. That was what I would use all day when I could. But it wasn't perfect. I started on the journey to create something that could blend powders and keep your drink cold. So, I took what I loved from shaker bottles and replaced what I didn't love. I added insulated, kitchen grade premium stainless steel to keep drinks cold or hot. I loved the easy-open pop top. I wanted a handle on it as well so it was easy to carry. I took all my favorite things and put them into one cup.

Through my wife's business, I've been able to incorporate the ability to customize Ice Shakers and do bulk orders fast for customers.

I've had to learn that you cannot conquer the entire market overnight. You can't just throw money at it. Most of your success will come from relationships and figuring things out.

I have a family, a wife, and kids, so working a hundred hours a week doesn't work for me anymore. That forced me to put people and processes in place, which takes time!

Learning from My Dad

My dad has 32 years in the fitness industry, and over that time, he has built 17 retail stores. He wanted to be a mentor to me in sports and business. At first, I didn't listen. It took time for me to realize the value of his wisdom. When the pandemic hit, things slowed down. There were no processes in place. There was no budget. I could only come in the store when half of my employees were there because of the new COVID restrictions and my kids at home. With the way things were, I realized I had better figure things out pretty quick.

It was time to figure out how to do this the right way and to build the team. I went back to my dad and said, "How'd you build your business to 200 employees? That's insane." At the time, I was trying to manage eight employees. I asked, "How'd you get there?"

My dad said, "I asked you from day one. What's your game plan? What's your budget? What's your forecast? How are you incentivizing people? Tell me that first, and I'll tell you how to fix it."

That's exactly where I was going wrong. First, there was no team. It was me making every decision and me with all the responsibilities. I thought that was how it was supposed to be because it was my business. Finally, when it couldn't be like that anymore, I was forced to delegate, which was one of my dad's keys from day one.

When I started to share the responsibility, I realized that people responded well. They felt like they were part of a team. They could make their own decisions. They loved it and they wanted more.

Next was figuring out how everyone could win. I had to start figuring that out with the whole team. We had a fulfillment team that wasn't feeling like they were winning when we made sales. They didn't have a piece of that pie or input on the goals we had set. We had to realign all the goals, and rather than just certain individuals, we had to incentivize everyone as a team.

Once we did that, I would walk in with a big sale, and everyone in the entire company was pumped. That's when I knew we had figured this thing out.

You can follow Chris Gronkowski on IG @chrisgronkowski and go to Iceshaker.com to order your own Ice Shaker. You can order from Chris and his wife's company at EverythingDecorated.com.

Tweetable: One of the big lessons is to show up with confidence, have fun, and know what you're talking about!

RANDY WILSON

How Robert Kiyosaki and Jim Rohn Changed My Life

Randy Wilson is a successful husband, father, entrepreneur, author, speaker, and results coach. His passion is helping others live the life of their dreams through financial education and personal development, which aren't taught in school.

Get Up, Go to Work, Do Your Job

It was a day just like all of the rest. I showed up to work, took my normal lap around the perimeter of the store, and checked in with my night grocery manager to see if there were any issues that needed to be handled immediately. After a quick conversation, I continued my lap around the store and greeting my team.

As I was covering my office manager's desk while she was on her break, I looked up, and in walked my supervisor. It was about 9 AM, and a visit this early wasn't normal. I greeted him, and we shared small talk. He then told me to finish covering the manager's break and we would connect afterward.

All kinds of thoughts stirred in my head: *What brought him into the store so early?*

We met down the back aisle of the store, near the dairy department. He was acting a little strange. We had a great relationship, and it was obvious to me that something was just not right. He looked me straight in the eye and said, "Let's go chat in your office." I knew something was really going on now.

I walked in first, and as I was approaching my chair, he closed the heavy door behind him which made the loudest BANG. My heart and my mind raced. *I think I'm about to get fired.*

He began to speak, and I focused on every word. He cut right to the chase: the company had decided to close my store. I had 30 days to liquidate my inventory and lock the doors for the last time.

I Thought I Had It All Figured Out

I was 30 years old and one of the youngest store managers for a regional grocery chain in Indiana. I was never good in school, but I had a great work ethic which propelled me quickly through the ranks of the company. I would work days, nights, weekends, holidays, through family functions, and kids' birthdays—it didn't matter. Whatever was needed to make my store succeed, I was willing to do.

I never questioned anything. I did what I was told, and up until that moment, I believed that was the best thing to do for my career.

But that morning with my supervisor, I began to question everything I had done. I realized that it didn't matter how hard I worked or how much time I put in. At the end of the day, I was just a "number" and the business owners were going to make decisions I had no control over which would impact my life and my family tremendously.

Realizing these facts for the first time was very uncomfortable. I was brought up to believe that you work hard for the same company your entire adult life, move up whenever you can, and be satisfied with being comfortable. My parents modeled this philosophy growing up, and up to this point, I had followed the plan exactly.

Now, I knew in my heart there had to be a better way.

As I look back, there have been a few moments and decisions that have completely changed my life. The unexpected visit from my supervisor was one. Going to the library soon after was another.

The Search Begins

As I mentioned earlier, I was never good in school. Being forced to read was one of my least favorite activities, so my being in a library seeking answers was ironic. I started there because it was the only place I could think of that possibly would have some of the answers I was looking for.

I didn't know where to begin. All I knew was I had to figure out how to get out of my JOB and start to take control of my life. My first thoughts were that I wanted to be wealthy. At that time, I really didn't even know what that word meant. None of my friends or family were wealthy, that I knew of, so I wasn't sure what I was even looking for. I went to the section that seemed to make the most sense—the personal finance section. As I was scanning the shelves, one book JUMPED out at me—Robert Kiyosaki's *Retire Young Retire Rich*. The title alone was exactly what I was looking for, so I immediately checked out the book and dove right in.

From the first page, I was learning things that I had never learned before such as mindset, assets vs liabilities, leverage, and the different quadrants of cash flow. I was completely blown away and frustrated that I had never heard any of this information in school or from anyone close to me. I began to question everything I had believed in terms of work and business and began seeking others that might be able to shed a little more light on how these ideas could actually be applied in my life.

I began reading and listening to as much as I could possibly find. It was as if my life had just started over. All because someone made the decision to take my store away from me, and all because soon after I decided to go to the library, I was exposed to a whole new reality of possibility that I had no idea even existed.

For the first time, I was excited and eager to learn all I could about both my financial and personal life. I was going to begin taking personal responsibility for the results I was getting in life. I decided that I was going to take the information and ideas that I was discovering and begin applying them. I wasn't exactly sure what the results were going to be, but I knew I was desperate to change my circumstances. It took a lot of faith to step out into the unknown, but I was sure that staying the same was not an option.

One big, scary move I decided to make was to leave my retail job. After my store was closed, I bounced around to a few different stores, working the same amount of hours, but without the same passion for the work. Knowing in my heart that I needed to move on, I took a job which gave me back more of my precious time. I used this time to study more and began applying what I was learning. Getting some good results led me to continue.

The Hidden Secret to My Success

Personal development was another fantastic thing that I discovered inside of that library book. Any success I've had can 100% be attributed to my introduction to personal development. Without it, I know I would not be where I am today. On page 131 of *Retire Young Retire Rich*, Kiyosaki talks about an audio program he used to help him escape being a corporate employee called *Lead the Field* by Earl Nightingale. Intrigued, I bought the CDs that same day.

This was when I was still working at my W-2 job with an hour commute each way six days per week. I took advantage of that time and played and replayed those CDs as often as I could, so much so that I wore through two different copies. The content I learned on those CDs completely changed my thinking and outlook. They were my first exposure to the personal development world, and I was hooked.

Earl's work then led me to discover Napoleon Hill and W. Clement Stone who were the creators of *Success Magazine*. Inside the pages of *Success*, I was introduced to Darren Hardy who led me to one of my personal favorite mentors, Jim Rohn. The words and wisdom that Jim Rohn shared have completely changed my life both personally and professionally. He shared nuggets of wisdom such as, "Work harder on yourself than you do on your job" and, "In order for things to change in your life, you have to change," and, "In order to have more, you must first become more."

The amount of wisdom he shares in his audio programs and books is tremendous, and these quotes are just a few of the highlights. Jim Rohn has had such a positive impact on me and my family that I know for a fact that I wouldn't be where I am today without him. I truly wish I could thank him personally. Unfortunately, I can't do that due to his passing in 2009. So, to carry on his legacy, I do my best every day to live through the wisdom he shared and to share that wisdom with as many people as possible in hopes it will positively impact their lives as it did mine.

My Dad Didn't Know

As I continued to study, I started to see some positive results. I was so excited. I decided to share the ideas and principles I had learned with my father. I idolized this man, so much so that almost everything I had done in my life ran through a filter of "What would my dad want me to do?" Discovering this wisdom from others actually made me frustrated that he hadn't shared these ideas and principles with me. It became clear in the beginning of my journey that applying what I was learning was going to make a huge difference in my results.

As I began to share, he was soaking the material up like a sponge. We'd go to lunch and talk for hours about a new personal development concept I'd discovered, business, or the economy. As much as I looked up to and loved my dad, we never had a very good relationship outside of talking about work and sports, so this was a lot of fun.

A few months later, he called me and said that he had some exciting things to show me. I invited him over because I was curious about what he was so excited about. When he got to my house, I could tell something was up. He looked like a little kid: excited, happy, and just beaming with positive energy. We sat down at the kitchen table, and he showed me a manila folder about an inch thick. He then opened it up and began to share with me different investment opportunities he had discovered. He ran me through the numbers of each opportunity. You could tell he had spent a lot of time on this by the amount of detailed notes. At that moment, I realized that the reason I hadn't been exposed to personal development and financial education was that my dad didn't know. No one had ever shared the wisdom with him until I had a few months before.

Unfortunately, six months later, he was diagnosed with cancer, and he passed quickly soon after. I'm glad I was able to share what I had learned with my dad before he died. Growing up, I worked very hard to get him to tell me he was proud of me. Looking back on that night in my kitchen, I believe he was proud of me for the discoveries I had made and the results I was getting.

Since his passing, I've continued on my journey learning, applying, pivoting, and moving forward. I love that I get to share this wisdom with others and help them discover new possibilities. I want to share what I've learned with as many people who will listen because I know that if it can help me and my father, it can help everyone.

It All Begins with Self Education

I've discovered that we all have infinite potential inside of us, and learning how to tap into that potential is key to designing a life of joy and happiness. I've learned through this process of personal development that the harder I work on myself through studying, networking, and skill development, the "luckier" I am. The best and most exciting part is that I'm in control of the outcome. The outcome will be based on my effort.

My hope for you is to discover, as I did, that you are one thought, one idea, one connection, one book, one smile, one hug, one song, one decision, one leap, one pivot... away from creating your best life, and for you to courageously step into that gap—the area in your life where you don't know what you don't know. The gap is where all of your hopes and dreams reside. If you have the courage to begin filling it with the knowledge and wisdom from others, you will reach the other side and begin living the life you desire.

To find out more about Randy Wilson and the financial education and personal development programs he offers, go to randywilsononline.com. If you'd like to connect directly and continue the conversation by email, go to randy@randywilsononline.com or Instagram @randywilsononline.

Tweetable: Whatever you do, don't get to the end of your life and look back to find woulda, coulda, shouldas. The world needs you to show up and deliver your gifts. Decide, take action, adjust, grow, achieve.

VICKIE "SUNSHINE" CORTES

Building Hope in Puerto Rico and Beyond

Vickie "Sunshine" Cortes is an instigator of big things. She is the founder of Hope Builders, a nonprofit disaster relief construction company. She is a mentor, coach, speaker, and facilitator of transformational retreats focused on empowering women who want to transform their lives to impact the lives of others.

Hurricane Maria Hits Puerto Rico

On September 20, 2017, Hurricane Maria, a Category 5 storm, ripped through the tiny island of Vieques, Puerto Rico at speeds of 175 MPH, leaving catastrophic devastation in its path. Over 400 homes were completely lost and more than double that were massively damaged. People on Vieques were already struggling prior to the storm, and now their homes and livelihoods were lost.

I had purchased a home on Vieques a few years before Maria. I fell in love with the beauty of the island and even more so the people. There is something special about the Viequense community.

The night of Maria, I felt helpless as I watched the weather reports from my home in Massachusetts. Hurricane Maria was going to be the strongest hurricane to hit Puerto Rico in 89 years. The last report before I headed to bed was that Hurricane Maria was sustaining winds of over 175 mph with gusts beyond 225 miles per hour.

The next morning, I anxiously awoke to see how the island made out and to make sure my friends were okay. I turned on the news, and there was nothing. There were barely any reports. All communication had been lost during the storm. All I knew was Hurricane Maria was really bad. My prayers went out to everyone in Puerto Rico.

Two days later, I was at the gym on the treadmill when I looked up at the TV screens that lined the wall in front of me. All I saw was the devastation Hurricane Maria left behind. On every screen, you could see stormwater and mud rushing three stories high through homes. There were homes without roofs or walls and homes completely flattened. I saw people walking the streets in absolute shock. It looked like a bomb went off.

I could feel the tears running down my face. My heart was broken. That very minute, I began to pray: *Dear Lord, what can I possibly do to help?*

And, it came to me. I was going to help rebuild Vieques.

I thought to myself, *What are you talking about, God? How am I going to do that?* I had 25 years of experience in the real estate industry selling new construction and investing in fix and flips needing minor construction and cosmetic repairs, but I was no general contractor.

I had no idea how I was going to accomplish this. I just knew I was being called to do it. I stopped my workout and headed straight home to put a plan together. That is how Hope Builders was born.

On the Ground in Vieques

I had never worked in the nonprofit sector, so I was flying by the seat of my pants. While everyone was trying to get a flight out of Puerto Rico, I was trying to get a flight in. Once I was on the ground, going door-to-door delivering necessities, Sonia Ventura, a 75-year-old woman with a heart and personality larger than life and founder of the nonprofit COREFI, agreed to partner with us and introduce us to the most in need, I quickly realized that nearly every home we entered needed repairs. I had raised just over $3,000 and knew this would not even buy the tools we needed.

I worked day and night to figure out how to get building materials. At the same time, I continued to meet friends and neighbors to help where I could. I witnessed people suffering without resources. I felt helpless. It was a blessing to be present, to be able to sit and listen to people as they shared their hearts with me. At that point, all I could give them was my time and my prayers.

I heard FEMA was holding weekly meetings on the main island of Puerto Rico for non-government organizations helping in disasters. To get there, I had to get to the docks by 5AM, take the ferry over to the main island, rent a car, and then navigate the traffic-filled roads with no traffic signals due to power outages. The meetings were held in churches deep in the rainforest of the rural mountain areas.

I began attending FEMA meetings bi-weekly. I was the only one at the meetings who did not speak or understand Spanish. I was fortunate enough each time to find someone who could speak English willing to translate. Through those meetings, I learned of a program where FEMA would give non-profit organizations free building materials to help speed up the rebuilding process.

On April 9, 2018, our first load of building materials arrived. On April 11, Katrina, her cousin Mike, one paid worker, a group of volunteers, and I began to work. Katrina, a woman who lived seasonally on the island, wanted to help the community and believed in what I wanted to accomplish. She helped raise money to put toward hiring a local for the team and chose to lead a group of volunteers.

Building in the States can be difficult, however, building on an island off of an island became a monumental test of patience and perseverance. Getting supplies on a regular basis proved to be extremely difficult. Due to island politics, trucks with supplies heading to Vieques were turned away. I finally felt the only way we were going to get building supplies to the island was by hiding them. We began renting moving trucks and having volunteers drive them, being sure not to tell anyone they were connected to rebuilding homes.

Having spent time in the community, getting to know those in need and understanding the need, we hit the ground running—or limping depending on what lens you looked through.

We could not afford to buy a work truck. The only vehicle I had was an "island car," an older model SUV. We would tie lumber to the roof and fill the inside with lumber running from the dash and out the back.

It would have been easier and less expensive to exclusively utilize volunteers. However, I recognized the value of hiring locals. I found myself constantly reaching out to people for help. I was able to find volunteers to help train our workers. The difficulty was finding workers who knew how to build. In a patriarchal society, it was extremely difficult to be a woman overseeing and working hands-on. That, paired with my inability to speak Spanish, at times made it feel like an impossible task.

I did not have systems and processes in place. We worked in reactionary mode. It was tough. It seemed like everything was an uphill battle. Everything seemed to take so long. Nothing happens fast in Puerto Rico except the passing of the day. The despair people were feeling was insurmountable. I found myself crying more than I ever had. I spent many nights crying out to God, wondering what I had gotten myself into and why I ever thought it would be a good idea to try to rebuild homes.

Through the grace of God, with the help of many volunteers and staff, over time, we were able to get grants and materials. To date, we have repaired and rebuilt over 270 roofs, installed hundreds of doors and windows, repaired crumbling ceilings, installed kitchen cabinets and countertops, and fixed electrical systems. We have assisted 1,058 people in making their homes weathertight, providing support and hope to those who suffered the devastation of Maria. We helped over forty people appeal and overturn denials for help from FEMA.

We have helped the emergency management department by repairing roofs and buildings and helping to build interior dorm-style bathrooms for their staff. In the event of a storm, they now do not have to walk outside to use the restrooms. For the police department, we donated the materials to build carports and a workshop for police cruisers. We helped the mayor by donating materials and volunteers for projects throughout the island.

Hope Builders was the only nonprofit organization repairing and rebuilding homes on Vieques. All our work to date has been done for free. We know our community and focus on elderly, bedridden, single-parent households, and families that need a hand up. Hope Builders continues to visit our clients and support them in finding resources to help them build a better future, and a stronger, more resilient Vieques.

South Florida and Another Storm

COVID and health issues changed the way I worked in Puerto Rico. I left Vieques in March of 2020 due to the pandemic. I needed to be home with my family. The following year, I purchased a mobile home in Fort Myers Beach, FL, to have a place to visit that was close to some of my family.

In January 2022, I had been in Fort Myers Beach for a week, and the weather had not been the best. My plan was to relax and heal from an illness I have. I had just come back into the house from putting some furniture I was giving away in the front yard when it began to rain. I went back out to put the items in the back of my covered truck. When I turned my truck on to back it up, the announcer on the radio said, "Tornado warning. Take immediate cover. Six minutes to touchdown in Fort Myers, Florida."

I looked around and wondered where the storm was. It was almost time for church. I loaded the furniture, walked inside, and started folding laundry before I got ready. Seconds later, my dog Tango started pushing into me. He stood in front of me and put his body around my leg. It felt like he was trying to pull me out of my bedroom. Then I heard a noise. I just knew it was the tornado.

I immediately began to think, *Where can I take shelter?* I'm thinking,

83

Where am I going to hide in a mobile home? It's going to be blown apart. I began praying, *Dear Lord, please keep everyone in the path of the tornado safe.*

I ran outside to get my bearings. The sky was a strange yellow color. I looked down the road. All my neighbors were standing there. They looked at me and pointed to where they could see the tornado. I yelled, "We all should be in a shelter not watching the tornado go by." I was not far enough into the road to see the tornado before it disappeared.

I ran inside, grabbed my phone, and called my mom and my dear family friend Marie to make sure they were okay. They both lived out where the tornado came from. Mom seemed alright, and Marie was taking shelter in a local grocery store. I got in my truck and drove over to the store. Everywhere I looked, I saw the devastation of the tornado.

After I knew my mom and Marie were okay, I began to drive home.

Before I knew it, I was turning into a neighboring mobile home park. Through the rain, I could see it was absolutely devastated by the storm.

I jumped out of my truck, went to police officers nearby, and introduced myself as the founder of Hope Builders, a disaster relief construction company, and let them know I was there to help. They were saying another tornado was going to touch down and they were evacuating us. I exchanged information with the district captain of the sheriff's office and immediately began going door to door, helping people out of their homes.

The majority of the people were elderly and in complete shock. They were all just waking up or still in bed when the tornado struck, leaving them no time to get into a shelter. People did not want to leave without their pets, so I was climbing through the soaked wreckage of what was once their homes to find cats and small dogs. I began loading people, pets, and any medicine they needed into my truck and bringing them over to the church, which would be a good shelter. I kept going back and forth until I knew everyone was out. I was drenched to the bone.

After my last run, I began calling the local Gavin's Ace Hardware and Home Depot, telling them that I was doing disaster recovery in the local area struck by the tornado and asking if they would help. I had a great response. I filled the back of my truck with tarps, gloves, rakes, chainsaws, and contractor bags, and I went door to door handing out supplies and helping people.

Change. Impacting Lives

Over five years after Hurricane Maria, Puerto Rico still has a long road to recovery. Thousands remain homeless and hundreds of thousands live in homes with leaking roofs or missing windows. To make matters worse, in 2020, earthquakes devastated hundreds of thousands of homes and businesses while COVID became a pandemic. Many are losing hope.

I would be lying if I said this work wasn't hard. It can be emotionally draining, and sometimes I wonder how I am going to continue. But there are moments, moments when I see first-hand how we have improved someone's life and how grateful they are because of some small thing we have done, that make me realize why I continue.

Our mission is demonstrating God's love building homes, communities, and hope. Our vision is strong, healthy communities where all people have access to safe, affordable, resilient housing. We will continue to repair and build homes to rebuild and improve lives. We will also continue to bring housing programs to and advocate for underserved communities not only in Puerto Rico but also in the States. We will continue to jump in when disaster strikes.

There are many ways you can help. Spread the message of Hope Builders and our important work through your social network. Volunteer. With your help, we can build homes and rebuild lives. You don't have to have construction knowledge, just a willingness to help. Last, but certainly not least, donate. No amount is too small.

I attended a conference with the great John C. Maxwell. He spoke about doing big things and serving others. He said, "When God calls, say yes, tell the world, and figure it out."

That is exactly what I did with Hope Builders. God called, and I said yes. I told everyone who would listen what I was going to do and I figured it out as I went. I am going to challenge you to do the same thing.

As I continue this work, I am called to another purpose. I know there are others with a longing to grow and find their own path to help the world. I have found my path, and it is now my mission to support others in doing the same through coaching and mentoring.

Do you have a longing to do something big? Something that will truly impact your life and the lives of others around you?

If so, I challenge you to also say yes, tell the world, and figure it out!

Vickie "Sunshine" Cortes specializes in life-changing coaching, mentoring, training, and retreats that will help women not only impact their lives but also the lives of others through personal development and leadership training.

www.vickiesunshine.com
vickie@vickiesunshine.com
To support Hope Builders, visit:
www.hopebuildersinc.org/donate

Tweetable: Say yes. Tell the world. Figure it out!

JACK LANGENBERG
Making a Difference

Jack Langenberg is an industry speaker, real estate investor, and co-founder of Sapient Capital Group. He has invested in over 4,500 units across 20 multifamily properties. Having led Global M&A at a Fortune 500 company, Langenberg has negotiated complex transactions around the world.

Important Questions

The crowd cheered as I smashed a sledgehammer into the windshield. Satisfied with the spiderweb crack I made across the glass, I stepped aside and let my friend take a turn.

One swing at a Japanese car cost five dollars at the county fair in Flint, Michigan in the summer of 1982. It was fun, but something did not feel right about it. As a teenager, I pondered, *How could a town that had produced dozens of professional athletes love competition in sports so much but utterly despise competition in the auto industry?*

My father, an automotive engineer, shared with me his thoughts on competition from Japan. At the time, his viewpoint was quite novel. Citing advancements in both quality and pace of innovation, he credited competitive pressure from Japan as a catalyst that forced American automakers to produce better cars. He felt it was important to understand Japanese design and manufacturing concepts. I remember my father posing the question, "What would it be like if Japanese and American engineers worked together?"

My father's view was not shared by the two laid-off autoworkers in Detroit who took out their frustrations on Vincent Chin, a Chinese American. The details I read in the newspaper articles about Chin's murder disturbed me. While sharing my feelings with my parents, I asked them, "How could they hate someone, who they didn't even know, so much that they beat him to death?"

Our conversations about the crime included themes like ignorance, fear, and racism. We also talked about the importance of understanding others and making a positive difference in the world and how each person has the responsibility to do both. As a fourteen-year-old, there was a lot I did not understand. At that time, I wondered, *How would I make a difference in the world?*

Early Opportunities to Make a Difference

My first significant opportunities to make a difference occurred while I was in high school. Working as a lifeguard and swim instructor at the YWCA, I taught inner city kids to swim. Taking part in a child's development by helping them overcome fear of the water and become a competent swimmer was fulfilling. Knowing that I taught hundreds of kids to swim is deeply gratifying. Through this experience, I began to develop the ability to see the world from other perspectives and to identify and examine stereotypes.

Around this same time, my high school English teacher, Rick Morse, helped me and a group of classmates found a clown club. We learned to juggle, perform skits, make animal balloons, and of course, apply clown makeup. Our mothers learned to sew clown costumes. After some practice, we became competent enough to perform at local festivals, hospitals, pre-schools, and senior living centers. It did not matter that we weren't professional clowns; what mattered was that we could make people laugh and bring them joy.

During this time, I became more curious about Japan. My interest grew in major part through conversations with my grandfather, a World War II veteran who flew a P-40N Warhawk in the Pacific Theater. On the 40th anniversary of the end of the war, he traveled back to Japan with my grandmother. Unlike many from his era, he did not harbor animosity toward the Japanese people. The purpose of his trip was to see how the people of Japan rebuilt their country and to experience them as allies, trading partners, and friends as opposed to wartime adversaries. The photographs of the people he met in the cities and countryside drew me in, and his stories truly captivated me. We spent hours together at the kitchen table or on the front porch talking about Japan. I dreamt of living there one day.

Naked Rice Planting in Japan

The first step toward making that dream a reality was to learn Japanese. I began that daunting task in 1986 as a freshman at the University of Notre Dame. As Dave Barry said in *Dave Barry Does Japan*, "The method of learning Japanese recommended by experts is to be born as a Japanese baby and raised by a Japanese family, in Japan. And even then, it's not easy." The next best alternative is to live in the countryside of Japan, which I did for two years.

I chose the provincial town of Mito in Ibaraki Prefecture because no Americans lived there. In fact, everyone I met there had never met a foreigner before me. No one spoke English, and that was just fine by me. In that total immersion environment, my language skills improved rapidly.

Nonetheless, I made many linguistic errors. When I helped the Watahiki family plant rice at their farm in the mountains, I made a slipup that followed me for quite a while. Since rice planting takes place in early April, they wore knee-high boots to protect themselves from the ice-cold waters in the flooded rice fields. My size twelve foot was far too big for any spare boots. Not wanting to miss out, I offered to plant the rice *ha-daka*, which I thought meant barefoot. I could tell by everyone's facial expressions and laughter that I had said something wrong. . . .

Consulting my pocket dictionary, I saw that *ha-dashi* meant barefoot but what I had said, *ha-daka*, meant bare-naked! Even grandmother Watahiki did not let me live that one down. When it came time to bring in the fall rice crop later that year, she asked me if I wanted to harvest the rice naked. We all laughed. Being able to laugh at myself was important because I accidentally created a lot of humorous situations at my own expense.

Working and Living in Tokyo

Within ten years of swinging that sledgehammer into the windshield of a Japanese automobile, I was fluent in Japanese and working in strategy and finance for General Motors in Tokyo. We were not selling GM cars to Japanese consumers. Our vehicles were too big, and the steering wheels were on the wrong side. However, our electronic components were sought after by Toyota, Honda, Nissan, and other Japanese automakers. Together, my Japanese colleagues and I grew our sales from zero to over $300 million in only a few years. The fact that some of those components were manufactured in Flint, Michigan made me feel like I was making a difference in my hometown from the other side of the world.

That side of the world was my home for seven years. During that time, the once exotic sights, sounds, and smells of Asia became familiar, even ordinary. More important than my memories of the many places I experienced were the friendships, insights, and perspectives I gained from all the fascinating people I met. I learned to not only tolerate people who think, look, speak, or act differently from me, but also relish their differences. I also came to appreciate that all people have feelings, needs, hopes, and dreams, regardless of their background.

From Japan to Harvard Business School

The story of my business success in Japan must have intrigued the admissions committee at the Harvard Business School. I vividly recall my hands shaking when I opened their letter. My eyes locked on a single word that would change the trajectory of my life: Congratulations!

Over the course of two years, my 880 classmates and I read, analyzed, and discussed at length nearly 500 case studies. Each case covered real-life situations faced by business executives leading companies. As we discovered, the objective of the case method was not to reach consensus but to understand how different people use the same information to arrive at vastly different conclusions.

I came to understand that complex problems are best solved by bringing together people with different viewpoints to explore options and take decisive action. I also learned that successful leadership is not about power, authority, and influence, but about the ability to inspire. Those discussions and the lessons I learned at Harvard Business School prepared me well for my twenty-year career as a C-level executive.

Making and Keeping Promises—The Key to Being Trustworthy

One of my favorite leadership roles was head of global mergers and acquisitions at Kelly Services, Inc., a Fortune 500 company. My team and I traveled the world looking for companies to buy. I met many incredible business leaders while helping Kelly enter new markets to serve customers abroad. This role helped me develop deep expertise sourcing and valuing acquisition targets, understanding seller motivations, as well as negotiating complex transactions.

The most challenging acquisition I completed involved helping Kelly Services expand into Japan by buying the Sony Corporation's in-house temporary staffing division. Naturally, Sony would not trust a newcomer to buy the company outright. Creativity and trust were required to make this happen. The creative part included a unique three-step acquisition strategy. The first step called for the creation of a three-way partnership between

Kelly Services, Sony Corporation, and Temp Staff (a large Japanese staffing company). The second and third steps called for Kelly Services to buy out Sony and Temp Staff after accomplishing mutually agreed-upon objectives. We built trust by making and keeping promises no matter how difficult it became.

Trust among colleagues, customers, buyers, and sellers has been a consistent theme throughout my career. However, investors require the highest level of trust, and it must be earned before they invest. I came to appreciate this fact while serving as chief financial officer of two companies with toplines over one billion dollars.

Several years ago, my entrepreneurial spirit pulled me toward real estate. My appreciation for investor trust has grown with my real estate portfolio, now 4,500 units across twenty apartment complexes. I am satisfied knowing my role as a professional real estate investor provides me with a way to make a difference in many lives. I am driven to perform by my respect and appreciation for the trust my investors have in me.

Passing Down the Mindset of Making a Difference

One of my proudest moments as a parent was seeing a desire to make a difference develop in my children.

In April of 2020, after watching a news story about struggling renters who lost their jobs due to COVID, my son Nick, a high school junior at the time, wanted to help. The cynic in me wanted to point out that we were in lockdown, and he was just seventeen. I am glad I kept my mouth shut. From his bedroom, he searched the internet for charities that offered rent assistance, called them, and made a list of the steps renters needed to take to obtain rent assistance.

Through his individual effort, he helped twelve families secure assistance. What really impressed me was Nick's plan to think bigger. He scaled up his rent assistance project by recruiting fellow members of his school's National Honors Society to extend help to struggling renters in other cities in Texas. Together, he and his classmates made an enormous difference for over 50 families by helping them secure rent assistance. I am proud of Nick for his creativity, determination, and leadership.

I am grateful to my mother, father, grandfather, and teachers for instilling in me a desire to understand others and make a difference in the world. Whether as a swim instructor, clown, executive, or father, I have positively impacted the lives of many people. Now as a multifamily deal sponsor, I impact the lives of investors who trust me to protect and grow their wealth, residents who live in the communities, and staff who help me operate the properties. Understanding that I have both the opportunity and ability to make a difference in their lives fills me with a strong sense of purpose.

Jack Langenberg co-founded Sapient Capital Group to offer joint venture partnerships and passive investing opportunities. Sign up for his e-book which covers 7 insider secrets of why large endowments, institutions, and other savvy investors choose multifamily real estate. https://sapientcg.com/connect or jacklangenberg.com

Tweetable: Trust among colleagues, customers, buyers, and sellers has been a consistent theme throughout my career. However, investors require the highest level of trust and it must be earned before they invest.

GREG ZLEVOR

Leading with the Heart, Not the Ego

Greg Zlevor, president of Westwood International, has worked with Johnson & Johnson, the Singapore Police Force, Volvo, General Electric, and many other high-profile companies, co-authored five #1 bestselling books, and shared the stage with greats including Jim Rohn, George Land, and M. Scott Peck.

EGO: Three Letters That Can Hold You Back

If you're a crossword puzzle enthusiast, you likely know that one word that pops up over and over in the famous *New York Times* puzzle is "EGO." It's been the answer to over 30 different clues over the years, ranging from "self-image" to "star quality," "big head," "I," and "Claudius." Any word that has that many definitions and interpretations is invariably an indefinite term. It also indicates that ego is one of those concepts we toss around a lot in conversation. Yet, sometimes we aren't really in agreement on what we're talking about.

So, when I ask you—When you're at work, do you know how to deal with your ego?—you might have to ask right back: What do you mean by ego?

I define "ego" as the conscious self that you are aware of. Saying both "conscious" and "aware" sounds like a redundancy, but think of it this way. You're likely aware that there's a lot about you that isn't part of your conscious self. The more awareness you have of that, the further away you are from raw ego thinking. Your raw ego is your impulses, immediate desires, reactions, and how you protect, defend, or promote yourself. Your raw ego is your instinct toward self-preservation.

Here are a few examples of the ego playing out at work:

- You're in a meeting, and one of your colleagues criticizes an idea you just had and suggests it won't work. You get defensive. Instead of asking a question to build understanding, you cut them off, restate your position, and move to the next topic.
- Bonuses and raises are coming up. You feel the need to ensure management sees you. You mention how well you are doing while

subtly shading a colleague. You position yourself for a raise while diminishing a peer.

- You're pitching a client. Rather than inviting teammates into the creative process as you develop the pitch, you refuse to let anyone see your work. After all, they might take credit for "your" work, right? You go it alone rather than expand your work and improve the pitch with additional input.

All those scenarios depict the ego taking control. And none of them are great scenarios—not for you, your boss, or your colleagues.

Self-absorption ruins the very thing it wants to promote. Ironically, raw, unfiltered, immature ego energy often creates the opposite of its desire. The wall or shell that raw ego manufactures slowly dissolves or destroys that which it intends to protect.

Making Friends with the EGO

Letting the most toxic version of your ego take over isn't good for your professional present or future, nor is it good for the people you work with. So, what can you do?

Harnessing the raw ego ensures that you, as a leader, can run a functional and successful team in a transformed business world. As M. Scott Peck said, "One's limits are one's ego boundaries." Shatter the boundaries your ego is arbitrarily putting in place for you, and suddenly, your limits to successful leadership fall away.

Here's a basic checklist for how you, as a leader, can start improving how you manage your ego.

1: Understand that you will never truly drop the ego. You can't make an egoless team nor do you want one. You're better off making room for the ego, in a mature way, and this is one of the key transitions in most people's development.

This is important for two reasons. One, while you as a leader can grapple and wrestle with your own ego, and you can institute exercises and processes to help your colleagues and employees do the same, ultimately, it's only your own "re-ordered" ego that you control. If you don't take the time to "see, befriend, and re-order the ego," your personal raw ego orders you. We must deal with our own ego first.

The ego isn't bad, it just needs to be acknowledged and "re-ordered."

Unfortunately, many people think they're getting past their ego when what they're really doing is denying the existence of their ego while justifying "egoic" behavior. This is incredibly unhealthy. You must make room for your ego through awareness, not justification. Understanding this is one of the key transitions in most people's development as mature individuals and professionals. Trying extremely hard to eliminate ego is giving it undue attention. Giving the ego "space" or room to exist, without allowing it to run the whole house, is healthier and wiser.

Paradoxically, a healthy, wise, and trained awareness utilizes the ego to serve itself and the world. The ego isn't something so big, scary, and powerful that you must squash it out. It's a significant part of you that teaches you how to monitor, feel, and express your energy, dialed to a calculated and precise force, at the right target. A wise mind and heart, acting from awareness, acknowledges the ego without giving it undue authority.

Great leaders work on their own ego while guiding the collective to do the same.

The first step toward a healthy relationship with your ego is to be able to notice, perhaps through a meditation or mindfulness practice, when your ego is taking over and getting defensive. Fear, irritation, anger, or anxiety often spring from the ego. Instead of trapping us, these feelings can lead to freedom. Awareness is the beginning of freedom. The negative emotions originating from the ego can produce dysfunctional and destructive behavior. An awareness practice curbs and eventually eliminates this pattern.

I like to recommend breathing exercises to my clients to help them develop a sense of self-awareness that can help with a nervous and overactive ego. Here's an example: When you feel your heart rate racing as a work situation becomes more stressful, close your eyes and inhale for four counts. Hold your breath for five counts. Then exhale for six counts.

This combination of slow breath and precise counting (4-5-6 breathing) will help center you in a way that will allow you to ask yourself a few important questions. What is this feeling? What label would I give it? What is this feeling telling me? What is important to me right now? This pause and breathing creates space for a wise answer instead of an emotional reaction. This practice helps re-order the ego.

2: Get comfortable enough with your ego that you don't feel the need to insert it everywhere. You may be surprised that an unhealthy ego is fundamentally a defensive mechanism, not an offensive one. Ever heard of the term "fragile ego?" The people at work who seem the most egotistical are often the most insecure, not the most confident. That boss who randomly yells at subordinates isn't projecting authority; he's likely projecting a vulnerability that he isn't willing to address. Fragility needs serious protection.

Ego is most often a suit of armor that you rely on and hide behind, rather than a fundamental part of your personality.

One of my favorite business thinkers, Raj Sisodia, author of books like *The Healing Organization*, has said that once you're comfortable with your ego, you don't feel the need to project it everywhere. Raj says that when we get to a place where we don't have to defend, promote, or protect anything—the instinctive actions when the ego is in control—we can be more open and make a bigger difference in the world.

Getting comfortable with the ego means making room for difficult feelings. I recently attended an extended silent retreat with my son. At the end of the retreat, we stood in the parking lot waiting for our ride. As the minutes passed, I got frustrated. I texted the driver. He apologized and said he was stopping for gas. I turned to my son and complained, "What? Now he's stopping for gas when he's already late? Don't you think he should have planned for that?" My son turned to me, held out his clenched fist, then slowly opened his hand. Calmly, he whispered, "Let it go."

Grappling with difficult feelings helps ensure you're addressing stresses and insecurities in a healthy rather than toxic way. A friend redirects us. A smile shifts us. A new perspective alters my thinking. Taking a walk calms me down.

3: Learn to take the maturity of your ego into the collective. As a leader, it's important for you to take the management of your own ego into your team at work and the broader organization you work in. As with just about everything in business, it's a team effort—it doesn't matter what you do as an individual if there aren't others along for the journey.

Recently, I was leading a workshop for a division of a major pharmaceutical company—specifically, the clinical team. They're the group that tests products. They're a critical piece of any healthcare or pharmaceutical company's research and development. This company's clinical team was struggling. The leaders were experiencing difficulties with everything from communication to productivity, and morale was low.

So, in our kickoff session, I had the team—a group of about a dozen leaders —sit in a circle, and I asked, "How are things going?"

First of all, the top executives and supervisors of the team chose to sit on the outside of the circle rather than within it. That's a red flag that the leadership doesn't see itself as part of the collective... and is likely a sign of fragile ego, because they felt the need to publicly validate that they're different.

Then, one of the senior leaders sitting in the circle—let's call her Janice—turned to another senior team leader, who I'll call Mike. Janice said, with contempt, "Mike, you say things are getting better, but they're not. In our last two meetings, you've been rude and cut me off. You aren't listening to my ideas. You're a bad listener." Her venting went on for 30 seconds. Mike wanted to respond right away, but before he could, I jumped in to ask a question.

I said, "Janice, did what you say get you closer or further away from your goal?"

There was a long pause, then Janice said, "Probably further away."

Then I asked what her goal was. And she said, "I'd like to be respected. I want everyone to be respected. I want us to make better decisions. This company and this team are suffering because we're not getting our work done quickly. We don't trust and respect one another."

She was right. Unfortunately, she led with her raw ego.

Here's the problem. By calling out Mike as rude rather than engaging him in productive dialogue, Janice was setting herself against Mike and undermining the team's ability to operate as a collective. In stressful situations, we often resort to blame, justification, excuses, or tribalism—banding together with the people who agree with our opinion, often in opposition to others in our organization—because our ego, our sense of self-preservation at all costs, is taking the lead.

Even though everyone is on the same team, discord and tribalism ensue. These differences trigger a protective mindset that is more "us vs. them" rather than "us vs. our challenge." Potentially functional groups stop communicating effectively when contempt creates subgroups.

No wonder this team wasn't getting its job done. Awareness and a healthy, re-ordered ego hadn't been ingrained as a value for this team, and as a result, toxic egos still lashed out at one another and prevented cohesion, collaboration, and growth. Moving teams away from protectionism or tribalism and toward "growthism," as we might call it, is how the purpose-driven company of the 21st century thrives.

It's on leaders to ensure tactics for managing the ego and developing a mature relationship with it are offered as resources to every member of a team, not just the leaders themselves. Appreciative inquiry can be a crucial philosophy here. Focusing heavily on the negative breeds blame and tribalism. Assessing and digging into what's working creates the appreciation and bonds that can lead to growth.

Leading with Heart

The final step to a healthy relationship with the ego at work is to ensure that you're operating from a mindset that helps you and provides resources to those around you—especially those who are on your team or reporting to you or otherwise looking up to you. In a corporate world where we are seeing an increasing desire to be driven by a higher purpose, it's imperative.

"People face challenges all the time, and then they come to work and we add to those burdens by the way we lead, manage, or organize," Raj Sisodia said. "Done right, business can be a place of healing. People can leave at the end of the day, mentally, physically, emotionally, spiritually, and socially in a better state than when they came in."

The first move to ensure your organization is headed toward that better state? Address the ego. Yours first. Then empower those around you to do the same. There is a fundamental disturbance from and with the ego when the ego's perspective is the center of the world. A roughshod ego amplifies "dis"-ease. An ego with no wisdom or heart is deplorable. An ego empowering the heart is unstoppable. Let's be unstoppable. Let's do the work to re-order our egos.

Contact Greg Zlevor if you're looking to bring leadership development or training programs that will help your organization reconnect with its core meaning and instill a sense of hope and shared purpose. gzlevor@westwoodintl.com | westwoodintl.com

Tweetable: An unhealthy ego is a defensive mechanism, not an offensive one. Ever heard of the term "fragile ego?" The people at work who are seemingly the most egotistical are the ones who are the most insecure.

NANCY LUNTER YATZKAN

Tax-Smart Investing for the Win!

Nancy Lunter Yatzkan is an entrepreneur empowering others to take massive action and create financial freedom so they can live life on their terms. As the Director of Operations at KOR Capital Fund, she provides investment opportunities in energy, real estate, and technology to help investors reduce taxes, earn passive income, and create generational wealth.

"Whether you think you can, or you think you can't . . . you're right."
– Henry Ford

The Rug from Under Me
"Sorry, I can't help you. . . . Your money will not last very long, and I don't feel comfortable working with you in this situation."

Was I hearing this financial advisor correctly? After a 21-year marriage with more money than we ever needed, how was it possible that now in my 50s I had to worry about my financial security?

Childhood: "Work Hard and Save Your Money!"
I grew up with blue-collar, hard-working parents in a suburb of Chicago. My three siblings and I were raised to believe that if you are going to do a job, do it well. Get a good job, work hard, and save your money.

My mom's family moved from Ireland, and as the oldest daughter, she worked hard from a very young age. At 84, she is still a proud and hard-working Realtor that seizes every opportunity life offers. Her days are filled with travel, theater, concerts, and the many charitable organizations she is active in. Not one to dwell on setbacks, she taught us through example to "pull up on your bootstraps and keep going!"

My dad's family moved to Chicago from Czechoslovakia. They came with very little money but a strong entrepreneurial spirit. Through the years, he and his family opened a preschool and owned multifamily apartments and a hotel for truckers. Skilled at solving problems and mechanically-inclined, my dad provided for our family by working as a pipe fitter for the city. His integrity and strong work ethic have always been at the core of who he is.

He will still tell anyone that will listen how he loved every single day he served as a cryptographer in the Air Force.

Every Day Is a Birthday and a Reason to Celebrate

His greatest strength was and continues to be his undeniable ability to find joy in simple things. He passed on to me the belief that "every day is a birthday and a reason to celebrate." This positive influence has been one of the best gifts I have received. It is with me daily and sets the tone for my life.

My mother and father's 64-year marriage has been and still is a testament to teamwork, strong work ethic, love of family, a strong faith, and equally as important, the joy that comes from playing a heated game of euchre or bridge.

Grand Enterprise, Inc.

After studying economics at the University of Illinois, I was about to accept a generous job offer in sales from a well-known company, just as my parents had hoped for. My career goals were big, and they included all of the fun and excitement that Chicago offered: street fairs, art shows, concerts, and the lakefront. When I heard the job was based in a rural town in Illinois rather than the exciting, bustling city of Chicago, the opportunity seemed less appealing, so I politely declined.

Through a series of serendipitous events, my sister and I decided to embark on an entrepreneurial journey together; Grand Enterprise, Inc. was born. We had the opportunity to represent a new product in the health and wellness market, AquaSoothe (now HydroMassage). In the early '90s, the concept of wellness and heart attack prevention was trending. This new invention provided a powerful heated water jet massage, reduced stress, tension, and muscle tightness as well as improved circulation, all while remaining dry. Now, 30 years later, Hydromassage has expanded into Wellness Space Brands, which focuses on experiential wellness products and is a staple in fitness clubs and wellness centers in over 30 countries.

Everything about this endeavor was challenging and NOT the safe and secure 9-5 job I was told was the way to go. The company we represented was a start-up, which meant we were responsible for marketing, sales, the scheduling and setup of trade shows. Not to mention, the installation, service, and repairs of the 400-pound equipment. Thankfully, all of my childhood lessons provided what I needed: confidence I could solve the problems that arose each day, the resourcefulness to rewire electrical panels from 110 to 220 volts, and the ingenuity to run to a hardware store in the middle of a trade show to buy a soldering iron and repair the crack in the tank that held the 25 gallons of water. Most importantly, I had the fortitude and optimism to embrace the fact that I was in way over my head as a 22-year-old and persist anyway. I had big, audacious plans for my future, and creating my own destiny and financial freedom through this unconventional post-college route was worth it because I learned invaluable lessons I would unknowingly need for my future.

Marriage: Living the Dream (So I Thought)
While building my company, I met a man and after three years of dating, a whirlwind of travel and fun, I was married in 1998. My husband was older than me, divorced, and a father of two sons. He sold his business just before we were married and retired young, at age 40. We enjoyed an amazing lifestyle, funded by passive income from investments and multifamily real estate he owned before our marriage and some that was acquired after.

We agreed that I would walk away from my business to raise our children and take care of the home—he would manage the finances.

As with most things I do, I gave 100% to my role as a stay-at-home mom. Our house was always the hub for class parties, meetings for charities, and many parties with our friends. My plate was full with volunteering for several local organizations, being classroom mom, event planning, and fundraisers.

Left in the Dark
Although our family never had financial concerns, I was consistently uncomfortable not being privy to the details of our finances. I had always been fiercely independent and wanted to know exactly how my retirement accounts were structured. As time went on, it was clear that there were two sides to my husband's personality and it was better for the kids and me to keep things peaceful. After eight years of asking to be more involved with our finances and continuously being assured I had nothing to worry about, I reluctantly stopped asking.

I agreed with the idea that "to those that much is given, much is expected." In response to our affluence, I devoted a lot of time and energy to organizations that helped women and children in need. My plan for after my kids were grown was to travel with Doctors Without Borders, helping those that didn't have access to medical care. I took classes to earn a certification as an operating room patient care technician so I could bring value to these medical missions.

Divorce: I Felt Like A Complete Failure

When my husband asked for a divorce and I had to accept that my marriage was coming to an end, I felt like a complete failure. I was always able to make the best of every situation—how could I not repair the most important part of my life?

I was fixated on the idea that our two children, 13 and 16 years old at the time, deserved the strong family foundation I had. Once I accepted that one person cannot save a team and that this was indeed happening, I was committed to doing my part in being the best-divorced couple we could be. I asked my husband to join me in honoring our marriage and the beautiful children we created by making the divorce procedures as amicable and pain-free as possible for all of us. What we verbally agreed and what actually happened were in complete contrast.

Nothing Prepared Me for This

I have often been accused of seeing the world through rose-colored glasses, but nothing could have prepared me for the shock of what I was about to experience.

While I had been assured throughout my marriage that finances were nothing I needed to worry about, it turned out the reality was nothing like I expected. There were plenty of investments, multi-family properties, a strip mall, ownership in a Chicago high rise, retirement accounts, and three family homes, but none had my name on them. I had no partial ownership in anything.

Learning during the divorce proceedings that my name was kept off 100% of our assets was soul-crushing. This included our primary home and income-producing properties from our 21-year marriage. My attorney assured me that the accounts were structured in such a way that there was no way around it. I felt betrayed.

I was in utter disbelief. It didn't make sense. I had given everything I had to my marriage and our family. I knew it was imperative to free myself from the controlled and unhealthy world I had been living in. I was intentional in doing what was needed to receive a one-time settlement instead of ongoing maintenance (alimony), knowing that otherwise, I would never truly be free.

I Had Less Money Than Was Spent in a Typical Year

The financial advisor pointed out that after paying off my remaining divorce bills and buying a home in our community for me and the kids, the money that remained from the settlement would not last long—in fact, I had less money left than we spent in a typical year. I immediately stopped spending any money that was not absolutely necessary and then quickly got to work on my personal growth and financial education.

Growth: Personal and Financial

This was all happening as the world slipped into the turmoil of the COVID-19 pandemic. I know that time was very hard for many. For me, it was a time of self-discovery and nonstop investment in my financial education. I came to terms with my part in co-creating my situation. The red flags were there—why did I ignore them? Why did I cover up what was really happening behind closed doors? I accepted the fact that people may do things to us but we also play a part in allowing those things to happen. It was time to heal and move forward. I no longer feel anger. Instead, I feel empathy for those with such internal pain that can lead to hurting others.

This Setback Was My Biggest Blessing

If I didn't experience something as gut-wrenching as I did, I would never have had to dig deep to see what was holding me back. My journey of self-discovery has brought clarity. I had to look deep within myself to understand what allowed me to blindly trust when my instincts told me not to. I was able to reclaim my inner strength and confidence, and now I can move forward with compassion, strength, and joy. It was important to separate who I am from my experience, untangle the emotions, and let go of the darkness in my heart so I could begin again.

I acknowledged that all the years of walking on eggshells gradually took me further away from who I truly was. I lost my enthusiastic, playful spirit. Thanks to the opportunity the pandemic presented, I had plenty of time to find myself again. It feels amazing to be back!

I had over two decades to make up for and had to start rebuilding my financial security in my 50s. I needed to think big. There was no value in wasting time sulking. I knew that our very affluent life was funded by the passive income from real estate, so that was my plan. If I wasn't reading a book by Kim or Robert Kiyosaki about real estate investing or Tom Wheelwright about tax strategies, I was listening to podcasts and audiobooks on financial education.

During my marriage, I had spent over a decade going back and forth to our Clearwater Beach, FL, home, and I knew the area well. Also, with no state income tax, Florida would continue to be attractive to snowbirds and those relocating from states with higher taxes. After thorough research and networking, I found the right business partner to invest with in the Tampa/St. Petersburg, FL, area.

KOR Capital Fund, My Mentor, and Beyond

Baskal Korkis, his wife, and their kids live in the Tampa area. He and I spoke regularly. Unfortunately, he made it clear that he didn't take investors. He was a one-man show. He bought his first property when he was 19 years old and remodeled and refinanced his way into 23 doors by the time he was 23. He continued to advise me and offered honest, straightforward advice on how best to create passive income and equity growth with the money I had. Most importantly, he helped me to start trusting people again.

Watching his Instagram posts, I saw every decision he was making in his remodels: the materials, the strategy, and the value each decision brought to the overall value of the project. I agreed with every decision he made, and his philosophy matched mine: "Invest in the front end, save in the back end… make a lot of money." Those were basically the words my dad said his whole life: "If you do a job, do it well. Don't cut corners. It will only cause problems later." After some time and some persistence on my part, Baskal allowed me to invest in one remodel project.

After establishing a two-year relationship and enjoying the financial success of my first real estate investment with him, I asked if we could allow others to join us. Baskal has established all the necessary teams and tends to underpromise and overdeliver. We are aligned in our values of honesty and integrity, we share an unbridled sense of optimism, we like to keep the process fun, and we agree that nothing is worth compromising our values. I felt selfish keeping this amazing opportunity to myself.

To our mutual benefit, Baskal and I decided to scale the business, working together to share what we do and help everyone achieve more.

I Was Born for This Moment

Financial freedom to me is being able to do what I want when I want. It is true that money is not the most important thing, but it does affect everything that IS important.

After finding myself in an unexpected financial situation, I chose to not let the experience define me. Rather, I chose to think big and create an exciting future through education and taking action. I had many plans to travel to exotic destinations with my kids, live in various interesting locations, and experience unique adventures, and that hasn't changed. I made the mistake of putting my financial security in the hands of someone else.

Now my goal is to help others take ownership of their financial futures, especially women who find themselves in unexpected situations.

I have found what I was born to do and now I am having so much fun growing the business with my partner and sharing the financial education and opportunities I have benefited from. We all have the opportunity to assess our situation and, if it doesn't align with our goals, take massive action to create the life we want for ourselves!

Connect with Nancy Lunter Yatzkan at nancy@korcapitalfund.com to strategize on tax-smart investing, passive income, and investment opportunities to accomplish your long-term goals. Visit www.korcapitalfund.com/ThinkBig to receive a 6-Part video course, "How To Outsmart Inflation & Taxes" and discover how to preserve your wealth with strategic investing.

Tweetable: Every day is a new opportunity to celebrate and take massive action to create the life you desire.

GLADE POULSEN

Learning I Matter
From the Farm to the Global Stage

Glade Poulsen has known dizzying highs and stomach-dropping lows. Through it all, he keeps digging—and trying to inspire. From a high school graduating class of 34 students, he has gone on to build multiple international businesses. He continues to excel in sales, entrepreneurship, and mental performance coaching.

A Long Time Ago

One week before my seventh birthday, my mother died after a two-year battle with breast cancer. My father was left with eight children and a mountain of debt. In those days, insurance companies could cancel policies at will. And they did. Everyone felt bereft and though I never felt unloved, I missed out on the affection and tenderness only a mother can give. I spent a lot of time by myself on the farm. Almost every day, I would walk into an empty house after school and shout, "Anybody home?" to hear nothing but crickets. Sometimes, as silly as it was, I would call for my mother. "Mom, where are you?" Did you know that silence can slice like a razor? I'd begin to cry, because—and there's no other way to describe it—I hurt.

I don't like loneliness. It's too raw—too familiar. Now, looking at vacant walls and empty corners, the old ticker wants to throw up its arms and say, "I can't take this again." I feel dismissed, alone, broken, and tired. So, I sit and listen while a voice pounds a question in my head: *Who am I?*

Growing Up

I was born and raised on a farm in Idaho. Adversity hit me then and has felt free to revisit throughout my life. I have made mistakes and enjoyed more than my fair share of wins. Early on, I vividly remember my sister asking my father, "Daddy, are we poor?"

Dad, who didn't say much, said, "No, we just don't have any money." When my mother died, she left Dad with five boys and three girls. I was the caboose. In truth, I liked the notation but being the youngest was difficult. My eldest sister had recently married. The rest of us were at home.

Our closest neighbors lived more than a mile away. We didn't have much interaction with others except on Sunday when we went to church.

I knew I was loved, and I knew I mattered as a member of the family, but there was not a lot of hugging, nurturing, luxury, or communication. No one sang lullabies to me at night. Every day, I got up, did my chores, went to school, and spent a lot of time inside my head.

I drove my siblings nuts with all my questions. I was the annoying little sibling whose favorite question was, "Why?" I wanted to understand why about everything!

"Why can't I go with my brother? Why do you have to plow the fields in the fall?"

After a while, the family grew weary of my questions and delivered the stock response, "Because!"

I'd then respond, "Because . . . why?"

The next answer won't surprise you at all: "Because I said so!"

The Runt of the Litter

My older brothers were active in sports in high school. With forty or so kids in each class (150 in the entire school), you didn't have to be Tom Brady or Kobe Bryant to start on a team. But I didn't know any better. I thought my older brothers, and my sisters in cheerleading, were awesome. We were a competitive family. No one let anyone win anything. I was routinely crushed! I was too slow, too small, too young . . . you name it. I simply could not hang with the older kids. I constantly sought approval. I wanted to do the "big boy stuff."

I wanted to drive the tractors. Sometimes I went out, started a tractor, hooked up a plow, and took off over a field. Never mind that I was not strong enough to pull the lever to lower the blades, so I wasn't really doing anything but making ruts. I wanted to see my dad beam with pride. I wanted to show him what a big, capable boy I was.

The farm, with little female nurturing and my competitive brothers, toughened me up. So did following in their athletic footsteps. TV, sports, and farming were my life. After about a half dozen years of hearing nothing but "because," to soothe my curiosity, I looked for answers on TV, the playground, the ball field, church, and the locker room. John Wayne, Dick Butkus, the Bible, and my self-talk were how I learned.

I quit asking my family questions. I retreated into my head and developed mindsets based on what I gleaned from the limited mediums I could find.

The Bird Leaves the Nest

High school was fun and eventful. I played on a lot of teams and enjoyed every minute. After graduating, I attended college for a year, then completed a two-year mission in Denmark for my church. I learned a new language and saw a bigger, broader world.

I returned to the US and college. When I completed my degree, I sent resumes from Boston to San Diego. My only offer came from a rec center, handing out towels for minimum wage. Ah, the glorious life of the recently graduated! But there was one thing I knew I could do—*sell*. After a summer hawking pots and pans in Texas, which is a long story, I started selling modular homes on straight commission.

I didn't know anything about the construction process, but my mission in Denmark had taught me how to meet, greet, and have a conversation with people. I was good at asking questions and figuring out what folks wanted. Within a few months, I was outperforming my boss. I listened to audiotapes whenever I had a free moment, and my truck became a traveling library.

My sales career was on an upward trajectory. I stumbled upon books by Stephen R. Covey, Zig Ziglar, Napoleon Hill, and Og Mandino. I was fascinated by the stories and principles of highly effective people. Earning a lot of money by helping people was something I had never learned about in college or on the farm.

Within a year of finishing school, I got married. In the blink of an eye, we had four beautiful daughters. The responsibilities of fatherhood and marriage pushed me towards maturity, and my burning desire to escape the scarcity of my upbringing drove me to succeed. I started winning every sales contest—earning awards became a way of life. I wanted to give my wife and daughters every material thing I had lacked as a farm boy. My drive was unstoppable.

And my ego swelled.

What Goes Up Must Come Down

My wife and I agreed she would stay at home to provide the stability and care I had missed. No child of ours was ever coming home to an empty house. My income continued to rise. Before long, I could provide much more for my family than I had ever imagined possible.

Life ran along. I chased it with vigor and enthusiasm to prove I was somebody. I proved I could do big boy work. I was a big dog! And I was determined to continue to excel.

I was the big fish—and I wanted a bigger pond, so I moved our family to Arizona. I believed if I mastered my mindset, created a vision, and had the work ethic I learned on the farm I could accomplish anything and be the master of my fate.

Once I got to the big leagues, I crushed it. I stood toe-to-toe with players from big cities and Ivy League colleges. I decided to leave the corporate structure and build my own business. I wanted to be the boss.

That's when, for the second time in nearly 20 years of sales and entrepreneurship, a significant recession rocked the nation. I had built a large construction business—over 150 employees. And everything disappeared like an anchor dropped into the middle of a lake. Before I knew it, my daughters and I were sitting on the backroads of Arizona selling all the toys, nail guns, ladders, and compressors anyone would take off our hands just so the kids could have lunch money for school.

The relentless pursuit of my own goals, ambitions, and entrepreneurship had dragged my wife and daughters onto a financial rollercoaster that had jumped its tracks. No one had ever mentioned this possibility. I didn't know anything about the dark side of entrepreneurship. Almost all successful entrepreneurs endure their own financial and relationship hardships, but none really taught how to avoid the pitfalls. I had focused so much on my personal agenda and my determination to become "Daddy Warbucks" that I failed to pay attention to the one person who was supporting the entire family structure—my wife. She finally told me she wanted out.

When the divorce was finalized, I didn't have many options. My once sterling resume had crumbled into dust. Searching for options, I came across the direct sales industry. The possibilities of building a thriving international team intrigued me. I jumped in and found success again after a lot of effort, a journey I share in my book *From Sugar Beets to Shanghai*. In that time, I learned a lot, and I was fortunate to marry again.

Five years later, my new wife and I stood on stage in Hong Kong while 5,000 cheered and fireworks erupted. I built sales teams in over twenty countries and climbed to the top of the financial ladder, a testimony to achievement, perseverance, and tenacity. The little farm boy from Idaho "done good!" My success in the business world exceeded my every expectation and dream.

Once again, my home situation proved to be an Achilles heel. The foundation of home life requires and deserves fastidious attention from everyone involved. Neither my second wife nor I spent enough time filling the emotional tank. And when the needle bounced on "E," the specter of divorce rose up, took body form, and punched me in the mouth again.

Fall Down Seven Times, Get Up Eight

It's time to start over, assess, correct, and try again. *Who am I?* Well, I am not the man I was. I have learned a lot about priorities. The secret to success, at least for me, is not avoiding adversity, but learning something from every setback and then leaning in.

My four daughters and 11 grandchildren, along with my siblings, are my biggest cheerleaders and most faithful critics. I turn to them for wisdom and advice. Stuff does not make for success. Joy does.

Every life will encounter adversity. But someone has been there before and knows the way out. Now is the time I find out how much I have learned over the years. I have studied all the greats and I have worked with fabulous people. Are the principles of personal development I have long trumpeted thoroughly ingrained in my life?

As I look at my wall, I see three words. Mindset. Vision. Habits. A good stool has the steady foundation of three legs. I have built my life on that trinity of principles—and now it's time to revisit them.

Mindset is your motor. If you don't care how and what you do, no one else will. In *Miracle*, the dramatization of the 1980 victory of amateur US hockey players over the mighty Soviet National Team, Head Coach Herb Brooks says, "This is your time. Now, go out there and take it!" Even as I write, I am retooling my mindset, becoming more positive, and working to be intentional, empathetic, and focused.

Vision is your compass. As Proverbs 29:18 says, "Where there is no vision, the people perish." If you don't know where you are going, all roads lead there. Dreams, goals, and ambitions will pull us through even the toughest of times. I carry little cards with me everywhere I go. Each one has a word or phrase on it, something to remind me of the direction of the course I have set and the goals I intend to accomplish today, tomorrow, and in the days to follow.

Nothing good happens unless you perfect your **Habits**. You can know where you want to go, but you will continue to spin your wheels unless you have discipline etched into your everyday activities. Establishing good habits saves you the time of bypassing bad ones and makes decisions easy. You know what is right and effective before you have to think. I have removed negative thoughts, negative habits, and negative influences from my life. Every day, I read, pray, exercise, journal, make calls, check my course, and try to help at least one person.

These are not chores. They are my way of life. I am a farm boy from Idaho who adversity has hit more times than I care to remember. I am a man who has made mistakes and one who is grateful to have enjoyed more than his share of wins.

There is work to be done . . . a mindset to recalibrate . . . a vision to overhaul . . . and habits to revitalize.

It's my time.

Connect with author, entrepreneur, and sales trainer Glade Poulsen at glade@gladepoulsen.com or 208.608.2345. Glade specializes in coaching individuals, teams, and groups.

Instagram / Facebook: @gladepoulsen
linkedin.com/in/gladepoulsen

Tweetable: A good stool has the steady foundation of three legs. I have built my life on that trinity of principles: Mindset. Vision. Habits.

DR. ERIC N. SHELLY

My Next Adventure
Helping Others Create Financial
Independence Through Investing

Dr. Eric N. Shelly works with investors and healthcare professionals in projects targeting high yields and tax advantages. Focused on the clean energy technology space, he now manages over $100 million in assets. Eric transitioned from a 30-year dental business to his current consulting career.

Selling My Dental Practice

As I approached my mid-fifties, I knew I had to reduce the number of hours I spent at the dental chair. After 25 years in dental practice, the physical toll of maintaining the odd positions required in treating patients created back pain and carpal tunnel syndrome that affected the quality of my life. I knew I would not be able to continue this type of work long into the future.

I loved dentistry and serving the patients, my team, and the profession. What would bring me the same level of fulfillment? I needed to develop a new, massive, transformative purpose that would give me the same drive dentistry did.

When considering how life circumstances often lead you to your best opportunities and purposes, I always remember one eventful rafting trip. From this experience, I learned a lot and I went on to apply those lessons to my new, transformative purpose.

One early morning, toward the end of dental school, I met some friends for a whitewater rafting trip on the Cheat River in West Virginia. It was late spring, and the water was surging from recent rain.

There were at least 20 teams getting set for the thrilling ride while the gray skies threatened rain. We adjusted our wetsuits, helmets, and life vests, and prepared for the Class IV rapids.

Our 10-man raft, powered by seven dental students, two instructors, and our river guide, was fourth to cast off. We spent the first thirty minutes at a smooth and gentle pace, practicing maneuvers at the command of our guide. The first roaring, Class I rapid required minimal maneuvering and was perfect for getting everyone's adrenaline pumping. As we entered the rocky canyon, the ride became more technical. We spaced out the rafts to avoid interference as we maneuvered between rocks, eddy currents, and waterfall drops.

Launching My Next Journey

Similar to how I started my rafting adventure, in developing my new transformative business purpose, I had the insight to start slow and develop my new skill set and expertise. I started attending real estate masterminds. The first mastermind I joined was actually designed for dentists in my exact situation.

I knew I had to create passive income to replace the income of my practice. I knew that my savings were far short of the amount my broker recommended for retiring at my current lifestyle. Testing new skills with like-minded dentists worked very well for me. Within months, I was able to navigate complex deals and work with others to create a business that helped me and other dentists earn passive income to replace our practice income. Each project became more complex and involved more and more colleagues investing with me, just as each set of rapids required more maneuvering and teamwork.

On the river, the next obstacle was Coliseum, normally a Class III rapid with a 12-foot drop but swollen to a Class IV fall this day. We lined up the raft and went over the drop. The raft ended up in a vertical orientation. Dental students were falling out in all directions. I was immediately sucked into the churning water.

I eventually popped up right beside the raft and grabbed the rope attached to the perimeter to hoist myself in. However, in an instant, the raft shot down the next set of rapids. I was flailing, desperately hanging on. I assumed I would be less likely to be pushed into the rocks if I had the raft in front of me and held on tight.

At a calm spot in the river, I again tried to hoist myself into the raft and saw my friend Rick inside, sprawled on the floor. He came over to pull me up as the raft rotated. I saw Rick's eyes widen as he looked ahead: two boulders about 20 feet apart and a 10-foot waterfall in between. I was not going to make it into the boat in time. Holding onto the rope and taking a deep breath, I decided the safest place was under the raft, away from the rocks and hopefully in the deepest part of the falls. I felt the launch and then the raft land on me at the bottom. After a bit of disorienting churn, I emerged and, with a lot less energy, attempted to pull myself into the raft. All of a sudden, Rick curled my 200-pound body up, exclaiming "Dude, you're alive!"

During this part of the river journey, I was thrown into different situations that required me to take advantage of the circumstances presented to me. In each scenario, I would evaluate and respond accordingly. Using the same process in my business, I would evaluate opportunities and circumstances and follow where they were leading me.

After a few years of masterminding and acquiring assets, the circumstances were right to sell the dental practice to my partner. With that sale, I was able to replace my practice income with passive income from my assets and investing business and retire myself from dentistry.

Finding the Greater Purpose

I was also making progress on finding a massive transformative purpose. Investing was as interesting to me as the dental profession, but I wasn't finding the element of service at the same level. Yes, real estate investing improves housing conditions and provides places for people to live, but for me, that alone did not drive me.

I began to see opportunities to help my colleagues break free of their practices, as I had, by providing them passive income investments.

I found an investment opportunity in the energy space which involved purchasing and operating a new carbon capture technology that was environmentally friendly and great for building a compelling investment structure. The tax benefits solved a problem for most doctors, who are high ordinary-income earners, and it provided good passive returns as well. With an investment offering such as this, I would be able to help my professional colleagues become financially free and able to pursue their own massive transformative purpose.

Just as I had decided to commit to this great opportunity in early 2020, along came the COVID-19 pandemic.

The lockdown had quite an effect on my fundraising business. I was solely dependent on going to live mastermind and investor meetings where I could connect and network with my potential investors. The lockdown essentially "knocked me out of the raft." I was left to grab onto the rope of social media and Zoom calls to maintain contact with existing investors and meet with new potential investors. I built Facebook and LinkedIn groups and was able to create content for webinars. Social media was the raft I was clinging to through the choppy ride. I was able to leverage the raft to protect myself.

When you are at risk, take advantage of any protection or opportunity available. During the COVID lockdown, investing capital was the last thing investors wanted to do. The great opportunity for my capital raising business was several provisions of the CARES Act involving IRAs and 401Ks. I was able to take advantage of these provisions with a new deal structure that brought many investors back.

It Takes a Team

You can always accomplish more with a team. That day, I was not able to crawl back into the raft myself, and I gladly accepted Rick's help. We were the only raft with a crew at that point. All the other teams were in the water or walking to catch up with their rafts. We started retrieving rafts and getting them to the rocky riverbanks to await their crews.

Floating in a calmer section of the river, we had managed to pull in two raft mates and recover two paddles. As we finished retrieving the rafts, we saw a solitary rafter bobbing in the current. He was weakly calling for help. We were able to reach him and pull him aboard. He was exhausted, and we grew concerned that he may become unconscious. If he passed out and needed CPR, we would be unable to do it on the raft, so we quickly got him to the river bank where he was able to step off the raft but went unconscious, collapsing, as soon as he stepped onto the rocks. We checked his vitals, and his pulse was very hard to discern. One of my friends was shaking him to elicit a response. A slap to the face was enough to render him conscious.

He was conscious, but this was still an urgent situation. He needed medical intervention, and we knew we would not be able to take him out on the raft. We needed to call an airlift. We continued to monitor him until the helicopter arrived.

We needed everyone in that raft, as a team, to take care of that exhausted rafter. Had I not held onto the raft through that set of rapids and over the waterfall, I might not have been in the raft, and we may not have been able to get him to shore and revive him.

Had I not taken the opportunities of the CARES Act and "hung on" while building a social media presence, I may never have finished that capital raise fund. If that would have stopped me, I would not have gone on to help 200 investors get $100 million in tax deductions. I believe that you are presented opportunities that will lead you to bigger things if you are just willing to accept and develop them.

Once the compromised rafter was on his way to the hospital, the crews regrouped and floated the rafts out to the take-out point down the river. We spent the rest of the night sharing experiences and celebrating the successful rescue.

My rafting experience was filled with lessons of starting small and working up to greater complexity, taking advantage of opportunities, accepting help, and working as a team to achieve a greater outcome. Those same lessons I was able to apply to my current massive transformative purpose and the business that grew from it.

Riding New Opportunities

My carbon capture investment opportunity became my primary business focus. It started in 2019 with the opportunity to raise $2,000,000 during the last two months of the year. A month later, I was offered the opportunity to raise another $6,000,000 for six more CO2 scrubbing units. This was quite daunting at the time. I didn't think I had a big enough list of investors to accomplish this but I knew, given this opportunity, I had to try.

By March, I had $1,700,000 raised and another $2,000,000 committed just as the country went into lockdown. The commitment suddenly disappeared and my main strategy of personal networking at investment events went away. During that time, I was fortunate to be part of another mastermind group, The Real Estate Guys Inner Circle. Because I was able to lean on this group for ideas and opportunities, I was able to weather the COVID lockdown, and that put me in a position for something really big.

Scaling Through Leverage

The key to scaling your business is the strategic use of leverage. With innovations such as using leverage to magnify the tax benefits, we were not only able to close out the six million dollar fund, we also closed a total of seventeen million dollars worth of equipment.

The goal for the following year was to deploy 40 CO2 units. We knew we had to scale up our infrastructure to handle the accounts for that many units. To leverage my team, I brought on my nephew as an executive assistant, my close investor friend John as an investor relation expert, a fractional CFO team that could scale with us, and Organize to Scale, an integration team to handle data storage, social media, and back-office technology platforms.

I also needed to expand my list of investors to be able to scale up the capital side. The best leverage strategy for increasing potential investors was asking for referrals of like-minded investors and finding influencers and connectors such as accountants, tax planners, and business sales specialists. These influencers allowed me to connect with their clients to provide significant tax savings, creating a win/win/win scenario.

The final leverage strategy was to partner with other syndicators/sponsors to bring the investment opportunity to a group of new investors previously outside my reach. The result was the deployment of 52 additional CO_2 units, bringing the total to nearly $100,000,000 in capital. Without the help of my fellow mastermind folks, I would have missed this huge opportunity. As with the lessons of the river which resulted in saving a life, my team and I are in a position to help many investors.

I have now helped over a dozen investors create enough passive income to allow each of them the freedom to tackle their own great transformative purpose. I know many of my dental friends and investors are able to go on more mission trips, work in community clinics, and provide pro bono care in their practices as a result of their newfound financial independence.

I realize, in a lifetime, I cannot do nearly as much charitable dentistry as a group of financially free dentists unleashed toward their own transformative purpose. To help them achieve their financial freedom as my massive transformative purpose is the best leverage strategy I could ever hope for.

Contact Eric N. Shelly to discuss your tax mitigation or cash flow needs at 484-883-2223. Visit the website to join our mailing list www.freedomimpactconsulting.com. For a free report on our projects visit carbon@freedomimpactconsulting.com

Tweetable: The key to scaling your business is through the strategic use of leverage.

RAVIN S. PAPIAH

Your Way to Think BIG!

Ravin S. Papiah is highly-decorated in the professional speaking, direct selling, and network marketing industries and is passionate about helping others reach their highest potential. He is a founder-partner, coach, speaker, and director of the Maxwell Leadership Certified Team, Gitomer Licensed Trainer, Canfield Certified Trainer, and Distinguished Toastmaster.

A Way to Think Big

My life has been a real roller coaster, especially my early childhood in Mauritius. Being born a sick child, I had to fight for the things that were normal for other children. Simple things like being able to play outside were a big stretch for me, and I had to think big to be able to at least try!

I did not know the concept of thinking big. I didn't read the book by David Schwartz, *The Magic of Thinking Big*, until 2008 at the age of 33. The book states, "Set your goals high, then exceed them." For me, playing outside, running, and sports were out of reach for me, and thus were beyond-high goals. Not being able to aim for physical goals because of my poor health, I took refuge in reading and aimed to read tons of books compared to my friends who hardly read at that tender age of six. I believe this is where my concept of thinking big was born.

During my school days, if there was an area where I excelled, it was my studies. I earned 100% in my subjects. I saw studying as an escape from my health issues. I would always be studying chapters in advance, trying tougher math problems, and making sure I was ahead of the curriculum, not to compete with my friends, but as a makeshift path because of my health and physical weakness.

A Dilemma for World Book International Mauritius

Fast forward to the '90s. I was working as a regional director for World Book International in Mauritius. I was responsible for the sales and sales force management of the company with another regional director. I had already won seven International Championship Awards for my personal and team performance. We were killing it year in and year out, both at the national and international levels.

Our sales kept increasing, which was one of the criteria to qualify for world championship awards and overseas trips. Then, in 1997, sales dipped and did not increase over sales the previous year. As a result, that year, despite our team achieving the best sales at the international level for our category, we were not qualified to take part in the international championship awards.

For five consecutive years, we had been at the pinnacle of success, hitting the highest awards at the international level and making our country proud. For Mauritius, a small island with merely 1.2 million in population, to beat bigger countries like the US, India, South Africa, the Philippines, and others, claiming international awards was an out-of-this-world achievement. And we had done that not for one but five years running. So, not participating in a sixth year was unbearable for me and my team.

Our sales numbers were amazing, and despite those numbers being the best numbers in the world, because we had not increased our sales over the previous year, we were not recognized as the best. That was heartbreaking for us, and our team was broken. The motivation, the excitement, the desire, all were gone.

1998 started slow with sales figures lower than we had ever imagined. As the team leader, I must admit, my reaction to this miss was a feeling of defeat and failure. It was like an ice-cold shower. It showed in my demeanor, and my attitude translated to my people.

An Opportunity to Change the Game

In early 1998, we received notification that the World Book International president, vice president, and their spouses would visit Mauritius. Since Mauritius was a top sales producer of World Book International, the chief executives made it a must to visit at least once a year on their way to Africa and India. I was given the responsibility to pick them up from the airport in my BMW and drop them at their hotels.

Our airport is in the south of the island and their hotel in the north, about an hour and forty minute drive. After the arrival procedures were completed, I welcomed them and got them comfortably seated before hitting the road for the long drive.

The president, seated next to me, started the conversation. We talked about the business, the weather forecast, and our gala dinner and awards night happening during their stay.

Then, an idea struck me. Should I talk about my concerns? I had thought hard about my team's situation and even discussed it with my local superiors, but they were not too excited to discuss the matter with higher-ups at World Book International. Still, I thought it was unfair for our team to hit the best numbers in the world in our category and not be recognized. I understood that beating your previous year's sales was a criterion to compete, but a team just could not sustain continuous positive sales growth year after year. If the numbers are still the best worldwide, and you are denied the opportunity to compete, it breaks the momentum of the team, and thus breaks the ongoing growth pattern. Growth is driven by people, and when the people are broken, growth in turn breaks down. If not attended right away, this can create a downward spiral.

For me, this was a fight to keep my team motivated towards continuous growth. So, while driving and chatting, my mind was at war. Should I break protocol? Would my superiors be cross with me? I was hesitant. And then, the president said to me, "Ravin, your 1997 performance was brilliant!"

This was it! I seized this moment and replied, "But it broke my spirit and that of my team!"

All four of my passengers were stunned, and I heard a common "Why?" stated in a surprised tone. I thought, *Ravin, this is your moment to share. Just do it.*

I was thinking of my people and the future of our business. I was thinking for the future. But, speaking to the international president and vice president about established company rules in the absence of my local business owners and senior management executives was not an easy decision. I realized being bold was my only solution. What could I lose? I could get a NO, but what if I got a YES?

So, I shared the dilemma with the president and vice president. First, I suggested that every salesperson, at any level, could attend the conference if they achieved a minimum sales quota. That would motivate more salespeople to achieve that minimum, which would increase sales worldwide. Second, I recommended that when a contestant did not satisfy a particular criterion of positive growth, in place of eliminating the contestant from participating in sales competitions, points should be calculated to determine the winners with the negative growth accounted for. This would avoid demotivating top producers.

Both executives listened to me intently. I could see them thinking deeply. After I shared, they both reassured me they would think about it.

The President's Announcement

Two days later was the gala dinner and awards night. The president was seated next to me at the same table. He smiled at me with a knowing look.

It was then time for the presidential address. The president started his speech, glanced at me, and announced, beaming, "I have good news for you—in fact, for every salesperson around the world—because someone here among us dared take the first step to correct an unfairness."

To my utter bewilderment, the president acquiesced to both of my requests. Going forward, everyone who achieved a minimum sales quota required at their level would qualify for the overseas conference trip, and everyone who qualified could also compete for awards, with changes made to account for negative growth. The president further told us that as he made his announcement, every team in the world was reading these changes as well, heralding a positive wind of change. WOW! That was a phenomenal night that completely changed the lives of thousands of salespeople around the world, including mine and those of my sales team.

Think Big Campaign '98

After the president left for the US, I was back to work, wondering how I would motivate my team to get back on track, flying at our usual height and even higher. The computer craze was starting to hit our shores, and encyclopedia sales were becoming more and more challenging. I created the 1998 Think Big Campaign. The goal was for us to think big again, bigger than before. The new changes solved the demotivation problem but also brought the possibility of comfort, as salespeople could now target only minimum qualification numbers and still attend the conference. I wanted my team to win at national and international levels.

We created a unique pin with the words THINK BIG CAMPAIGN '98 on it with the World Book International logo. Everyone was to wear the pin throughout the year to demonstrate their commitment to thinking big. We hosted recruiting campaigns, held training sessions to train everyone on high-level recruiting, and then we trained the recruits on product knowledge and sales techniques.

1998 turned out to be a big year. Hundreds of new salespeople joined us, many existing salespeople advanced ranks, and we produced one of the finest annual performances ever. But you know what? The bold changes that

I had to be courageous to ask for, that were eventually given, and that were benefitting the entire world—we didn't need them at the end of 1998. Why? Because, in the end, we did achieve an increase over the previous year!

Think Big Your Way

Thinking big has always been my driver. It all started unconsciously, when I did not even know the concept. THINK BIG is the vision that things can be better in the future than they are today. I started with me, when I was just a school kid who wanted to become more than I was. I wanted to be what every other child around me was, like everyone else. YOUR "think big" may not be doing something that will stun the world. NO, your "think big" is something that will stun you, that will make the whole difference to you and your life even if it looks ordinary to the world.

Being a normal child was not a given for me. I had to fight for it. I had to THINK BIG to find the way. People always ask me how a super shy guy like me became an international public speaker. Let me tell you that hard work and perseverance have paid off for me and continue to do so.

As a certified trainer, speaker, and coach of the Maxwell Leadership Certified Team, Gitomer Licensed Trainers, and Canfield Certified Trainers, and as a member of the Kyle Wilson Inner Circle, I now help entrepreneurs, executives, and corporations build businesses for people by people. For this to happen, developing the essence of leadership in every individual is instrumental. My certifications coupled with my higher academic qualifications and my engagement with Toastmasters, Rotary, and BNI provides me with experience, knowledge, tools, and platforms to help individuals who desire growth and success but do not know where to start or how to do it.

I help you to think big! Think big YOUR way. Stun yourself with your performance, and eventually, the world will surely be stunned. It happened for me, and I know, it will happen for you too!

Connect with Ravin S. Papiah, professional speaker
and trainer, in The Life Defining Leadership group on
Facebook, on LinkedIn, on his website
www.johncmaxwellgroup.com/ravinsouvendrapapiah,
or by email at ravinpapiahleadership@gmail.com.

Tweetable: THINK BIG is the vision that things
can be better in the future than they are today.
Think big YOUR way. Stun yourself with your
performance, and eventually, the world will surely
be stunned.

LUCELIA CHOU

A Waitress from Venezuela to NYC with a Big Dream

Lucelia Chou is an educator who turned her passion for investing into a teachable career. She leverages the power of YouTube to share her financial literacy content, making education free and available to anyone seeking it. She is a real estate investor and successful YouTuber with over 362,000 subscribers.

Girls Are Meant to Be at Home

I was born in Venezuela to Chinese parents. I am the oldest of five daughters, so my parents were extra strict with me as I needed to set an example for my younger siblings. I grew up in a small Venezuelan city, Maracay, surrounded by the four most dangerous neighborhoods in the area.

Growing up, my parents didn't have much. They eventually saved enough money to open up a restaurant. It was mostly a family-operated business. My dad handled the customer service, my mom handled the money and the accounting, my uncles were the cooks, and my sisters and I were the waitresses. The city I grew up in was small enough that all my elementary school teachers used to hang out at my parents' restaurant for happy hour.

That was my first job. My dad ran a tough shop. We all worked long hours with no breaks. Food was fuel and had to be inhaled because we had to get back to work. My dad took no breaks in life. Everything was work, including the holidays. Valentine's Day, Mother's Day, Christmas, and New Year's were the busiest and most profitable days of the year—everyone in the family had to work.

The restaurant business demanded a lot of time from the family. My mom was physically very ill by the time she became pregnant with my youngest sister. So, I became the new "her" in the business at the age of 10.

Life as a Business Owner

Working full-time in the family business taught me a lot. For starters, being a business owner wasn't easy. It wasn't just about cashing out profits. It was about long hours of hard work, making sure the invoices and the staff were paid, and ensuring the business had what it needed first. There were months we weren't able to meet our operating expenses and I saw my parents asking the restaurant staff (my uncles, the cleaning staff, and the additional waiters who stepped in when the sisters were in school) for a bit more time to pay them. The restaurant staff understood and were always loyal to us. From that moment on, I learned that relationships were everything in business. As business owners, we are nothing without the team that supports us. And as the staff, we need the company that hired us to do well so we can continue to be employed.

At an early age, I never wanted to be a business owner because I despised the unappreciated, long work hours. My dream was to become a well-educated woman who held an executive role on Wall Street and be able to build happy memories during the holidays with my loved ones. I thought the reason my parents were putting long hours in the family business was that they didn't have the opportunity to go to school. I strongly believed that my life would involve shorter working hours if I had a formal education under my belt.

My mind was set on becoming an executive on Wall Street, so everything I did in my early years was to prepare for that moment. Since I grew up in a Spanish-speaking country, I made sure I excelled in my English classes. I also made sure I read every book on business and leadership that was available at the time.

I moved to the US at the age of 17. I arrived in New York City in late September 2002, a little over a year after 9/11. Moving was tough. I felt like I was abandoning my family to fulfill my selfish goals.

Big Apple Dreams
My first job in NYC was in a jewelry store in Manhattan's Chinatown. I started cleaning the bathrooms but quickly got "promoted" to sales since I spoke three languages. I enjoyed the additional responsibility but would have appreciated a pay bump to match. I met people who had worked there for over 10 years making only $50 a day for an 8-hour shift.

I had just turned 18. I ran the numbers and realized that at $50 a day, I was never going to be able to bring my family to the US, much less buy them the houses and the fancy cars I had in mind for them. When the reality of those numbers hit me, I got very scared. That job was a true dead-end job.

But within two months, I unexpectedly got fired!

Getting fired was the best thing that happened to me. I had no other choice but to be out of my comfort zone. Back then, I had a roommate who was all about credit and working the least amount of hours for the most bang! So I started learning from her.

I opened my first credit card when I was 19, and with my roommate's advice, I got three jobs that paid extremely well for a kid in her early 20s without a college education. I put myself through my undergraduate studies thanks to the knowledge I had on credit cards. With the financial assistance of those cards, I was able to proudly major in finance with a minor in mathematics! Every semester, I would pay my semester upfront with my credit cards, and throughout the semester, I would pay the cards down with the income from my three jobs.

It was a long, exhausting journey, definitely no different from the long exhausting hours worked at the family restaurant. Yet, this journey felt harsher because I was alone in NYC. There were times I thought that my family was right. *I must be a princess. I can't do anything. What was I thinking, dreaming about getting to Wall Street? Maybe I should find myself a nice guy to marry and have him support me and my family financially.*

Those were common thoughts during college, especially year five. I was supposed to graduate in five years or less, but I almost failed a class in my (then) last semester and it dragged my GPA down. I blame sleep deprivation. I stayed an extra year to bring my GPA up to graduation standards and earned my degree in six years while working full-time.

Graduation Crisis

I finally graduated in 2009. I worked so hard all of those years only to graduate in the middle of the financial crisis. It felt like a joke. At that time, Wall Street was in a lot of heat, so my job search didn't go well.

I stayed grounded, but my fears grew stronger. I was also frustrated! I planned so hard for graduation. I never planned for what was going to happen after. I believed Wall Street firms would come fight for me. But they never came. That frustration took years to overcome. I felt entitled, that a job was owed to me because I went to school. It took me more than 10 years to learn that life doesn't owe me anything. If I wanted something, I had to earn it.

I realized that I had two choices: go back to Venezuela and admit that I was a useless princess and a financial burden to a husband OR suck it up and keep pushing in the Big Apple, even if that meant working 10 times harder.

I chose to do the latter.

I realized that college wasn't enough. My degree was only one part of the equation. I needed to keep building my skills. So, I decided to take a taxation course at H&R Block and a bartending course.

My taxation course came in very handy. I was able to get a part-time job at a small tax consulting business. But that job was only temporary. The real benefits came later once I became a million-dollar business owner. I never thought that a taxation course would matter so much in my future. It was one of the most valuable courses I have ever taken. My accountants love talking to me because I get them. I understand their language, and I can sometimes be even more meticulous than they are with the company books.

The bartending course was excellent too. During the crisis, a lot of people turned to parties and drinking. I was making good money. At one point, I even considered quitting my pursuit of Wall Street. Who needs Wall Street when you are making all this cash? But, life had different plans for me. A few years later, I landed a job at the Federal Reserve Bank of New York.

Learning Doesn't Stop at Graduation

The Fed taught me a lot. It was very intimidating at first. I felt like an impostor. I met people who spoke six languages, some of whom spoke better Chinese than me! A good percentage of the people at the Fed held PhDs. Some of them even had three PhDs. I came to the equation with only an undergrad degree, which took me six years to get.

I worked extra hard. When my bosses gave me feedback that I lacked business communication skills, I was disturbed. I couldn't understand what the leaders wanted. However, I knew I could learn it. After work, I would devour lots of business writing books.

My career at the Fed was cutthroat. I realized a boss in a suit could be a lot worse than my dad on the days he would yell at the restaurant. With my dad, you could see the heat coming. But in a nicely polished suit, it's almost always a surprise. There were only a few spots at the top. I thought the women at the Fed were going to support me, however, the women I thought were my mentors took advantage of and claimed credit for my hard work.

Simultaneously, I learned a lot of professional skills at the Fed from great people who took me under their wing and taught me how to navigate the corporate world in an efficient and ethical manner. I didn't want to become the kind of leader who would be unethical. I stand by that philosophy today.

In my five years at the Fed, I was able to finish my master's degree with the cost of tuition and books fully reimbursed by their education program. I will always be grateful to the Fed for that.

During that time, I was also able to purchase my very first property in Alabama. My sister accepted a job offer there, and as the big sister, I wanted to make sure she found a safe place to live. So I made the trip with her to Alabama to hunt for a rental apartment. When we found "the one," the Realtor told me the property happened to be for sale, so I bought it as a safety net for retirement. My plan was to leave NYC at retirement and move to a more affordable town without worrying about paying rent.

Momentum Came Knocking

Two and a half years later, the same Realtor contacted me to offer another apartment in the same building complex. I told him that I would buy the unit if he could find a lender who was willing to finance my purchase with zero money down. Honestly, I was kidding. I didn't know how to say no, so that was my polite way of doing so. But then, my Realtor found the lender who offered exactly what I asked for! I had no idea how that was possible, but I went for it because I could not picture myself working at the Fed for another 10 years. I realized that I didn't have to save money for another decade to be able to buy another property, and I liked that! That was the moment I began to actively pursue real estate.

Later that year, I learned that I was able to buy that rental without a down payment because of a cash-out-refi, a mortgage that allows you to pull equity out of a property you own. That same year, I repeated the cash-out-refi process again to build and grow my portfolio of 24 properties.

I was so passionate about what I learned about investing that I couldn't wait to share it with the world. Investing changed my life and my family's lives for the better. I realized that if an immigrant like me could do it from scratch, everybody can do it. All they needed was access to the information that I had acquired over the years thanks to the great samaritans who crossed paths with me and helped me grow. It felt selfish to keep all that information to myself.

So, towards the end of my career at the Fed, my boyfriend Anthony and I co-founded Novarise. Novarise was born on YouTube in December 2019. Our company is all about educating and empowering people through financial literacy.

As of today, Novarise has over 362,000 subscribers on both its channels (English and Spanish). The company has a global online presence and has impacted over 10 million lives for the better since its inception. Our dream is to turn Novarise into a legacy that outlives Anthony and I so that future lives and generations continue to benefit from our informational content.

I feel very honored that our followers have welcomed us to be part of the change in their lives. Some say we all have a purpose in life. I am very fortunate to have found mine: help others change their lives through financial education. Because of that, I decided to leave my corporate life to embark on this amazing journey as an educator and learner of life. I am very grateful for all the lessons learned in my earlier years and very excited for the ones that will come from this new journey. To keep my family proud, I am still grounded, residing in my 900-square-foot New York City apartment with Anthony while working (some) holidays and weekends, and we love it!

Watch and share Lucelia Chou's YouTube channels with someone you know will benefit from her content: Novarise Invest (for content in English) or Novarise Latino (for content in Spanish). Visit novarise.com to get to know more about her team, company's mission, and story.

Tweetable: Whatever you don't know you can learn.

PHILLIP WARRICK

From College Dropout to Financially Free Through Real Estate Investing

Phillip Warrick, certified high-performance coach, creative real estate investor, and serial entrepreneur, teaches entrepreneurs, investors, and professionals how to create passive income and achieve financial freedom through real estate investing. Phillip and his wife Lindsey have four children and one grandson.

Thinking Big Since High School

In 1997, when I was a senior in high school, I wanted to purchase a house and go to college. My desire was to rent out rooms to roommates. I figured those rented rooms would pay the whole mortgage allowing me to live in a house for free. This was my first idea of rental arbitrage, or better yet, ownership arbitrage.

I knew from an early age that I was going to be wealthy and successful because I was told I would be. When I got this idea in my head, I asked my father, "What do I need to do to buy a house?"

My dad was a missionary in Brazil for 10 years who turned entrepreneur. Some would agree that running a church is a business as well. The best advice he could give me was, "Son, you need to save 20% for a down payment, to qualify for a home loan."

I decided I would wait one year before going to college, continue working, and do everything I could to save up that 20% down payment.

Falling in Love with Lindsey and Real Estate

I met Lindsey our senior year of high school and she fell in love with me at first sight ;-). I decided she would be my wife and I would do everything in my power to convince her of the same. We dated, went to prom together, and were stuck like glue. We made plans to stay back for a year after high school while I worked to save up that 20% down payment and she went to community college before going to university.

One night, I was watching television, and a late-night infomercial came on. There sat the late Carleton Sheets on a barstool talking about his home study course *How to Buy Your First House or Investment Property with No Down Payment*. I bought the course, and I was hooked.

I had heard most successful, wealthy people made their fortune through real estate investing. Or, if they made their wealth through business or earned income, they held that money in real estate as a hedge against inflation and to grow and protect it. And, as a high school senior, I didn't have much money or great credit, so I thought this would be a good path to take.

I remember like it was yesterday: my buddy on a Saturday morning trying to get me off the couch from watching this training. He said, "Come on, man, that won't work, they're just trying to sell you. You're wasting our Saturday." Well, I wasn't so sure it was a wasted Saturday. I believed I could have success buying houses. I stayed committed and would spend countless Saturdays over the next several decades devoted to my self-education.

Chasing the Cheerleader

I have to admit, when I was a senior in high school, I was a little rough around the edges: running with the wrong crowd, smoking mary jane, and partying a little too much. Somehow, someway, Lindsey put up with me. We were an interesting combination: high school cheerleader dating an entrepreneurial-minded burnout. Nobody thought we would make it. Shortly after graduation, Lindsey's mom decided to send her to Stephen F. Austin State University, three and a half hours from home, most likely to get her away from me.

Like the in-love, 18-year-old teenager I was, I packed my bags and chased her. I got a job in town, rented an apartment, and enrolled in a community college close by. We ended up breaking up after the first semester, and I dropped out of college.

I was heartbroken. I moved back home, but I continued paying the rent on my apartment so I wouldn't ruin my credit. On recommendation from my dad, I took a job at a bank and worked there for about six months. It was the best job I'd ever had, but I decided I should go back to school.

I enrolled in community college, but I dropped out after two weeks to move to Colorado with my friend Todd. School just wasn't for me, and I wanted to get to work. We took jobs as housemen at a local ski resort, but two weeks later, I got a phone call: My dad had cancer. I cut my "ski bum" dreams short to be with my father.

Dad was diagnosed with pancreatic cancer in January and passed away in April at the young age of 44. This forced me to grow up fast. The last words I spoke to my father were that I would take care of my mother.

After dad passed, my mother was tasked with running and operating the sign company dad had started. I realized she needed help. I took over the business operations and soon after was able to purchase the business from her so she could retire. Mom became my first private lender and has lived off her investment income since then, allowing me to honor my commitment to Dad.

Not long after Dad passed away, Lindsey and I found our way back together. Finally, in 2001, I married my prom date. Shortly after, we had our first daughter Raylea. Since, we've had three more children, two daughters ReAnna and Emma and our youngest son Andy. Today, we are blessed with our first grandchild.

Saturdays Are Still for Education

"Formal education will make you a living; self-education will make you a fortune." – Jim Rohn

In 2002, I joined the Real Estate Investment Club of Houston (RICH) where, on the first Saturday of every month, 500+ real estate investors and vendors gathered to teach real estate investing. I went to seminars and trainings, devouring all the information I could get my hands on. Soon after my first flip, my wife and I bought our first home and started buying, renovating, renting, and flipping houses. We flipped three to four houses per year until December of 2003 when we decided to take the leap, sell the sign business I had purchased after Dad passed away, and go all-in as full-time real estate investors.

It was a struggle back then to learn from experienced investors. Everything was a big "secret." We didn't have Google, YouTube, and online courses. If you wanted to learn more, you had to buy books, pay thousands of dollars to attend live training seminars, then if you really wanted to get ahead fast and skip the learning curve, pay for coaching and mentoring. I stuck with it. I hired coaches, I hired mentors, and I kept "wasting my Saturdays" on my self-education. I went to every training seminar I could get to as fast as I could, paying thousands of dollars every year to learn, grow, and succeed doing deals. Today, I still attend trainings on a regular basis. In fact, I am honored to often lead real estate investing trainings, sit on expert panels, and coach up-and-coming real estate investors.

Burn the Boat

We went strong in real estate investing from 2004 until 2008. We did every type of transaction from pre-foreclosure, short sale, owner finance, subject to, lease option, hard money, wholesale, and full rehab. We'd buy, renovate, rent, refinance, and repeat before people coined this the BRRRR method. In 2008, before the market crashed, Lindsey and I had 57 houses on the books and were living the good life. We had two lake houses, luxury vehicles, and were feeding our family of six. Life was good and getting better all the time.

Then, just like that, just like almost every other real estate investor I knew at the time, we got hosed. We ended up underwater with a ton of vacancies, and we couldn't handle it. We ended up losing houses to foreclosure which led to frivolous lawsuits which turned into some pretty heavy financial burdens and losses.

Financially and emotionally, 2011 was the worst year of our lives from the effect of the 2008 banking collapse. I became depressed and even suicidal. By the grace of God, we held on and managed to hold a handful of properties. In November, we purchased back the sign business we had sold in 2003 and persisted until we were able to regain our ground. We were very close to filing bankruptcy before the dust began to settle.

We let a few years pass without new acquisitions, managed the real estate we had left, and revived the sign business. Then at about the same time as all the other real estate investors, we started getting back in the game.

Go Big or Go Home, Airbnb Short-Term Rentals

In 2017, all the real estate gurus that had quit teaching after the crash started to make their way back into the education space. I started seeing emails from all my real estate guru friends promoting the Airbnb formula. I took an online eight-week training course to learn how to profit from AirBnb on properties I didn't even own. That sounded good to me because, after the sting of the crash, I wasn't sure I wanted to buy real estate anymore.

In November of 2017, we started Epic Property Pros LLC.

From 2017 to 2020, we accumulated 17 vacation rentals using rental arbitrage and properties that we owned. We slowly furnished each property. Everything was going great, but I started to wonder why I was renting houses instead of buying.

I realized I prefer being the owner over being a tenant. Arbitrage did not resonate with me anymore. I did not like the idea of paying down another landlord's mortgage while he was enjoying the tax benefits, principal pay down, appreciation, and other benefits that come with owning investment real estate. I slowly started to shut down the rental arbitrage properties. I was no longer going to fix up houses I didn't own. I was going to get back into buying real estate using the BRRRR method.

When COVID was in full swing in 2020, all our vacation listings suddenly went vacant. Airbnb offered guests full refunds for canceling due to travel restrictions, and just like that, I was living in fear of repeating the 2008 crash. Never could I have planned for complete vacancy. Due to this uncertainty, I was able to get out of my rental arbitrage properties, working things out with the landlords to let us out of the leases early because we couldn't pay rent with vacant houses. One by one, we shut down the remaining rental arbitrage properties, used the furniture to furnish the houses we owned as long-term rentals and converted them into short-term rentals. While the world was on lockdown, we were working around the clock, and thank God, people started booking again.

Finding the Money to Grow to the Next Level

It was actually quite a feat to keep adding one property after another considering that I did not have verifiable income because of all the tax write-offs created by rental real estate. This was good strategy, but I could not qualify for traditional financing due to being self-employed and the paper losses created from rentals.

I searched and searched until I finally found a lender that would qualify me based on the property's debt service coverage ratio and fund my property purchases up to 80% of the purchase price. Remarkably, they also do cash-out refinances up to 75% of the appraisal value on property owned for 12 months or longer. This is a non-qualifying loan, for self-employed borrowers and investors. We only have to prove the property is a good investment and the rental income will support the debt service. As long as I have 20% down or 25% equity, I get a 30-year fixed rate loan at a decent interest rate compared to the 8-15% hard money rates I had grown accustomed to.

One by one, I refinanced houses that I had purchased with seller financing, hard money, and private money loans into 30-year fixed rate loans. This allows me to pull cash from equity and deploy that cash into new houses I plan to keep, all while lowering our monthly payments and increasing our monthly positive cash flow.

Before 2008, I qualified for stated income loans. After 2008, those loans disappeared. I didn't believe I would ever qualify or find a lender that could replace those coveted stated income loans. But, in the last 12 months, I've refinanced multiple properties in my portfolio with interest rates in the 4-7% range. After investing since 2001, I am blown away by how these resources have absolutely changed the trajectory of my real estate investing career.

In 2021, I partnered as a broker so that I could offer these loans and bring these awesome products to my coaching and consulting clients. I'm blessed to offer what has been game-changing for me to my real estate investing clients and students.

Today, we're looking at prospective properties every single day, and we continue to grow our business and portfolio one property at a time.

We provide property management, next-level real estate coaching and consulting, and exclusive purchase opportunities to our students and partners, and manage Airbnb short-term rentals through Epic Property Pros LLC.

Since getting started in 1997, I've learned how to navigate the up and down cycles of real estate. I believe anybody can and everybody should invest in real estate at some capacity. I understand not everybody wants to "quit their job in 90 days" to become full-time real estate investors like me. I coach and create custom-tailored plans to fit an individual's needs. Some people might want to invest passively and put investment capital to work. Some might want to flip a house to create big chunks of cash they can put into other ventures or get out of debt. Others may want to do long-term rentals or short-term rentals. I believe I can help anyone find the best plan out of the thousands of ways you can do real estate investing. Everyone needs a custom roadmap to reach their own personal desired destination, and anyone can get there faster with more efficiency with a coach guiding the way.

My desire is to use my 20+ years of experience to continue helping people shorten their learning curve and achieve financial freedom starting TODAY.

Contact Phillip Warrick, with over two decades of real estate and entrepreneurial experience, to learn more about creating passive income through real estate investing and start your journey towards financial freedom. Ask about a complimentary investment consultation, one on one coaching, and group mastermind coaching.

phillipwarrick.com | phillip@phillipwarrick.com

Tweetable: I believe anybody can and everybody should invest in real estate at some capacity. There are many paths to reach your unique dream. How can you shorten the learning curve to get you to your dreams faster?

DAVID IMONITIE

How to Positively Impact a Billion People

David Imonitie is a sought-after speaker, author of Conceive, Believe, Achieve *and* Believe Nation: The Belief of a Nation, *and founder of Believe Nation and the I Believe Foundation. He has had a global impact through his humanitarian efforts, inspired millions, and helped bring billions in revenue to multiple organizations.*

Childhood

I was born to two amazing parents in the United States. When I was about six weeks old, we moved to Nigeria, where my parents grew up. So, I consider myself originally from Nigeria. My life consisted of church, school, and tennis. My dad, David Sr., played professional tennis. He was number one in Africa for a very long time. It was fun to grow up with a celebrity.

In 1993, when I was 10, my mom made the pivotal decision to move us back to the United States. We packed up myself, my mom, my two sisters, and moved to New York.

We were there for seven years. As a young kid from Nigeria not familiar with this country, it was challenging. My accent was different. People butchered my name. But eventually, I adjusted and things got better.

We moved to Houston, Texas, then I went on to college in North Carolina. That's where things got really bad, or so I thought. Now, I think what I thought was so bad at the time was God putting things in place to put me in the right position.

After my sophomore year, I dropped out of school. At 21 years old, I was introduced to relationship marketing and the direct sales industry. That was my first introduction to Jim Rohn. I'd listen to *Building Your Network Marketing Business* over and over again. I felt like I knew Jim. That was the start of an 18-year journey of personal growth and leadership. Starting with this audio, my personal growth and my belief system developed to where, now, my ability to impact people is what brings me the biggest joy.

The Power of Autosuggestion

I remember listening to an audio by Mark Yarnell about the quantum leap. Why is it that so very few people ever make the quantum leap? There's a secret to it. There's a reason many people don't grow to earn $100,000 a year. And if someone ever gets to $100,000 a year, there's a reason they don't get to a million a year. If they ever do get to a million a year, there's a reason they don't get to a million a month. I'm so glad, ecstatic, that I found out what that reason is.

It's a practice everybody knows but very few practice every single day. Autosuggestion. You're only going to believe what you hear. What you hear on a consistent basis is what you're going to believe.

I decided a long time ago that I was not going to set limitations on what was possible. People struggle to get to $100,000 a year because they have set a limitation that they can't get there, or that it's difficult to get there. And people that do get there, they do the same thing—they set limitations on why they can't get to a million a year.

Once I learned about this principle at age 21, it took me some years to understand it. I didn't make my first million until I was 27. There was a maturation process that each of us have to go through and, more importantly, grow through. It required putting in the work, mental and physical work. It required going to every event, reading the books, and listening to the audios, over and over and over again. It required constantly searching for the right information. Finding a mentor was huge. Once I did, I had close proximity to what I had been believing in, dreaming of, and hoping for. There was someone physically in front of me who had the life I was dreaming about. I think that's when things really started to take off.

Success requires both rewiring how you think and goal setting. You have to rewire the way you think to accomplish the goal. Some individuals may say, "I don't really set goals anymore. It's really more about purpose." I don't disagree with that, but I can promise, before anyone gets to that way of thinking, they set a lot of goals.

I don't speak to people from where I am today. I speak to people from where I was when I was stuck, when I was living with my dad, when I had a thousand dollars to my name, when I didn't have a car, and when I didn't have a driver's license. I speak from that place. And I show what I did to get to $10,000 a month, then $100,000 a month.

These principles work in finance, but they also work in your relationships with your family, your friends, and your partners. They also work in your relationship with God. The strategies are the same. It's just a matter of deciding to utilize them in that area of your life.

Leadership

Leadership is not one size fits all. For me, leadership is about influence. For me to have influence with someone, I first have to have a relationship with that person. In that relationship, there has to be trust. The people I lead, naturally, come from different phases in life. Some people may be just starting out as entrepreneurs. Others have been entrepreneurs for 20 years. So, I use different strategies for different people. It's not cookie-cutter. I tell people, "I don't know what's best for you, but I want what's best for you. I'm only going to speak to you from a place that is going to benefit you based on the experience I've had."

It starts with love. I don't think you can lead people unless you love them. And every leader must have discipline. Family goals, business goals—it's impossible for you to succeed without discipline. Through discipline, you gain experience. Then, I believe every leader has to have results, not personal results, but a track record of people they have helped along the way.

At the level where I am today, it's about building a culture of growth, unity, and trust. I've learned to give people a break and to understand that growth is a process. Not everyone is going to walk and run at the same time. I think it takes two to five years to really develop a great leader. Most people are not willing to pay that price, and that's why a lot of people don't get the prize.

My Pyramid of Belief

My secret sauce is belief. I call it the pyramid of belief. My foundation is my belief in God. I had an encounter in 2010 that forever changed my life. I was in tears for nine days because I knew for a fact that I had encountered God.

That belief in God led to the second part of that pyramid—belief in myself. I have so much belief in Him and I know He's in me. That automatically leads to me believing in myself. So, I don't set limitations on myself. I don't think realistically. My life's not realistic today. I wasn't thinking realistically when I was living with my dad and had a thousand dollars to my name. I was thinking out of this world. Now, I'm living out of this world.

The third part of the pyramid is my belief in people. The same God that's in me is in you as well. So, if I believe in God, I believe in you. My goal is to bring to your awareness the power that's inside of you. Once you accept this reality, you can start the process of reconditioning yourself to only think big.

A belief is created three ways. It's created through the words we speak, the images we look at, and the emotions we have. How do I find the right words? I have words in my home. In my office, I have a sign: "I positively impact the lives of a billion people." I have images all around me. In my closet. At my bedside. In my shower. Everywhere. I'm constantly creating the future. I see it all the time. And then, my emotions are of loving gratitude.

Once I've created this future, what are the skills I need to master to get there? I can't say I want to earn a million dollars and not be skilled at what it takes to make a million dollars. So, I start that process. But, I'm not starting the process from a place of *Is it going to work?* No. I already believe that it has worked. Now, I'm just doing the work.

What's Next

You may be looking at your life, saying, "Man, things are falling apart." The reality is that He's orchestrating things for your good. Even things that you think are bad, He has something great in mind that will come from it. I've had to remind myself of that over the last 18 years.

Never stop, because the world is always attacking. You've got to keep your mind focused on where you're going, your purpose, your goals, and your vision, to impact other people.

Every single day, I give value to people, and every day, I give love and have gratitude. I don't have to think about it. It's automatic in everything I do. In every conversation I have, through the images around me, through what I consciously and subconsciously see, I'm taking care of my spirit so my body can go do what it needs to do. Prayer is something I do all throughout the day. When I worship, I'm showing gratitude. My spirit, my mind, and my soul have to be fed. It's not a daily ritual, it's just the way I live.

Impacting a Billion People

In 2013, I had just come off a multiple seven-figure year. I felt fulfilled by my success because I had been fighting for so long for what I considered success, financial success. But there was a level of, I wouldn't say emptiness, but it wasn't just about the money anymore. And so, I wrote down the goal to positively impact the lives of a billion people.

What I actually wrote was, "Lord, when they see me, I want them to see you. When they hear me, I want them to hear you." I've been on that journey for nine years now. I know for a fact, I have been able to impact millions of people. And it's going to get to a billion, because really, my goal is to work with a thousand leaders who then each go out and impact a million people. That will get us to one billion.

That's why I started Believe Nation, to create an opportunity to make a difference in the lives of others through the power of belief and through the heart of the leader.

We want to help people with their spiritual awareness and their emotional strength. I know that your faith and your belief system are what will allow you to live the life you truly want to live.

Learn more about David Imonitie and his programs at believenation.com. Follow him on Instagram (www.instagram.com/davidimonitie) and Facebook (www.facebook.com/davidimonitie).

Tweetable: You may be looking at your life, saying, "Man, things are falling apart." The reality is that He's orchestrating things for your good. Even things that you think are bad, He has something great in mind that will come from it.

SHANNON ROBNETT

Zero to Sixty . . . Million Dollar Portfolio

Shannon Robnett is a developer, builder, syndicator, blockchain enthusiast, and philanthropist. As active CEO of Shannon Robnett Industries, he vertically integrates all aspects of investing. Shannon and his wife Jessie travel the world looking for opportunities to combine real assets with cash flow and freedom.

Hit Hard

"Boss, I hit a bridge with this house."

This is not the start of any phone call you want to have. But there Billy was, with the bedside manner of a wounded grizzly bear, delivering the news in the middle of my Sunday afternoon without preamble.

"Say that again, Billy. You hit a bridge?!"

"Yeah, boss, I did. Down here in Weiser." Billy was some 20 miles off route hauling a 16' tall mobile home with two pilot cars. And even with flashing lights and signs everywhere, he had proceeded, at 60 miles an hour, to remove the roof of the mobile home with a 14' high bridge.

In the fall of 2013, this was starting to seem like just another day. Nothing was working. Like it was for so many during this time, the struggle to survive was real. As I drove out to the crash site, I kept thinking to myself, *How did I get here?* And more importantly, *How do I make the madness stop?*

The last five years had just seemed to go from bad to worse, starting with the Great Recession. I lost my successful construction business when the housing market busted. My marriage of twelve years fell apart. I had tried to put together several other businesses, but nothing seemed to stick. Then, I co-founded a logistics company with a buddy of mine from high school which built a transport business to supply the Bakken oil boom—the only bright spot in the economic picture of the Pacific Northwest at that time. But business problems were not my only problems. Like they say, when it rains it pours, and the Robnett household was in the middle of a deluge.

If You Don't Have Your Health . . .

In 2011, I had a second neck surgery that left a few side effects, including fainting spells. One of the falls left me with three broken ribs. I don't know if you have ever tried to climb into an old cab-over semi, but doing it with three broken ribs is excruciating. While I continued to try and drive to keep our trucking company ahead of the orders, the pain grew too intense and I resigned myself to the work of growing the company.

The growth was good and the ribs healed, but cash flow was always a problem. December 2012, I took a trip to see one of my largest customers in Utah. After dropping off Christmas gifts at his office, my kids and I had decided to go skiing, as Park City was close to my customer's office. Our final run before lunch, I did something I had done many times in my twenty years of skiing—had a gnarly spill. But this one was very different.

After a moment of trying to get my skis back on and figure out where I was, I realized I had done something pretty major to my right leg. I had blown out my knee. And I was uninsured!

After a slow drive home in blizzard conditions with my sixteen-year-old son, Devan, driving, reality set in.

That business meeting we were in Utah for led to more orders, the need to purchase two more trucks, and the need to hire more drivers. And there I was, barely able to get around on crutches, trying to find a surgeon who would take me on as a broke and uninsured patient. I began the process of enrolling in a pre-existing condition insurance program and tried to figure out how I was going to work and raise three kids in this condition. Most days, I would push through without taking any pain medication because of what it did to my mental capacity, only to overmedicate in an attempt to find a level I could live with in the evening. I pushed harder to find success in business but wound up further in the grips of prescription drugs to survive.

Was It Ever Going to Get Better?

Pushing harder to keep all the balls in the air continued to take its toll, and by March of 2013, I existed only in my living room La-Z-Boy. The only solace I felt I had was the pain medication that I received by the buckets. It seemed there was nothing my doctor wouldn't give me and in abundant supply.

While still attempting to be a father and business owner, I was slowly sinking into a drug-induced fog that consumed me 24 hours a day. I had almost resigned myself to this, but I couldn't quit on my kids.

As March became April, a break in the darkness came with the approval of my insurance plan. The last thing they needed was my 2012 taxes. I humbly showed a $30,000 annual income. I had finally sunk low enough to get help. I had often heard people say, "I was broke, but not broke enough to get any help," and now I knew what that meant.

The doctor asked me why I had waited four months with such a severe injury. I told him, without insurance, no one would fix my knee if I was broke. After moving a few things around, he scheduled surgery the very next week. Things were definitely starting to change.

I left the hospital in the care of my sixteen-year-old chauffeur. Devan said, "You seem to be making a habit of getting stoned and needing a ride, Dad." It was the first time we laughed in a long time.

My right leg had lost over 35% of its muscle mass and had been confined to a 12% range of motion for too long, and I had to rebuild it in physical therapy. The doctor assured me that on the therapy regimen, the chronic pain would also subside. But it didn't, in fact, it got worse. As I attempted to change my gait, a herniated disk and my sciatic nerve were at war, and the only thing that kept the peace was the pills. So my spiral continued.

I was a cobbled together wreck, and mentally I was worse. I went from bed to physical therapy to bed. On the odd occasion I felt good enough to drive a trucking route, I was right back in bed from the fatigue and pain. I had seen several surgeons, but they said it was too big of a risk to get into that disk space. Through acupuncture, chiropractic care, stretching labs, and back to the pain management doctor, I had trouble staying in front of the pain and often found myself over or undermedicated with disastrous results. My smorgasbord of remedies included morphine, oxycontin, and tramadol in doses that were starting to cause seizures.

Under the Knife

Finally, I found a surgeon that had a new procedure he felt would fix me. I was willing to try anything at this point.

We were all more than a little concerned on the day of the surgery that our expectations were too high or that there would be complications. These things were not easy to talk about, but the air was thick with the questions.

To be honest, I had an impending feeling of despair. As long as the surgery was a future promise, the outcome was a wonderful thing that *could* happen. The night before the surgery, I was an absolute mess trying not to overthink. I was having a really hard time staying optimistic.

Although I didn't feel ready, the time had arrived. I looked at the woman who had been there through all of this and hoped there would be a future for us. Then, I was wheeled away to surgery. I remember praying for a chance to be free of the pain, have a normal life with Jessie and raise our kids.

Surfacing from unconsciousness, I began to notice that the ache, the deep pain that I had been living with for over a year, was not there. I couldn't believe it. I was not in pain! I was flooded with joy.

When I was released from the hospital, I was not only pain free I was also drug free, and life was going to be grand. When I tried to put on my shoes, they all were deformed and I realized my gait had gotten so bad from my atrophied leg and foot drop that I could not wear them anymore. So new shoes were in order! With this surgery, there was no physical therapy, and my life was perfect from the day I walked out . . . until the following Sunday.

Really, God?

The following Sunday, Billy drove the house into the bridge. I realized life was going to keep coming. Dealing with the bridge disaster seemed to take forever, but it was a turning point in my thinking.

Even though my physical pain was gone and I no longer needed the drugs, I was having a hard time adjusting to "normal" uninebriated life. Life was full of trials. I felt that if I kept the trucking transport company going, the stress of constantly having to hire new drivers and training would truly kill me. Cash flow was still very tight. Some months, I was only getting partial pay on our loads and was struggling to operate with no cash. Every time $100,000 would come in, I would throw it at the $110,000 pile of bills.

But slowly, I began to see the freefall of the previous years halt, and like an overloaded airplane, I started to claw for altitude. I pushed on and drove harder, expanding all the way out into Indiana. I purchased a couple of newer trucks and ran cargo trailers when the weather was bad.

Just when I thought we seemed to be coming out of the bottom of the pit, my biggest contract stopped paying. I had shipments that needed to go out, but literally no money for fuel to get it there.

I was at the breaking point, and from the cab of my truck, a broken, sobbing man, I called my dad. He tried to tell me I could stop it all at any time. I argued that I was not a quitter. He begged me to just hit pause and evaluate. I said I would, and with one final act of determination, I pointed the truck for North Dakota.

As I drove, I had time to think. I began to wonder if battling drivers, cash flow, changing tires on the side of the road, and missing my family was going to be my life forever. I decided that there had to be a way out.

By the time I left the natural gas flares of North Dakota in my rearview mirror, I began to form a plan. Seventeen hours later, I climbed out of the truck with a very clear understanding of what was to come. Several months later, the trucking company was sold. Jessie and I were getting married and buying a house for our Brady bunch. Life was getting better.

Now What?

I went back into construction. It was the thing I knew best, and the market was starting to improve. I had a family of nine to feed, and after the wedding and the house purchase, I once again had very little money to my name.

I secured my first contract to build a mini storage facility and was on the hunt for more. Out of the fires of determination, grit, and tenacity, Phoenix Commercial Construction was born. I quickly found myself in a familiar environment, bidding work and looking for projects to build. I knew I had to get back into development. There were demons of self-doubt to face, but I had conquered bigger problems.

In development, I needed a project, then I needed a partner. I found several of each and began to build my portfolio of successes again, one partnership at a time. I found an old building that needed a facelift. Those profits rolled into a five lot industrial subdivision. I picked up an infill lot that I rezoned for 36 multi-family units. I partnered with an oral surgeon to build out another warehouse complex the next year.

As I strung together small successes, my confidence continued to rise, allowing me to try the truly audacious. I put a $1.8 M parcel of property under contract and went shopping for funding. I was able to find one of the most amazing people to partner with, and in January of 2022, after five years of work, we were able to sell the project for $64 million dollars.

We have since founded an investor relations group that in less than two years has raised $35 million in equity for numerous projects. With over 500 units of multifamily under development and $175 million in projects on the books, Shannon Robnett Industries now includes a property management company, an equity raising piece, as well as our latest venture of digitizing real assets on blockchain.

The Clouds Parted

I often find myself wondering what would have happened if I had given up. What would my life look like now if I had stopped my forward progress? Like Robert Betty said, "Our character isn't defined by the battles we win or lose, but by the battles we dare to fight." And fight you must, regardless of the outcome, because growth comes from the struggle along the journey.

I have never really considered myself to be an exceptional person, only one of exceptional determination and grit. We rarely see these qualities until we have truly traveled to the ends of sanity and tested the limits of endurance. Only then can a person look back at the gauntlet to see where their character was forged.

I have a dollar for every mistake I ever made. It's those mistakes and failures that led to the lessons that have led to the money! No one can expect that without failure you will ever get the winning formula. So, fail often, fail gloriously, and become a student of these lessons to become the winner you are designed to be.

Find Shannon Robnett's podcast @ *The Robnett Real Estate Rundown* or go to his YouTube Channel: Shannon Robnett. LinkedIn: Shannon Robnett or Instagram: ShannonRayRobnett and learn more about what he has going on at Shannonrobnett.com. For more information on Shannon's investment deals contact him: shannonrobnett@gmail.com

Tweetable: No one can expect that without failure you will ever get the winning formula. So, fail often, fail gloriously, and become a student of these lessons to become the winner you are designed to be.

DR. ASHLEY BLAKE

Changing Lives with Food
Founding an Intensive Pediatric
Feeding Clinic

Dr. Ashley Blake is a clinician, entrepreneur, certified coach, trainer, and speaker. In 2021, her pediatric therapy center was selected as a Michigan top 50 company to watch. She hopes to inspire others to follow their dreams and achieve their goals by taking one small action step every day.

Serving at the Highest Standards

The first in my family to go to college, I earned my PhD while growing a family of four. Then, I founded Encompass Therapy Center, a pediatric therapy center in Bay City, Michigan, where the highest-caliber professionals serve clients with different speech or neurological diagnoses and developmental delays.

Our vision is to provide children and families with the highest standard of care and the best treatment outcomes, even if it takes going the extra mile. We have found success through persistence, hard-working team members who go above and beyond the standard, and a leadership team committed to rising above challenges to build a game-changing company. Teamwork has allowed the therapy center to grow and fulfill the lives of those we employ and serve. In 2022, Encompass Therapy Center received a Michigan 50 Distinguished Alumni Award: Great Place to Work.

Food and Family

From the start, Encompass Therapy Center has included feeding programs within our therapy practice. The diminished quality of life for children with limited feeding skills and oral motor delays and their families is evident in the families we train and serve. Families must make difficult choices to adjust to having a child that does not accept, chew, or swallow new or, as we call them, challenging food items.

Families learn to avoid certain triggers related to food to avoid behaviors. Sometimes this means only being able to eat at two restaurants or not being able to eat out at all. Many families are unable to share one family meal and instead have to prepare multiple meals to fit each family member's limits and needs. Parents are often scared to expose their children to new food items when choking and vomiting have been common responses to new food. Parents and family members, including siblings, sacrifice social experiences to ensure that their child is safe and happy when that child does not have the feeding, oral motor, and developmentally appropriate behavioral skills with food that are typically present.

Parents often report being sad or frustrated that their child will not try or accept new foods. Most families want their children to have the positive experiences associated with food, like birthday parties, and to build the skills required to develop into healthy and accepting adults.

The concerns, wants, and needs of parents led my team and me to create the Encompass Pediatric Feeding Clinic.

In 2018, I was overseeing a feeding program for a client with one of my supervisees. During this learning process, colleagues commented on the significant impact feeding programs have on children with neurological disorders such as autism spectrum disorder. In just a short time, we were implementing feeding programs with multiple clients experiencing behavioral and oral motor deficits that were hindering their positive experiences with food. These individualized programs were having a direct impact on clients and families.

We wanted to expand our program to help children needing more intensive feeding services, and we hoped to expand our clientele to include other developmental and neurological disorders in addition to autism spectrum disorder. Families needed more access to care, and perhaps we could create a solution.

We had purpose. We had passion. We knew exactly the WHY, the WHAT, and the vision we were looking to create. But the HOW was still undefined. The Encompass team knew the impact we could make in the lives of children and families, but we had to think BIG by taking small action steps every day to see the future feeding therapy program come to fruition.

Step by Step Success
There was one day when two leadership team members sat in the conference room for eight hours debating the finer points of a plastic measuring

spoon: what measurements needed to be included, what shape the bowl and handle would take, where the company logo would fit, the color. . . . The detailed minutiae seems ridiculous, but deciding these crucial details was one of the very many important steps in achieving our company vision and serving children in need.

Amy Lee, assistant clinical director of Encompass Pediatric Feeding Clinic, said to me, "I remember the day you looked at me and another team member and said, 'I want you both to go to the conference room and learn everything possible about current feeding therapy programs in the state.' I remember thinking to myself, *This woman is for real.* We are not just talking about the day we will open a feeding clinic but actually putting the vision in motion."

I feel Samantha Borowiak, operations director of Encompass Therapy Center and Pediatric Feeding Clinic summarized it best: It was a whole new world of professionals, service codes, billing, documentation guidelines, and contracts.

I knew that with the team's ability and commitment to persist through challenges, we would be successful. The Encompass Pediatric Feeding Center has begun the process of changing the lives of many individuals, and it has also cultivated new professional characteristics within our team. Each team member has had to grow, and they have been willing to do so because the team has the same goal—to provide excellent, life-changing services to children in need in the Great Lakes Bay Region.

Every time we talk about the moments we have spent together building this company, it brings back great memories and laughter. We remember every small action step taken in the two years of due diligence. Research, learning, advocacy, hiring, training, and ultimately, developing a sustainable pediatric feeding clinic was our mission and goal.

The Vision Achieved, Changing Lives

In 2021, the grand opening of the clinic was the realization of our vision turned reality. We started with outpatient feeding therapy services while we continued to develop the medical intensive feeding program.

It required a collection of skilled disciplines—a pediatrician, pediatric gastroenterologist, pediatric dietician and nutritionist, board certified swallowing specialist, speech therapist, occupational therapist, licensed master of social work, licensed psychologist, board certified behavior analyst, and behavior technicians. Finding each of these professions in our rural area presented my colleagues and me with a challenge. It required my team to research and connect with medical, psychological, and social services professionals to learn about their services and ability to be a part of the grand vision of our very own local feeding therapy program. We wanted to be the program that professionals in our area could rely on for their patients in need of referral.

We want parents to have hope and understand that they have a team of professionals dedicated to changing the lives of children and families. Encompass Pediatric Feeding Clinic started with a passion to help children learn the skills necessary to accept and eat food items that would improve their quality of life. Utilizing a behavior-based approach, we teach children the skills needed to be successful accepting, chewing, and swallowing a healthy variety of food items.

Victory! Victory! Victory!

My team and I have created the only pediatric feeding clinic in our region which provides resources and feeding therapy services to families and children requiring outpatient or intensive feeding therapy services. This program allows parents in our region to receive services for their child without traveling long distances or having to take a work sabbatical. What started as an idea is now the victory of providing quality of life services to children and their families. It is one of the best feelings to be part of something that is changing lives for the better.

I am beyond proud to be called the leader of this amazing vision that became reality. Commitment, teamwork, belief in the vision, and lots of hard work ensured that each step of the long journey to victory was completed! A community of professionals has come together to provide vital services and improve the quality of life for our clients. Our dedicated team does not take this privilege of serving these families lightly and promises to ensure that our clients receive the best care possible.

Dr. Ashley Blake is the founder and CEO of Encompass Empowerment Team and Encompass Therapy Center. Her teams are ordinary individuals committed to making an impact on the world by taking one step forward every day. Connect with certified coach, speaker, and trainer, Dr. Ashley Blake and her team at anblake@encompassempowerment.com or on the Encompass Empowerment Facebook page.

Tweetable: The amazing, passionate experts on my professional teams consider themselves ordinary individuals conquering big goals by taking one small step every day!

DAVID KAFKA

Get Out of Your Own Head and Think Big

David Kafka is an honest real estate agent and broker in Belize. He educates people on moving to Belize, buying property, development, and starting a business in one of the fastest-growing Caribbean countries. David volunteers with animals, the Placencia Village Fire Department, and Believe in Belize as a health program manager.

No Silver Spoon in My Mouth

Growing up, I always had what I needed but nothing else. My dad brought my mom to the US from Germany and then left us. She was in a new country with two children and couldn't speak the language. It just so happened we lived next door to a Christian woman who taught my mom the Bible and English at the same time. My mom worked and worked hard to provide for my sister and me as a secretary. I was always embarrassed by hand-me-downs and clothes from K-Mart. I wanted to shop at the malls in stores like Sears or JCPenny.

If I wanted anything outside of the necessities, I would have to work for it. So, I started working when I was 13 at a friend's tackle shop and restaurant in Hopkins, South Carolina and cleaning offices with my best friend's family.

I was never afraid to work, and I appreciated everything I had. But I never thought I would do big things. I wanted to be a truck driver or an electrician, happily working 9-5. Thinking back on my own and with the help of a therapist, I think I struggled with low self-esteem or that I was always wanting to do the "right things" so that people would like me.

Life worked its way out to where I did electrical work. I also volunteered at the Ashley River Fire Department in North Charleston, South Carolina. And wow, I loved the feeling of helping and making a difference. Soon, I was applying at Mount Pleasant Fire Department, South Carolina. I got the job and was loving the career. But I wasn't making a lot of money. We do not do the job for the money, but the money is needed to survive.

I looked at my brothers and sisters in the fire service. Some had side jobs, some had their own company, and some were retired from the Armed Forces and starting another career. I liked the idea of additional income and started a landscape company.

I just wanted a few jobs on my off days to make more money. Well, with my work ethic and my desire to please everyone, I did pretty well for myself. I started to grow and grow, and then the big thinking kicked in. Maybe I could grow to having one or two trucks working while I was on the job. Maybe even bigger? Or could I grow this to a multimillion-dollar company? I had a big vision, but I still had a lot of self-doubts.

I grew to the point where I had crews to do all the work and great management staff. I was running the landscaping and irrigation side of the business and was phasing out of that to just manage the company when the crash of 2008 came, along with other challenges. I worked hard and continued to grow the business but started to feel like all I was doing was working to pay bills, pay employees, pay taxes, pay insurance, and on, and on, and on.

A New Beginning

In 2009, I sold my company, sold my investments, sold the majority of the belongings I accumulated over the years running the proverbial rat race, and moved to Belize with my wife, eleven-year-old daughter, and less than $20,000.

Not afraid of hard work or doing a good job for people, I started as an assistant in a real estate office in February 2010. Once I became an agent less than a year later, I was always in the top 100 agents in the Caribbean and Central America. By June 2013, I had the opportunity to buy the RE/MAX franchises for Placencia, Hopkins, and then, Corozal.

In truth, in all the time I worked in Belize, I'd never really thought about running one of the largest brokerages in the country. I was just plugging away, and the work came to me.

In my free time, I volunteered on the board of the Placencia Humane Society as well as the Peninsula Volunteer Fire Department. While I love to work, my heart is in giving back to the country I call home now, Belize, animals, and fire safety.

Goals, Do They Work?

I always knew I had a great work ethic and I am honest. But it was not until I met my mentors and found this thing called self-improvement that the game changed for me. They talked about not using your past as a club to beat yourself with but as a learning tool, about how your only limiting factor is yourself, and about the fact that you can do anything in your life if you put your mind to it. They also talked about this little five-letter word called GOALS. I learned what self-improvement does and how effective goals are. Plus, I learned if you are going to think, you may as well think BIG.

One of my life-altering moments was at a goals retreat. The end of my marriage was a hard thing for me. I thought moving to Belize would help bring us closer, but it didn't, and after 26 years together, my wife and I decided to get a divorce. Before the divorce, we were on and off a few times. The last few years have been good for both of us. I think we are better people now that we've faced the music, and our daughter is much happier as well.

Today, I am working hard in real estate and buying property as often as I can. I am learning a lot of excellent strategies like group investing (syndications), how to properly set goals (SMART goals), the principles of macro and microeconomics in real estate and precious metals, and so much more.

I am with a loving partner now, Meliza, and we have two boys together. She is outgoing. I am a big introvert. I like working, being with my family, and animals. However, being an introvert doesn't always serve me. Sometimes when Meliza wants to go out, I want to stay home. When I go to my mentorship meetups, sometimes I want to just talk to people I am comfortable with and sometimes I want to go to my room for alone time afterwards. All growth in life happens outside our comfort zones. If I want to do big things and help a lot of people, I have to learn to step out of my introvert comfort zone.

I love what I have been learning and being around a bunch of awesome like-minded people like myself. Some started a lot earlier than I did, some are starting later, but no matter our race, nationality, or economic background, we all get along, help each other learn, and work together.

Conquering Your Doubts

During the COVID-19 pandemic, my asset management company was not growing like I expected it to.

One day, I was voicing my frustration with one of my team members, Staci Gray. She told me, "You need to stop comparing yourself to other people and their success."

She pointed out that I had low self-confidence, and to get my confidence back up I needed to make little steps I could succeed in and build from there. She set me up with systems and tasks to help me get little wins. After a 90-day period, these little wins were big steps forward. Working 90 days at a time, in a year, we were accomplishing big things and building an asset management business.

As the head of an asset management company, the responsibility of taking care of my client's money weighed heavily on me. Every day I see Wall Street lose money on behalf of other people, and that is not me. I strive to treat my client's money better than I treat my own money. That is why I spend so much time in education, masterminds, and inner circles with my mentors. I always want to be learning, improving, and growing so I can perform well for the people I have agreed to take care of.

As my business grew, so did my thinking processes. I saw that you can think big and set goals and that goals do work. I want to be like Sir Richard Branson, who surrounds himself with great teams and has many companies that help him make his money so he can give back to what matters to him. Ingrained thoughts and self-limiting beliefs don't change overnight, but surrounding myself with a great team and continued work go a long way. There is no limit to what I can do.

If You Must Think, Think BIG

Today, in addition to running the asset management company, I am a selling broker of Caribbean real estate. We do not have enough agents in Belize to keep up with demand and allow me to stop selling, so I have a team and I sell.

My asset management company has over $7M in assets under management.

I have accumulated a couple of houses, a small resort in Hopkins Village, an older apartment building that needs remodeling, 34 units in Mahogany Bay Resort & Beach Club Curio Collection by Hilton, and over 600 acres of land.

Meliza, my girlfriend, and I have three art and gift shops in Placencia and San Pedro and are opening our next two stores in 2022. We are always keeping an eye out for opportunities to open other businesses we have in the works and teams to make those visions into realities.

Meliza's and my goals are to set up several businesses and spend time with our boys. I want to travel to see my daughter, Serena, and her husband as much as I can. I want to start supporting nonprofits to provide Belize with quality fire protection and set aside a nice parcel of land with a cattery to help provide a safe and suitable home to the large population of homeless cats in Belize. Anything I can do to enrich my family, serve my clients, and help the people and animals of Belize, that's what I'll be doing. I've learned that if you put your mind to it, you can do anything you want in life.

David Kafka will provide you with all the resources you need to understand and get comfortable with investing in Belize either passively or actively. For a free 30-minute consultation to see if Belize is right for you, reach out to him at calendly.com/davidkafka or by email at book@caribbeancapitalgroup.com. He is also on all social media channels.

Tweetable: An ordinary person with a passion for helping others, a strong work ethic, and lots of dreams must face his self-doubts and shortcomings and not just think, but think BIG.

THOMAS M. BARBA, PT

Failing My Way to My Big Goal

Thomas M. Barba is a physical therapist. Raised in Detroit, he graduated from University of Michigan in 1996 and now resides in Bay City, MI. Thomas founded Auburn Physical Therapy in 2003 and grew the practice to 14,500 square feet in four locations. Thomas and his wife Marie celebrate a blended family of four adult boys and enjoy reading, traveling to the Keys, and golfing.

The Conversation That Started It All

When I was ten years old, my grandmother suffered a stroke that left her very weak and unable to walk on her own. Since she lived with us, I was able to see firsthand the effects of physical therapy. The ability to help someone regain the ability to walk was intriguing to me at that young age. A few years later, I found out that my cousin was a physical therapist, and this ignited a fire inside of me.

Back in 1986, while in high school, I declared with authority that I wanted to follow in my cousin's footsteps and become a physical therapist! As I peeled my body away from the brick wall named my guidance counselor, the dream took a serious hit. Apparently, I was not smart enough for that profession and would be better served going into a more traditional service industry.

I took the opinion of my guidance counselor and turned it into motivation. I applied to physical therapy school in 1992. And . . . I failed to get in. I was not about to give up, so in 1993, I tried again and was accepted.

Keeping a Positive Focus

During my three years of graduate school, I was on top of the world. A classmate of mine and I discussed opening a physical therapy clinic. We made a sign that we put over the front door of our apartment that read "$100,000." This was our goal. We hit that sign before going to class every day. I did this for fun, not knowing that this was the beginning of envisioning what you want. This was thinking big back in 1993, as the average salary for a physical therapist was $40,000.

I made it a point that my learning would allow me to accomplish the goal of opening a practice and being my own boss. My grades were near the top of the class. I was ready to graduate and show myself that my high school guidance counselor was wrong. I was going to make a difference in the physical therapy world.

But wait, I could not work as a physical therapist until I passed the state boards. I went into the boards confident and ready, however, I did not pass. I waited the minimum required time of six months to take them again, and again, I failed. I had one more chance to pass or I was done.

I took this dreaded test for the third time. Going to the mailbox every day for six weeks for an envelope that would decide my physical therapy fate was heart-wrenching. Then, late one night, I went to the mailbox, and finally, there it was. I was hearing my counselor's voice saying that physical therapy was not in the cards. I opened it and could see the word "Congratulations!" I passed!

My self-esteem was restored. My confidence was flying high. I could now work as a physical therapist! I did it. There was nothing to stop me now. Right?

Following the Vision
I worked for a local hospital system in 1998. I knew that I wanted to open my own physical therapy practice, but I needed some experience and the perfect location. I quickly identified the location in the small city of Auburn, Michigan.

For three years, I drove through Auburn on the way to work. But I did not have the confidence to go open a clinic on my own. This was new to me. My safety net would be gone. Any money I saved would be at risk. I wanted this but was nervous.

I had a wife and three young boys, and I was comfortable. So, I did the next best thing. I went into my manager's office and asked if they would open a small clinic in Auburn. I would run this clinic and gain some experience in day-to-day operations while still having the safety net of working for a hospital system.

Well, that did not go as planned. My manager told me this would never work and the area would not support a clinic. I pleaded my case, but my idea was dead in the water. I was disappointed, to say the least.

As I sat there, my ego got the best of me, and words came out of my mouth without any control. —I quit.

There was no going back. I had just removed my safety net of a job and my dream of opening my own clinic. My head was spinning. *What did I just do? I have a wife and three young boys at home. How do I go home and casually say, Hey I grabbed milk, and I quit my job...?*

The time between when I heard the answer no, when I said "I quit," and all my thoughts was less than thirty seconds. Then I said, "I am going to open my own clinic in Auburn, and it will be the best clinic around."

My conviction was solidified by my manager's response of, "Auburn will not support you and you will be back in thirty days."

Sometimes You Need to Take a Step Back

After quitting my job unexpectedly, I still needed to gain experience.

So, I became a contract therapist. I traveled all over the state of Michigan for the next year working for various outpatient clinics. This was an invaluable experience. I learned what clinic cultures patients liked and did not like. I learned different managerial styles and the right and wrong way to interact with employees.

At the end of a year, I was ready to start my clinic, and I was going to call it Auburn Physical Therapy.

I needed to lease a location, hang up a sign, and start making a difference. Should be a quick process, right?

I hit my first obstacle quickly. It seemed no place in Auburn would work to start my dream. Absolutely no location worked . . . until I saw a dirt lot with a sign saying a small strip mall was going to open in four months. I called the number and signed a three-year lease for four hundred square feet. Now, I was committed and thinking big! I was going to make this work.

Well, that decision worked out. The strip mall was built on schedule, and within six months, I opened my doors with myself as my only employee. I was a physical therapy private practice owner in Auburn.

After two years of practice, the hospital system I had worked for also opened a practice down the street, solidifying my impulse to believe in my dreams and goals and continue to think big.

Thinking of Giving Up

In the next few years, I experienced some nice growth and opened an additional two locations in the area.

Things were going great, and I was planning more growth, when unfortunately, I went through a divorce which halted progress and jeopardized the practice. My wife lost her little sister in an automobile accident and went through a very challenging time. My wife worked the back office of the business including payroll, taxes, and human resources. Within a short period, I was left with 100% of the business as well as taking care of three young boys.

It would have been easy to close the business, but I still needed to be the difference in the physical therapy world that I envisioned early on. Not only for me but also now for my boys.

The next couple of years were satisfying and stress free compared to what I had experienced since starting my clinic. I had a few doctors that referred their patients to me on a regular basis, and one orthopedic surgeon sent me 99% of his clients. This was over several years and was truly a blessing on the practice. Fresh staff were hired and new equipment was purchased to keep up with the consistent growth.

Negative Events Are Not That Bad If You Follow Your Vision

At 7 AM, on the busiest day of the week, I received a text from a friend who said that my number one referral source, the doctor who was the vehicle for growth and expansion, and my friend, had suddenly passed away.

Just like that, I lost a mentor as well as a substantial number of referrals to the business. I had no time to grieve. I went from 100mph to a crash into a wall.

I had a busy day, week, month and now had to process and address this latest information. I thought, *What do I do? I have never been in this situation. I thought I had been through everything but this? This may be hard to come back from. Did I grow too big too quick?*

This major setback made me look at my practice and how I was doing things. I could not go through this again. I decided I would work hard at adding more referral sources, improving my community outreach instead of relying on physicians. I looked at the internal functioning of the practice and made things more efficient.

In a year, I was back to the same number of patients I had before the loss of my friend and number one referral source.

Business was going well. Hiring was increasing, and Auburn Physical Therapy was winning awards for best physical therapy company in the area. In fact, we were winning awards in adjoining areas where we did not have a presence but captured a market share. I was making the difference by giving back to the communities that we served. I was riding high and feeling great

. . . until a small little thing called COVID-19 started to make headlines. The pandemic eventually dropped my clinics from 100% capacity to 25%.

Of all the events that could have taken down my business, this was one that I had no control over. There were no decisions I could make that could turn it around. I was at the mercy of a virus and the politics that ensued. Or was I? *Why is this any different? Why not keep thinking big? If this is the end, then why not go out fighting?*

With time to think things through, I thought about what I could do that no one else was doing in my industry. I thought about what would allow me to take as much control of the situation as possible. *How about opening another clinic?* Was this thinking big or was it thinking dumb?

The amount of media coverage I received from this move was unbelievable. The limited number of patients that were seeking care at this time were coming to my clinics! I was able to get through the darkest days of COVID and came out further ahead. The clinics were up and running at full capacity even with the addition of the fourth location!

The Results of Thinking Big!

At this point, I received a call from a national physical therapy group that wanted to purchase my company, and it did not take long to realize that I had done what I had set out to do.

It was time to take the trials and tribulations that I experienced since that meeting with my high school counselor and do something else big!

I reaped what I sowed. Each setback over the years seemed insurmountable at the time. If it were not for the large goals I set, I would have settled for the low-hanging fruit and failed.

Now that I am starting other ventures, thinking lofty early really sets the stage for what is to come. When I sold the practice, I thought that would be the most satisfying moment. But I still had a nagging feeling. I reached the pinnacle of my profession yet was not completely at rest. Why?

The word is "drive." The think big philosophy will continue to drive me in every area of my life. Onto the next adventure. If you must think, why not think BIG!

Final Thoughts

I cannot say I was always a positive person. In fact, at an early age, I was more of the glass half empty kind of guy. But something changed inside of me during high school that is not easy to describe. What changed was a setback—someone telling me something I did not want to hear, that my vision may not happen.

I could have gotten mad or done something else, but I saw the positive in this advice. Maybe at that moment in time, I was not going to be a physical therapist as I planned. I was not angry, I was taken aback and forced to reflect. I came out seeing another side of the story. To change the narrative and to continue to follow my vision, I needed a positive attitude. Once I developed a positive attitude, doors opened wide for me, and my life changed.

I carried the principles of positive thinking, thinking big, and setting goals to another aspect of my life, one in which I was an utter failure—running. As a teenager, I could barely make it around a track once. I gave up. I was not going to be a runner.

But after succeeding in business, learning the powerful lessons of vision and thinking big, I set a goal to not only run around a track once but also train and finish a full marathon with my son Bobby. Using the steps I made for myself, I accomplished this goal in May of 2021.

The culmination of eighteen plus years of dedicating every day to building a practice and the dream of succession is finally a reality. This dream, which involved sacrifice and overcoming significant obstacles, has manifested as this abstract force that was supposed to leave me satisfied but has left me wanting more.

To get more information about Thomas M. Barba and his story or to inquire about his speaking on physical therapy clinic ownership, staying positive, and customer service, contact Thomas at thomasmbarba@icloud.com.

Tweetable: Have a positive outlook in any venture. If you see only positive things, the positive ideas will become clear. Envision what you want down to the minute detail, and it will happen.

MICHELLE KIMBRO

From Near Death to Creating a Successful Syndication Business

Michelle Kimbro is a successful entrepreneur and real estate syndicator helping others build and protect wealth through real asset investing that provides exceptional tax benefits. Michelle is mother of an equally successful daughter, Amber, and is an off-shore sailor with over 10,000 miles logged.

Calm After the Storm

It's 8 AM on Sunday morning. I'm sitting in my favorite chair, with a freshly brewed cup of coffee, watching the sun rise over Montana's Swan Mountain range. The sun is peeking above the horizon, painting pink and purple across the sky and reflecting in the lake. The snow glistens. The wild turkeys are crossing the property to feed while the deer bed down in the dense woods. The morning is beautiful and peaceful.

Not even six months ago, I was fighting for my life in a California hospital. A healthcare executive who started out saving lives in the dawn of the COVID pandemic succumbed to the virus.

Want to Buy Some Mud Tacos?

I grew up in Southern California and have always been an entrepreneur at heart. As a young child, I would invent different things to sell to my neighbors, anything from handmade necklaces to mud pie tacos.

I was the first person in my family to graduate college. After graduating with my MBA, I took a management position in the healthcare system, where I had been working for many years. I had numerous successes that improved the way the hospital system cared for patients, which resulted in better outcomes and national recognition. In spite of all the successes, I found myself feeling bound by the corporate constraints. Driving to the hospital one morning, I thought to myself, *There has to be something more to life than what I am living in the corporate world.*

Under the guidance of my mentors, Steve Curd and Siva Subramanian, I decided to pursue my entrepreneurial spirit and start a business consulting firm. My company took off, and we had success in leading Lean transformations and innovative projects that were nationally recognized by The Joint Commission.

On March 16, 2020, I was called to serve in my executive role in a different fashion: to help in leading the emergency response for COVID in my county in Southern California. I'd never have thought I would be leading teams in a pandemic. I worked with the public health department to streamline test results and contact tracing and assisted in procuring personal protective equipment for the county. After the unfortunate evacuation of a 100-bed skilled nursing facility, I saw the need to support these smaller facilities in obtaining medical supplies so they could safely continue to provide quality care for their residents.

I was able to start a company within two weeks, and with my contacts, I was able to distribute supplies quickly to these sites. We were supporting federal and international government agencies, state agencies, and medical and dental practices. The need and subsequently the business exploded.

I was working a disgusting number of hours weekly, and like most other healthcare professionals, I found myself burned out and again thinking there had to be something better for me in this life. I was helping others, which was very fulfilling. But, I was not securing my family's future, and with elderly parents, this quickly became a priority.

I had been contemplating investing in residential real estate for a while. I had read, listened, and attended everything in real estate education I could get my hands on. I was putting in offers on properties only to get outbid by all-cash buyers. This wasn't working and definitely wasn't scalable with one house at a time. I needed to think bigger so I could financially protect my family's future. So, I made the decision to go full-time in the real estate syndication business. I could secure profitable properties on a larger scale and help others create financial security for their own families in the process. Little did I know, the coming year was going to be anything but easy.

Falling from Grace

I had learned all I could about real estate syndication, and it was time to execute. I had to get around people who were already successful syndicators. I had a life-changing experience in Belize attending the annual Investors Summit hosted by The Real Estate Guys. I did and saw so many amazing things. I shared meals with fabulous people like Robert and Kim Kiyosaki,

Robert and Kara Helms, and Mauricio Rauld. I had the best walking talks with G. Edward Griffin, met my future business partners, Courtney Moeller and Jherie Ducombs, and even swam with sharks.

My parents and I had made the decision to consolidate households with the goal of maintaining their independence. They were still living in Southern California, and getting a bigger house in an area that would provide a better quality of life seemed like the sensible thing to do. We chose Montana. We had just purchased a new home in Montana and scheduled the big move when I returned from Belize and our world came to a screeching halt.

After arriving home from Belize, I came down with not only COVID but also mononucleosis and sepsis from the infections.

I had a raging fever of 104 degrees for days. I was losing strength. I was dizzy, not able to eat, and confused. *Michelle! Stop telling yourself "Just one more day and it will go away."* With 25 years of healthcare experience behind me, I knew better.

Not knowing I was sick, I had visited my parents earlier in the week. Subsequently, I infected my elderly parents. I had spent the entire previous year making sure they were protected from the virus. Now, I was the one to blame. I felt like the worst person on the planet.

My dad was quickly deteriorating, and I was helpless in quarantine at home. I asked my friend, Jeffrey, if he could take my dad to the emergency room to have him assessed. Dad was admitted to the hospital with COVID and required oxygen. Jeffrey then came to see how I was doing. I was deteriorating by the minute, and we decided to go to the emergency room. My oxygen saturation was in the low 80s, and I required immediate oxygen.

After twelve hours in the emergency room, I was admitted to the hospital. I could no longer sit up on my own without severe difficulty breathing.

I woke up one night to the nursing staff bringing in a new patient. I looked at my phone and saw a message from my daughter: They had brought my mother in by ambulance and she was being admitted to the bed next to me. All I could think was, *Great, now I have both my parents and myself in the hospital with COVID. You are SUPPOSED to be protecting them! You will never be able to live with yourself if something happens to them.* For days, I couldn't talk to my mother in the bed next to me because I didn't have enough air to get words out.

At that time, all I could do was prone, which means to lay on your stomach. It decompressed my lungs from my organs and allowed me to get more oxygen. The nursing staff was changing the bed linens and they needed to roll me to the side. I was no longer able to turn by myself because I was so weak. They began to roll me, and I became short of breath. It felt like I was drowning. I was panicking. Alarms sounded. A team of nurses ran in. I thought I was going to die. The respiratory therapist told me she was going to get the doctor.

All I could think of was my family and what were they going to do if I died. Everything flashed across my mind: my daughter's birth, her wedding, my parents, my dog, MY LIFE! The doctor came in and said I was not stable and they needed to move me to ICU where I could be monitored more closely. I knew exactly what that meant—they were considering putting me on a ventilator.

The last time my 93-year-old mother saw me, I was being wheeled out on the hospital bed with monitors, alarms going off, and a big tent over me. My heart broke into a million pieces right then.

My daughter had made her daily call to check on me. Through the phone the nurse was holding, I could hear her asking if I would be okay. I couldn't reassure her. I couldn't even speak to her.

I spent four days in the ICU with only 10% lung capacity. Every minute of every hour of every day that I was laying in that bed, I prayed to God: *Please do not let them intubate me! Please give me the strength to fight for my life, for my family, and for our future. Dear God, I'm not ready to go yet.*

Only You Will Get Yourself Out of This Mess

I always seem to rise out of the ashes. COVID was my fourth brush with death. While I was in ICU, I remembered what it was like being on a sinking 52' yacht in the middle of the Pacific Ocean in the black of night. We were racing from Long Beach, CA to Honolulu, HI, but had rudder failure. Two gallons of incoming water every minute and being out of reach of the US Coast Guard meant not only that we wouldn't make it, but also that we were completely on our own. I was fortunate that our team persevered and we made it to dry land with our lives.

I fought every day in the ICU. I got to the point where I could sit all the way up in bed and still be able to breathe. My labs were improving, and the sepsis and mono had resolved.

I could have no visitors; I was alone. My hair was matted to my scalp, I hadn't had a shower in weeks, and my skin was peeling. I just felt gross. On day five, the doctors said I was stable enough to transfer back to the Med/Surg unit. From then on out, I was not accepting anything other than "I'm just going to keep moving forward" and "I will be okay." I focused on little steps towards the end goal every day.

The moving company moved the contents of my and my parent's California houses to Montana. We were able to rent back my parents' house for 30 more days so they had somewhere to stay while recovering, but I was still in the hospital with no discharge date. I realized that nobody else was going to get me out of this mess, so it was up to me.

The doctors were amazed at how well I was recovering and said they had never seen anyone with my spirit. I would show them pictures from my daughter's trip for the move to Montana of the wild turkeys and deer on our new property. I told them I don't have time to be in the hospital, I had wild turkeys and deer that wanted to meet me in Montana. I refused to give up, even though at times it seemed easier to do so.

When I got out of the hospital, I was bruised head to toe from being a pin cushion for 19 days. Getting in the car felt surreal. I couldn't believe I was going home. I hadn't felt the sun on my skin in almost a month. I cried all the way.

Now You're Driving to Montana?
I had only 11 days to pull it together and get my family to Montana. I could barely get up off of the floor, much less walk 10 feet. I had no idea how we were going to get there, but the fact was we had to be out by the end of July.

I managed to get myself off of oxygen. I managed to buy a car and rent a trailer. On July 31, all three of us and our two dogs got in the car jam-packed with the last of our worldly possessions and drove over 1,200 miles to Montana.

I have no idea how we got there but by the grace of God. When I finally pulled into the driveway of our new home, I cried. I turned to my dad and said, "We did it. We're home, Dad."

Keep Moving Forward! Giving Back Hope
2021 was filled with many challenges and barriers in my life. I figured out how to make lemonade out of lemons! In the midst of the challenges, I

grew my medical supply company 55% and successfully started my real estate syndication business.

By the end of the year, my partners and I had successfully raised $1.45M in capital and closed on a syndication project in the energy sector. I have secured my family's future, and what's more, I have helped other families to build and protect their wealth through passively investing in real assets.

Throughout my life, professionally and personally, I have never been one to give up. I keep moving forward, removing barriers, and asking "how" it can be done instead of saying it "can't" be done.

This life has not been easy, and I have overcome many challenges. Purpose, resilience, determination, and courage have driven my success, especially in this past year.

2021 was another launching pad in my life. I am co-authoring a book. We have started on two more projects, assembled a rock-star team, and are on the way to becoming a world-class syndication company that helps others improve and enrich their lives through investing.

As I sip my morning coffee and look out over God's country, I'm grateful that I've been given another day to touch my feet to the ground. I am reminded of why I have survived all of these adversities in my life. I'm here to serve my higher purpose: taking care of my family, sharing hope, and helping others create and preserve wealth so that they too can enjoy creating memories with their families or simply enjoy a cup of coffee and a beautiful sunrise.

Connect with Michelle Kimbro to learn more about real estate and alternative investments that create passive income and provide exceptional tax benefits. Email Michelle to receive a free guide to Investing in Real Assets vs. The Stock Market.

Email: michelle@emprinvestor.com

Tweetable: Don't give up! Keep moving forward and figure it out. Don't tell yourself that it "can't" be done. Instead, ask "how" it can be done.

MARK HARTLEY

My Mom and Helping Others Through Grief Ministry

Mark Hartley is a minister, hospice chaplain and advocate, trainer, and coach. Through ministry, he has supported those grieving for over 30 years. He has a doctorate in grief ministry and trains people through workshops to help their grieving neighbor. Mark's passion is to ease the pain of end-of-life decisions.

No Lid

"All that I am, or hope to be, I owe to my angel mother," is a quote attributed to Abraham Lincoln. The impact of mothers on the lives of their children cannot be denied.

If you place fleas in a jar with the lid on, they will continually jump and hit the lid. After a day or so, they will learn the height they need to jump to come just short of the lid. Afterwards, you can remove the lid and they will continue to jump as if the lid is still on the jar.

My mom never placed the lid on the jar. Instead, she encouraged me to jump as high as I possibly could. She may not be present with me now, but she still encourages me to jump high because the moon is the goal. As Les Brown says, "Aim for the moon. Even if you don't make it, at least you will land among the stars."

The Early Years

Mom sat at the sewing machine piecing together quilt blocks. As she sewed, I sat on the floor behind the machine, cutting the blocks apart and stacking them. They had to be separated and prepared for the next pass through, making the blocks bigger, until they would all be sewed together creating a quilt top.

I would lay under the quilt as she, my grandmothers, or other ladies would spend time at our house quilting the pieces together and talking. My mom would buy math and word books for me to pass the time. I didn't know at this early age of four and five, she was setting me up to have no limits.

A couple years later, she began taking my brothers to town to play baseball. I was a year away from being able to play, but I begged Mom to at least ask if I could play. She asked, and they let me play. From this point forward, she traveled many miles to take me to practice and to watch me play. She made sure I was on time and had everything I needed.

The school district I attended was very small and didn't have a football team. As I began my sixth-grade year, I started to beg Mom to allow me to go to the school district where I played baseball so I could play football. This was before school choice, so that was not an option. The school district where I lived didn't want to lose any students because they needed everyone for the federal money. My young mind didn't know all these things then.

The summer before my seventh-grade year, Mom told me when football practice started and that I would be playing. I was an excited young lad. I was small but determined. I lived with my dad's brother and wife, my aunt and uncle, most of the time during school and went home on weekends. Mom encouraged me every step of the way. She didn't see my physical size but instead the size of my heart. She instilled in me passion and desire with no limits.

The summer going into my sophomore year, we had two a day practices. I would get up, ride my moped to town twelve miles, and have morning practice. Then I would ride home, load my moped into the back of Dad's truck, eat lunch, and go work with him in the woods until it was time to go back to afternoon practice. Each afternoon, as we got my moped out of his truck, my dad would tell me I should stay and work with him because I was too small to play. I was only about five foot eight and 115 pounds at the time. His comments just fueled me that much more.

I started as a sophomore. My parents bought box seats and didn't miss a game throughout high school. Mom had instilled in me that there are no limits to the determined mind.

It wasn't until I was in my late forties that I learned that Mom and Dad had turned my legal guardianship over to my uncle and aunt who lived in the school district so I could play football.

The Dreaded "C" Word

After I graduated, Mom didn't tell me where she wanted me to go to school. She let me choose and continued to support me. She worked at a bank and paid for my undergraduate degree.

My senior year of college, Mom was diagnosed with breast cancer. Waiting in the hospital during surgery was difficult. Many tears were shed. My mind was racing with all the "what ifs." Hearing the "c" word causes the mind to immediately go to a death sentence. I was not prepared for my cheerleader to die.

By God's grace, Mom came out of radical mastectomy surgery and came home on Christmas Eve. Mom never looked back, continuing to work and live life to the fullest.

In 2018, I went on to get a master's degree in theology and a doctorate for which I developed a workshop to help equip grieving people and their supporters with tools to help them shoulder the burden of grief. My years of pastoral ministry and hospice chaplain work helped me see the need. Many people are grieving alone. On many occasions, I had individuals say, "I feel abandoned."

Mom was not able to attend my graduation for my doctorate due to health issues. When I visited afterwards, she gave me a hug and said, "I feel like I had a part in your degree." The truth is, without her, my degree would not have happened. She had a huge part. She never put the lid on the jar. As far as I know, I am the first in the family to graduate from university and the first to have a master's and a doctorate. Mom was extremely proud of these accomplishments. I am her baby boy.

Nearing Home

I moved to Nebraska in 2009 to pastor and in 2012 began working in hospice full-time. Working and living 800 miles from Mom, I was not able to visit often. I called her every Tuesday though. This was a highlight of her week. It seemed she lived for it. If something happened, and I couldn't call, when I called the next day, she would let me know about it.

We all think about the day the call concerning our older loved one is going to come. It was a Tuesday. I called several times during the day but got no answer.

This was not uncommon. Mom and Dad would often be gone during the day on Tuesday. It seemed their doctor appointments were always on Tuesday. At about six in the evening, I called one more time, but there was no answer. I thought, *No worries, they went out to eat.*

About eight that night, my niece called and told me Mom had a heart attack and was in the hospital. She was still able to talk some but not much. I told her I would drive down right after the funeral I had the next day at three.

I called the next morning to discover Mom had deteriorated and was no longer communicating. By mid-afternoon, she was on hospice in the hospital. Before leaving home that morning, I packed my clothes, fully expecting to not return before we held Mom's funeral.

I arrived at the hospital just before one in the morning on Thursday. Dad was sleeping on a cot beside Mom. Mom had a breathing device on to help her breathe. It wasn't a ventilator. Shortly after I arrived, a nurse came in and repositioned the machine. When she did, Mom's oxygen level dropped very low, quickly. Having been a hospice chaplain for almost twenty years and having sat with a number of people as they took their last breath, I knew this was not good.

Through the night, I sat in a chair by her side, reminiscing about the individual who was my biggest cheerleader. She had driven me thousands of miles to play ball. She provided for me to go to college and get a degree. She cheered me on and told me I could achieve. She empowered me to continue to grow and never stop learning.

As morning dawned, I knew she wasn't going to get better, and she would not be returning home with Dad. For me, the decision was not hard. After living this many times with other families and thinking, *What would I do in this situation?*, I believed this was not what Mom would want. To keep her alive with the machine would be for us, the family, not her. She had been wheelchair-bound for almost 15 years. The last couple years, she had become legally blind. Now, she couldn't breathe without the help of a machine. The decision in my mind was easy: remove the machine.

Letting go can be difficult due to the impact the person has had on one's life. The greater the impact, the more difficult the release. I have walked this journey with many families seeking to make the "right" decision concerning their loved one. I have also sat with many families who, after their loved one has died, ask themselves, "Did I make the right decision?" When faced with this decision, each family makes the decision they can live with. There is no right or wrong decision. The decision from an objective perspective is easy, if the discussion happens before being in the situation. Don't be afraid to ask your loved one, "If you are in this situation, what would you want me to do?" From an emotional perspective, however, the decision is never easy. We don't want our loved one to leave us.

When Dad woke up, I sat on his cot beside him and said, "Dad, what do you think about letting everyone who wants to come see Mom come or call and say goodbye? Then, we take the machine off and let her go."

He looked at me and said, "The machine is keeping her alive?"

I replied, "Yes, sir."

He paused and said, "She doesn't want that at all."

"So, you are okay with taking the machine off?" I asked. He agreed.

All the grandchildren either came or called to say their goodbye. Before removing the machine, we sang her "Happy Birthday." It was, in fact, her 83rd birthday. At three o'clock, they removed the machine; she took her last breath on Earth fifteen minutes later.

She began her journey on Earth and ended it on the same day 83 years later. There is an idea in the Jewish tradition that when a person is born, God gives them tasks to accomplish, and if you die on your birthday, then you have fully completed the tasks God gave you. At least in my life, I believe she completed her task. There is no lid and no limits.

Passion Unleashed

The loss of someone or something we hold dear is inevitable. How we process this loss differs from person to person.

My passion is to help people walk through this process and find a greater purpose, how to use their loss for a greater good. I show people how to begin to think bigger than themselves and how they can help others as they themselves process their grief.

Our grief is intended to be used for a greater good. Grief isn't an obstacle to be overcome, but an opportunity to learn and grow to help others.

I love you, Mom. And as she taught me, I encourage others: Shoot for the moon!

Connect with Mark Hartley for your end of life or grieving questions. Schedule a workshop for those grieving or those who desire to help the grieving over Zoom or in your area at grievinghope@gmail.com or (402) 631-1156.

Tweetable: There is hope and healing in the midst of grief. Grief is not fixable, but a life long process to walk through.

SAKET JAIN

Laid Off to Financially Free
One Word Changed My Perspective

Investor, syndicator, tech enthusiast, and philanthropist Saket Jain works at Airbnb and is CEO of Impact Wealth Builders, LLC where he's passionate about achieving financial freedom through real estate. Over the last five years, Saket built a 2000+ unit portfolio (~ $200M) with his partners. When not working or investing, Saket loves time with his wife of 19 years and two daughters.

I Had It All or So I Thought

I was an Indian immigrant who thought he had made it in the US. Having worked at a top consulting firm, Booz Allen, having graduated from India's best engineering school, IIT, and having received an MBA from Columbia Business School, I was on top of the world. I was married to my sweet wife of thirteen years, and our two daughters were enrolled in a private school in Wisconsin. I had everything figured out, and nothing could have gone wrong. At least, that's what I believed.

Little did I know, life had another plan for me. I was informed that one of the divisions of my then employer was to be dissolved. I was part of that division. Yes, I was told that I was being laid off. While I had heard about layoffs before, I had never expected something like this would ever happen to me.

In a moment, all my future plans fell flat, and I was left wondering how, as the sole breadwinner, I would provide for my family.

My Lowest Point

My ego was shattered. I was devastated and could not come to terms with reality. A feeling of shame overpowered me, and the questions I consistently asked myself were, *Why me? Why now?*

I was pretty upset at my financial advisor, as he had never mentioned this gaping hole—having my job as a single stream of income—in our financial plan. Wasn't it his responsibility to prevent me from making such a financial blunder?

I was sad about being an immigrant and having no family support. I was ashamed of telling my mom back home in India that I got laid off. This was not part of my American dream.

I felt humiliated and defeated.

I was desperately looking for answers. We took our girls out of the private school and moved in with my in-laws to stop the financial bleeding. No matter which way I looked at the situation, I was only getting more and more depressed.

I couldn't comprehend why this would happen to me. I was a "good" guy and was always told that "only" good things happen to good people. I started thinking about people who had done worse things but their lives seemed perfect. I was convinced that this was not fair and that I didn't deserve this.

It was the lowest point in my life.

The Question That Changed Everything

It was not until I changed my question that I was able to see the light at the end of the tunnel. I switched from "Why me and why now?" to "Why not me and why not now?" Just one additional word—that is in its essence a negative word—made a defining difference.

This new perspective enabled me to shift away from a victim mindset and instead focus on how to use my current situation as fodder for my development. Reframing the question allowed me to look for the silver lining in what life had thrown at me and wonder what, if any, lessons were there for me to pay attention to.

I realized that instead of focusing on what I could have done, I needed to figure out what to do so this would never happen again.

Shortly thereafter, I promised myself that, moving forward, I would take full control of my family's financial future.

In Pursuit of Answers

In my search for answers, I started talking to my peers and friends. Everyone around me had no proactive approach to minimize the impact of such an occurrence. It was pretty clear that everyone had accepted the fact that they may lose their job at some point and that they can't really do anything about it.

I knew I had to look elsewhere for answers, as everyone around me seemed to have similar thinking as me.

I set out on a journey to challenge my own assumptions around financial wellbeing and learn from other individuals who had accomplished goals similar to mine. I relentlessly read books, listened to podcasts, and attended seminars where I could meet others with non-traditional perspectives on financial wellbeing.

In that process, I realized that my primary focus had been on growing my post-retirement net worth. I was paying attention to net worth instead of cash flow. I had believed that I needed to have a certain net worth to retire. On the contrary, I learned cash flowing assets can enable financial independence that can allow you to retire *and* build generational wealth.

Real Estate as the Answer

With this new perspective, I started to look for asset classes that would provide me with cash flow. I kept coming back to real estate.

Real estate investing was not new to me. My wife and I already had a few rental properties in our portfolio. However, up until that time, we had purchased real estate in anticipation of gains through appreciation. From the onset, the rent never covered the expenses, but we found solace in the fact that the properties were appreciating and that we were increasing our equity. Now understanding the importance of positive cash flow, my wife and I sold one of our condos. We redirected those funds towards properties where the rent far exceeded the property expenses (including the mortgage). We continued exchanging our non-cash flowing assets with cash flowing rental properties and grew our rental portfolio of single-family homes.

I now had a newfound clarity, and despite a lack of support from others around us, my wife and I firmly believed in our investing strategy. Although curious, our friends and "well-wishers" made several attempts to dissuade us from this path. They would share how much their portfolios had grown through appreciation and what we were missing out on. We appreciated their concerns and thanked them for their advice, but in our hearts, we knew we were on the right path.

As we continued buying rental properties, I discovered how favorable the US tax code is towards real estate investors. When I accounted for tax savings, our rental portfolio was yielding over 20% annualized return with relatively low risk compared to the stock market. I was hooked!

For the first time in my life, I had a crystal clear idea of how I could accomplish our financial goals. We stuck to our guns and continued on our path.

Transition from Single Family to Multifamily

While it felt like over a year, within six months of the unemployment, I was offered a great position at Airbnb. When I was hired, I was excited to receive a compensation package common at startups that included pre-IPO stock in the form of restricted stock units (RSUs).

I projected that when the company would go public, our portfolio would be too concentrated in Airbnb stocks and we would be subject to significant taxes. Thankfully, I already knew what I needed to do—go aggressive on our real estate holdings. Only this time, I would have to scale my acquisitions. Buying one property at a time would take a considerable amount of effort and time. This is when I discovered the power of multifamily—one building with multiple units.

I set out on the path to learn as much as I could about the multifamily asset class and networked with successful multifamily investors. We began investing passively in multifamily syndications with the eventual goal of becoming actively involved in this asset class.

Airbnb eventually went public. This time, I was ready and had a well-defined financial plan.

We now own over 2,000 units across several markets in the US, diversifying our portfolio and reducing our tax liability.

All Growth Happens at the Margin

I never guessed that losing my job would turn out to be one of the best things that ever happened to me. Although it shook me to my core, through that uncertainty, I found a path that was always present but to which I had kept my mind closed. Once I opened my mind, I had a newfound perspective on financial freedom and the power of cash-flowing real estate. We are grateful that our multifamily investments have pushed us on the path where the cash flow from our investments will soon exceed my W-2 income, enabling us to be financially free.

While the future remains uncertain, I am confident that my family will be able to weather any financial storm, and our financial needs will always be met.

Life really happens for you and not to you.

My Life's Mission

I firmly believe that financial independence is possible for all, and it doesn't have to be complicated or prolonged. It does, however, require commitment and some sacrifice. For most of us, fear drives our investing decisions—from investing in an asset class because of fear of missing out to hiring an advisor in fear that the world of finance is too complicated to understand. I have experienced the same emotions.

I addressed this trepidation by finding mentors, surrounding myself with people smarter than me, and focusing on improving my financial IQ. I would be lying if I said it was easy and without challenges.

While everyone can do it on their own, my wife and I have brainstormed extensively on how we can leverage our learning and help others achieve financial freedom without having to go through the emotional rollercoaster and upheaval. For that reason, we have launched Impact Wealth Builders.

At Impact Wealth Builders, our mission is to build a thriving community that grows their wealth together and positively impacts the world. As true partners, we will empower the next generation of wealth builders through financial education and opportunities to invest in cash flowing assets. As part of our commitment to the community, we have pledged to dedicate a portion of our profits towards educating underprivileged kids and enabling them to become the next generation of wealth builders. We firmly believe when a community of wealth builders focuses on growing their wealth, building a legacy, and uplifting communities, the positive impact will be transmitted across generations.

Connect with Saket Jain on www.linkedin.com/in/jainsaket to learn how you can get started in real estate passively and achieve financial freedom. For a free 7-day passive real estate investing course, send an email to freedom@ImpactWealthBuilders.com

Tweetable: I switched from "Why me and why now?" to "Why not me and why not now?" Just one additional word made the defining difference.

EVETTE RHODEN

I Fly on the Wings of the Storm

Evette Rhoden is a poet, author, path illuminator, photographer, and life coach who travels the world. Through poetry and photography, she relates her story. Her LifeScripts guides readers to gain a clearer vision of life and transcend the vision of their current self to release stress, shock, and trauma.

If I Jump, Will You Catch Me?

I grew up with my siblings in a home on a hill overlooking the sea on the North Coast of Jamaica. During summer days, we would lay on the powdery sand or indulge in the ethereal blue waters of the ocean. At night, as we gazed at the shiny, undulating waves, we pondered the mysteries that lay beneath.

My siblings and I went to church every Sunday. There, we sang hymns in the choir and recited poetry on special occasions. Poetry was an integral part of my English lessons growing up.

My mother, who had migrated ten years earlier, brought us to live with her and my father in New York one spring. From then on, my siblings and I set about discovering the city's charms.

I went to Brooklyn College and graduated with a degree in journalism, languages, and education. I wanted to work for the United Nations.

After seven years of working as a technical writer for an organization in New York, I abruptly decided to resign. Leading up to that moment, I was quite apprehensive. It was a huge risk since I was the head of my household.

I was living in an apartment in New Jersey with a beautiful balcony overlooking the river. A flock of pigeons used to roost on the balcony until one pair dominated the venue and started bringing twigs to make a nest. There, the female pigeon incubated her eggs. Each day, the male pigeon would bring food which she grasped with her beak. She was provided for as she protected her eggs. She never got up to fly away for a moment. I observed the process for a month until the eggs hatched. When the little fledglings were strong enough, the male pigeon exercised them by flittering their wings several times a day. When he thought they were ready, he prodded them off the balcony. I watched as they opened their wings and became airborne.

A day before I resigned, I walked along the riverbank and over the bridge, wondering how I was going to provide for myself. I started to pray. As I approached the end of the bridge, I saw a flock of pigeons pecking at some bread that was strewn along the path for them.

At that moment, a voice reminded me of these words from the Bible: "Behold the fowls of the air: for they sow not, neither do they reap... Are ye not much better than they," and "Consider the lilies of the field how they grow; they toil not, neither do they spin..."

I reflected on the fact that I never once saw the pigeons on the balcony save any food for the next day or pile up twigs that they did not use. Still, they were able to find everything they needed each day. *Am I not important to the Divine?*

So, I said to the Divine, "If I jump, will you catch me?" I trusted that, even though I didn't know how I would provide for myself, God would provide for me all that I needed. So, I wrote my resignation.

After I proffered my resignation, almost everyone I told disagreed with my decision, except one family member who shared with me a meditation practice which seemed to work. It opened up a connection that attuned me to more support. I started a practice of returning my mind and body to homeostasis.

Soon afterwards, I went on a job training course, and a month later, I started working in a new position. Within the space of five weeks, I was offered a position abroad.

Connecting to the Vibes of New York City

Over those seven years I had worked in New York, I had to find a way to distract myself from my arduous work environment and work dynamics. I would journey to the city during my lunch break, go to the cathedral to pray, then visit the showrooms on Fashion Avenue. I developed a database of fashion showrooms and collected many unique pieces that reflected my style and taste.

I indulged in arts and entertainment and attended many fashion shows, Broadway plays, and dance performances.

As I walked along Fifth Avenue one December to admire the credentialed stores ornamented in Christmas trimmings, I mused on the beautiful lights that illuminated the skyscrapers. There, entangled in the city's eclectic spoils, its hype, opulence, and decadence, I refined my interests.

Morocco, Saudi Arabia, and the Emirates

My new employers asked me to go to work in Morocco and the Kingdom of Saudi Arabia. It was an exciting chance for me to travel to new places.

I found Morocco expansive with green Mediterranean vegetation that seemed too perfect to be real. I enjoyed its intricate architecture, olive orchards, spices, and especially, the beautiful roses. I frequently visited the souks, or markets, which displayed the culture's superb artisanship.

In the Kingdom of Saudi Arabia, it seemed as if wealth directed the nation's creative expression. From the desert floor blossomed expansive oases, cornucopias of elegant expression through structure and juxtapositions of the finest materials from around the world. All this was ignited by the desire to be the best and to lead by showcasing the convergence of mind and money in quick actualization.

Burgeoning through the sands were palm trees that regaled the skyline, flaunting golden dates which garnished the dining tables. Each family's story of wealth was exhibited in luxury items culled from around the world or crafted locally by expert artists. Behind veils and abayas, women wore magnificent jewelry illuminated with brilliant stones, bedecking their hands, necks, and ears. These fineries complemented their latest haute couture fashions. Their grand reveal took place at dinner parties with families. Herein lay the true testament to wealth in diamonds, gold, and oil.

As a sign of the noblest intent, in the Kingdom of Saudi Arabia, the highest form of accommodation was conferred upon me in the words, "Treat her as you treat us."

The United Arab Emirates proved that great feats can be brought from streams of the imagination and imprinted onto the screen of reality. Geometric renditions of high-rise structures conforming to the architects' registry of order and concept of architectural reverence towered across the desert skyline as if erected to compete for the power of height and eminence. There, I spent some summers, Christmas, and a New Year's Eve.

A Path to Self Discovery

Having left the Kingdom of Saudi Arabia, my employer and I first took up residence in Beverly Hills, California. Our company was soon headquartered on a hill in West Hollywood with a fabulous view of the city. A home was created for me on that hill.

The architecture of that house was unique. Part of the roof and all the doors, except for the main entrance, were glass. At night, the moon and stars insinuated their friendship in a commendatory display of light through the glass ceiling and on the pool. I would often sit by the fireplace to bask in the energy.

At dawn, the sun would gleam through the verdant leaves, highlighting their hues. As it charted its course across the blue sky, it siphoned the last droplets of dew from the foliage. I marveled at the beauty of God's creation and scripted the poem "Look How Much I Have Loved Thee" in homage to the Divine.

Then onward, I started to offer up thanks. I declared I would write a book of prayer and praise. I started to write daily, consumed with connecting to the Divine and showing gratitude. I strongly believed my gratitude, rendered in the form of poetry, was accepted.

When it was time to transition to a new home, I decided on a New York beach town. I was quite excited to be near the beach, and I felt that hearing the continuous lull of the waves that etched their beautiful cadences in the wind would inspire me to write my praises.

Just before moving in, I had this eerie feeling about occupying that space and hoped that my premonition was totally unjustified. Alas, it was the onset of a storm.

Storms can represent a catalyst for a new path dictated by the Hand of Providence. I used to regard storms as petrifying, with damaging consequences and upheavals. They brought about changes abruptly. During these storms, I had to learn how to fly. Like the fledgling pigeons, I had to develop the strength of my wings.

As I settled into my apartment, I was happy to be reunited with many of the things I had collected over the years, especially from my travels. These I considered singular, unprecedented pieces. As a curator, I procured from those willing to share art from their minds' exhibits and displayed them in My Own Museum of Art (MOMA).

Nevertheless, others were more appreciative of the monetary value than the artistic value and started to pillage. Each time I left the apartment, I wondered what would be taken. By the end of my year-long stay, I grieved significant losses. The rest I had managed to save through ingenious contrivance or just pure luck. The memory of each missing piece plagued me. I was forced to transcend this using a moment by moment, breath by breath resistance, instituted by my quest for self-preservation since transposing myself to the next day was hard.

I had started reaching out to others for answers and healing tools. I found out that "My Guiding Light" was from within. I had to provide the answers for myself.

I started focusing more on my prayers rather than my rhapsodic praises. My poetry started taking on a didactic form. Others were connecting to it.

Reading the poems helped me deal with the shock and trauma of those "dark nights."

During these intense challenges, I felt insecure and afraid. I had to seek the light to infiltrate the lack of knowledge and unveil the answers that would facilitate my journey. I imaged representations and precepts by which to surmount these challenges and curtail the fear in my mind. From this revelation, I compiled several anthologies. For each topic I wanted to explore, I created LifeScripts and revisited them to uplift me or give me perspectives or shifts to transcend my concerns. I scripted a compendium solely dedicated to the theme of "Seemingly Lost Things."

I Fly on the Wings of the Storm

I was on my way to finding a new home again. I was ecstatic. After I left the trauma in that apartment behind, there were some good Samaritans who extended me the courtesy of accommodation. Shortly afterwards, I sensed the wind and thunder of another challenge brewing. I knew I needed guidance to develop the buoyancy to rise above the storm. So, I imaged the directives of the storm as wings to fly above or ride through the tumultuous motions it brought. I found myself scripting "I Fly on the Wings of the Storm."

During suffocating ravages, I looked towards elevating my view beyond the emotive experiences to entertain the glory and lessons at the end. Like the pigeons, I would be provided for each day. The Bible verse Matthew 6:33 kept echoing in my mind, "Seek ye first the Kingdom of God...."

I believe storms have many aspects. They are disruptive, but they can clarify the view, remove barriers, and prepare the path for progress and success. While experiencing these storms, I wrote and developed my LifeScripts, the precepts and stipulations for my well-being.

How They Helped Me

I believe these scripts could be a beacon of light for others, allowing them to experience their true identity as they awaken to their life's path.

I believe anyone can experience major challenges. It is not a matter of coming out unscathed but a matter of coming out with elevated wisdom and understanding.

Through the development of the anthology which I call *LifeScripts*, I have reached a greater understanding of myself.

Challenges motivated me to explore the gifts that I could offer to the planet and how I could support others on their journey. In my *LifeScripts*, I focus especially on themes that relate to consciously creating our days to contribute to the outcome of our lives. I was able to use tools recommended in my didactic poems daily. In that way, the new perspective lessened the stress of events.

Reading these poems helped tremendously to heal the trauma and mental stress I incurred. Having gotten through some harrowing experiences, I am willing to share my story.

To connect with Evette Rhoden and read excerpts from the *LifeScripts*, send an email to: eveedenj@gmail.com. For coaching on overcoming loss or managing stress, go to:

vetimore.wixite.com/Divineguidancenow or
eveedenj@gmail.com
facebook.com/evette.rhoden
Twitter: @canterbri

Tweetable: In the process of recovery, you can find many "Diamonds in the Valley" and use those gems to create a laurel to wear as a testament to your victory over adversity.

CRAIG MOODY

Uphill Climb
Developing a Strong Mindset
and a Seven-Figure Business

Craig Moody, business coach, writer, and speaker, has built and led successful businesses from scratch, including one with his daughter. Craig honed his skills through the John Maxwell Team and Darren Hardy High Performance Forum.

"Inside the infinite love of God there's a place for suffering."
— Fr. Thomas Keenan

Culture Shock

First thing first, this is my story. It's not meant to hurt anyone. This is what happened to me through my eyes and felt in my heart, my soul.

When I was six, my parents moved us to a small mining town in Eastern Arizona. My parents unloaded me at a friend's home and said they would be back after they packed up the Tucson house. I stayed on their couch alone, as I remember, as they would go to bed before it was dark and close their doors.

I was eager to make new friends, but the first two boys I met each challenged me to a fight. I hated our new church with no boys my age. And it was just weird. This was my introduction to my new life.

I ended up despising this town. It had a black cloud over it. I was always scared, the kids always seemed so mean, and people did not seem to be lifting each other up. In fact, the better you were at cutting someone down, the cooler you were. Bullying was an art form.

I found some solace in playing sports. Twelve straight years of football, several years of basketball, some baseball, golf, and track. I was an average athlete, but it gave me a much-needed outlet to burn pent-up anger and energy. Sports kept me somewhat focused on school, so I could eke out a C average and stay eligible.

My parents loved this small town. Any time I tried to convey my feelings to my parents, I was met with how lucky I am, occasionally followed by a story of true childhood pain. Anytime I really needed my parents to step into a bad situation with classmates, acquaintances, a teacher, or a coach, they seemed to make it worse, and somehow flipped it all back on me, as I interpreted it. Eventually, I hid most of my pain and fear from them. I thought the world would never change.

Relief and Hope

Every summer, we would travel to Northern Arizona University in Flagstaff where my mom was pursuing her teaching certificate. I loved it! The air was crisp and cool. There were mountains, pine trees, green grass, and a field house nearby where we could play basketball, tennis, or even pinball if we were lucky enough to have a quarter.

The other kids were friendly, each of us with a clean slate, a chance to be someone we were not. I was so happy there. In my junior high and early high school years, I met a girl from Western Arizona. She was a year older and gorgeous. She took me out on the NAU baseball field one night, and I came back a virgin no more. I remember families eating together in the cafeteria and the music. Everyone was so nice. However, each August, that came to an end.

After high school, I could not wait to leave and live on my own. My first choice was NAU, but my grades were not acceptable. My mom urged me to go to junior college in Phoenix. I thought, *Okay, at least I can get an apartment with friends.* However, my father said we could not afford the rent and I would have to live with my grandmother. After one very challenging year with Grandma, I eventually loaded up my car and moved to Flagstaff.

I went to NAU and applied again. I was accepted and paid for it on my own. For the first time in my life, I was alone. I loved my freedom, meeting new people, and partying. I dove into marijuana.

It gave me an escape from reality, the reality that my life was going nowhere and the confusion of the trauma of my childhood.

After two years, I dropped out and moved back home with my parents to a town I despised. I had utterly failed in life at that point. I got a few dead-end jobs and comforted myself with marijuana.

Looking back, God had a plan for me. At one of my jobs, I struck up a friendship with a kid named Eddie. One day, he asked me this question: "Who do we ultimately want to work for?"

I had no idea. Trying to be funny, I blurted, "Disneyland?"

He said, "No dummy, ourselves. We want to work for ourselves and own our own businesses." That thought had never entered my mind. Owning a business was for rich people, college graduates, people much smarter and wiser than myself. People with confidence, vision, and clarity. Not a loser like me.

I eventually made my way out of my hometown and back to Phoenix, more dead-end jobs, and bad decisions. I was surrounding myself with the wrong people, isolating myself in pity, boredom, and hate. Then, my grandmother that I had lived with passed away. My dad asked me to move back into her house to watch the place. I agreed. This became my ultimate rock bottom—no social life, jobs I hated, and people I despised.

I was constantly broke. I remember going to the bank one time and all I could withdraw was $1.75. I went to the store and got some Top Ramen. I remember the clerk looking at me like I was a total loser. *She was right*, I thought. I was a total loser. I went home, made the Top Ramen, smoked, and for the first time thought of suicide. I had a gun and sat on the bathroom floor. It was 1:30 AM. I just sat there and thought deep and evil thoughts. Then something amazing happened. I heard my dad's voice cry out "CRAIG." I threw the pipe I was holding in the closet, put the gun in my belt, and walked out into the bedroom, then the living room, then the kitchen. I looked out into the driveway, no cars. My dad wasn't there, it was just his voice, his love, and his pain. Truly a divine, angel intervention moment.

Elevating

Shortly after, I knew I had to leave and get back to the only town that brought me comfort. Flagstaff! A few days later, I did just that. I quit my part-time contracting job, loaded up my car, and left.

I stayed with friends at first. I was still going nowhere, but I was happier. I was mountain biking to work, rock climbing, camping, and doing more outdoor stuff that made me happy in my spare time.

After a few years and several jobs, I found a large printing company hiring in production. I liked the idea of earning a little more money working one job. I took the position—a swing shift, four 10-hour workdays.

Three years in, my back really started hurting. I would basically lay on the couch for three days recovering so I could work the next four. I went to the doctor and found out I had scoliosis. Intense pain forced me to get off my feet. The company had a call center. As I got to know the company structure, I could see that outbound sales consulting in the call center was where the money was to be made. So, I applied.

I met a beautiful woman there named Angela. She would eventually train me on how to operate the phones and navigate the system in the call center. Her mom also worked there, and I had mentioned to her that she had a beautiful daughter. A bunch of her friends and a few of Angela's friends devised a plan for us to go out. The rest is history. We fell in love, I joined the Catholic Church where I knew I had always belonged, and we were married in 1996. By 1998, we had two kids fourteen months apart. Ten years later, we would have a third.

The call center job was boring and a necessary step to get into sales. I applied for the sales position four times before I was accepted. Persistence paid off.

Momentum

Over the next five years, I developed relationships with clients and identified what types of clients led to new sales. Accountants were the best; they were constantly getting new clientele that needed new checks and envelopes. Contractors were great as well. As I got to know these people better, a few of them told me how much money they were making. I thought, *Wow, I must get on the other end of this call.*

Risk vs. Reward

My brother was a fraternity college graduate. He was more of a risk-taker, and he eventually returned home with his new wife, who was also a native of the town, and they started a family. He got into insurance and started his own agency. My dad had purchased a moderate-size commercial office building a few years earlier. My brother soon became one of his tenants. My family and I happened to be there one weekend when my dad got a call from a tenant. The entire lower level was flooded.

Six months later, my brother had sold his agency and was working for an independent agency across town. He called me and said, "Guess what? This office just flooded too."

I asked him, "Is there an industry for this?"

He said, "Yes, a carpet cleaning company owner dropped off his card for water extraction and structural drying."

One day, my brother called me and said he was sick of insurance altogether. He had checked into the water damage industry and found a new franchise out of Florida. They were trying to grow and were willing to fly out and meet with us and another guy.

I was scared. This would be leaving the comfort of my job, although it was no longer serving my needs, to invest in my own business. I had no confidence. My brother kept calling. "I'm gonna do it," he said. "Let's go to the training together." My loving wife believed in me and urged me to do it. We had equity in our home and could take out a second mortgage. Still, I had serious doubts. Deep down, I was a failure still. *What if this doesn't work? What if I fail? What would happen to the house? Our marriage? My reputation?* I was torn.

More importantly, at that time, our oldest was sick and required surgery. We were really scared, and I prayed so hard. After the procedure, the doctor said in addition to kidney reflux, he had a blood disorder. I was scared, however, after more education, we started to realize we were lucky. We would eventually take our child home, and he would live a long life.

My parents visited as much as possible. I was talking to my mom when she asked me what I thought about starting a business. I said it was just not the right time. Then she said the words I will never forget: "You're just not a risk-taker, are you, honey?"

The last afternoon before my son's discharge from the hospital, as I stretched my legs on the top level of the Phoenix Children's Hospital parking garage, I decided life was too short to not go for it! I called my brother and told him I was in.

Walk the Walk

The first few years were slow growth. My favorite part of being a franchisee was the conventions. I loved meeting new people in the same industry and listening to the motivational speakers. I started buying their books, and for the first time in a decade, I read a book.

Another franchisee introduced me to a leadership teacher named John Maxwell. I dove into his teachings. He was a former church pastor who saw a need for growing leaders. On the plane ride home after a convention, my brother and I made our first business plans on notepads. It took a while, but my business started to grow. I would have my entire team watch Maxwell's videos. I was loving it. I learned that to grow financially, we must first grow personally and professionally.

My first few full-time technicians were okay, but not great. I needed better people. Maxwell taught me that if you were a 4 on a scale of 1 to 10, you would only attract a 3 or lower. You had to grow yourself to a higher number to attract a higher number. I did just that. My first stellar employee freed me up to work on my strength, marketing.

It did not happen overnight. With debt, franchise fees, and a failing business, I was on a financial rollercoaster. "You are always so stressed," my wife would tell me. I was only stressed when it was really, really busy, or really slow. The problem with emergency restoration is, it is either really busy or really slow. There is rarely in between.

The Road to Passion

Ten years after my original agreement with the franchise, there was a massive exodus of franchisees due to the owners splitting up. I was able to buy my way out of the contract and start my own brand with additional services.

I learned over time that good business is a series of risks and decisions made daily. I kept thinking, *Once I do a million dollars in revenue in one year, I will have arrived.* Well, that year finally came. It felt good. I had a little breathing room, but not a lot. Budgets helped that going forward.

My mastermind group was amazing. One day, after explaining part of my story, my buddy Andrew said, "Craig, I have heard you tell this story several times, and I believe you suffer from PTSD." What he was saying was so freeing: you had trauma in your life, and it is okay to admit it and seek help. This was a huge milestone.

Andrew also told us about Darren Hardy. I watched him on YouTube. He was amazing. I read his books and joined his program. Through Insane Productivity, I learned how to stay focused, stay on schedule, and work hard. He was just what I needed, a no-nonsense, tough coach.

In 2018, I rejoined personal training and went on a diet fueled by Darren Hardy saying you absolutely need to do this to focus, get your mind right, and go to the next level. To get in shape, I told myself repeatedly Brian Buffini's axiom, "the power of a made-up mind." Eventually, I lost 50 pounds.

The next few years, I dove into insane production, even through the COVID-19 pandemic and having my youngest still at home. I built a solid management team, implemented better job descriptions, and grew the fleet. In a little over three years, I increased my annual sales by $2.4 million. I became debt-free, began traveling, and started coaching others. I developed a routine, and I hammered it: 4 AM wake and devotion, 5 AM workout, 6 AM inspirational writing, meditation, Darren Daily videos, podcasts, etc.

Everything culminated when I sold my contracting business in 2021 for more money than I could have ever imagined.

To quote John Maxwell, "It was uphill, all the way." It never got any easier, I just got better.

They say life is 10% what happens to you and 90% how you react to it. I know that had I not struggled so mightily my first 25 years, I would not have had the resolve to get to this level.

I'm nowhere near perfect, and I still have major struggles. I now seek to understand.

As parents, I believe we are truly trying to teach our kids to "learn life's lessons quicker than we did."

I am now following my passion through writing, coaching, speaking, and inspiring others.

To contact Craig Moody about his coaching, speaking, writing, and podcast platforms, email craig@thebizclimb.com

Tweetable: I learned that in order to grow financially, we must first grow personally and professionally.

BRIAN BUFFINI

Building Authentic Relationships Through Service One Person at a Time

Brian Buffini is the founder of Buffini & Company and has trained 3 million+ real estate professionals worldwide. Brian's most recent book The Emigrant Edge *is a NYT and WSJ bestseller. His podcast* It's a Good Life *has 13 million+ downloads. Brian and his wife Beverly are the parents of six kids and live in San Diego, CA.*

Put Your Name to That

Every episode of the *It's a Good Life* podcast ends with my mom sharing an Irish blessing. I was recently in Ireland visiting for her 91st birthday. She and my dad still live in the same little house my four brothers, one sister, and I grew up in. Ireland at that time was very poor. Everybody loves romantic Ireland. Well, in the late '70s and early '80s, Ireland was economically a third-world country. We didn't have much of anything. Five boys shared a nine-by-nine bedroom. It was a good life and a hard life.

We were house painters. We all learned the business and how to take care of our customers. My father and grandfather had a phrase; they'd say, "Can you put your name to that?" At the end of the day, they'd look at your work. And, if you couldn't put your name to the work you'd done, you had to do it over—whether the client saw it or not, whether they asked for it or not.

Deep in Debt to Making Millions

I took that principle with me to the United States and eventually applied it to real estate. I came over on holiday and had to stay after I got into a very serious motorcycle accident. They put rods and screws in my leg. I was in and out of the hospital for two years.

Fortunately, at the time, getting into real estate didn't require much financial investment. I just had to get licensed. As a Realtor®, I found that by doing work I felt I could put my name to, exceeding expectations, really pouring myself into people, and showing that I was going to put others' interests first and treat their money better than my own, I came out ahead. And then, I put some new school marketing techniques to it.

Within a short time, I was one of the top agents in the state of California. Within five years, I'd gone from a 19-year-old with $250,000 in medical bills and other debts to a 26-year-old millionaire. I came here with nothing and built what is today a pretty sizable multi-generational fortune.

On that journey, I found two insightful men who were hugely influential in my life and success—Jim Rohn and Zig Ziglar. Jim Rohn helped shape my philosophy more than any other person in my life. Zig Ziglar helped shape my attitude. The system I developed to generate referrals made me financially successful, but the wisdom I got from Jim Rohn and Zig Ziglar made me personally successful. It's because of them that I have it all. Many years after I was introduced to their work, the last time those two men were ever on stage together was at our event in Florida. I was very thankful Kyle Wilson, founder of Jim Rohn International, was there holding down the fort, taking care of Jim's affairs and the business side of the event.

Very First Real Estate Commission

I was at a Sunday open house 35 years ago in San Diego. I didn't have any listings, and the listing for this house was held by a successful agent who didn't want any part of it because it was in a rough part of town.

People were coming by, and this lady walked in the door—Ana D. I will never forget her. She was about 4'10" and probably about 300 pounds. She had some kind of sauce on her blouse and spoke broken English. She was asking me all these questions. I had just started in the real estate business. As a new agent, there were a couple of questions I didn't know the answer to. I said to her, "You know, I don't know the answer to that, but would it be okay if I got back in touch with you?"

When I drove my borrowed car back to the office, I got my answers and called her that evening. Her response was, "Huh, you called. You followed up." Then she said, almost under her breath, "They never follow up."

She said, "Young man, I am buying homes for my grandkids. I already know the house I want to buy. Bring a purchase contract. I'll tell you all about the house. You fill out the contract and represent me." I followed up, did the best I could, and helped her buy a home. And I was ferocious in following through on every detail.

Then, she asked me to help her buy another house. Over the next three years, she bought ten homes with me.

People always tell me that I was lucky. But, Ana said something: I was the one who followed up. I believe she was used to being underestimated, and I treated her as I would if she were buying a $10 million property, as I would have the opportunity to do for clients many years later. I poured myself into serving her, exceeded expectations, and then said, "Hey, if you know anybody who could use my help, please pass my name on."

Being the Utility

I developed a systematic marketing program that was about providing value to people. If I sold you a house, I would stay in contact with you forever— as long as you lived in the neighborhood. I would send you information on how to raise your credit score, how to protect yourself from identity theft, tax tips. . . . People came to count on me.

If you had a roof leak and I sold your house three years ago, I wanted to be your first phone call. If you were getting a refinance on your house, even though I was not a lender, I wanted to be your first phone call. If you needed a babysitter, a mechanic, an ear, nose, and throat guy, I wanted to be your first call. Long before Angie's List, I produced a yearly directory of the best trades and services in town that I trusted. I became a hub and a trusted advisor. I stayed in contact, provided cool marketing reminders about client parties I threw every year, and wrote personal notes, which to this day is one of the secret sauces of my success.

When I'd follow up with somebody, I'd ask how they were doing, we'd chat, and then I'd say, "Oh, by the way... I'm never too busy for any of your referrals." The average Realtor at the time was selling six homes a year. I was selling over a hundred. And I was doing so in San Diego where the prices are pretty decent.

Later, I bought real estate in San Diego. I still lived like an immigrant, however. I kept my expenses low and built my portfolio up to over 40 properties.

Launch of Buffini & Company

At the time, real estate speakers had slicked-back hair and looked very Wall Street. The leading speaker at the time had a phrase, "Find em, fleece em, and forget em." After about eight years working as a Realtor and investing, I would be asked to guest speak at real estate conferences. Nobody really knew me because I didn't do much public advertising. I didn't have a radio show or personal brochures, yet I was selling more homes and making more money than anybody. So, I would be asked to speak. At these conferences, I'd come up for Q&A, share a few things I was doing, and afterwards, there would be a line out the door to talk to me.

As I did more of this, my wife said, "This business has been a blessing to us. You really need to give back." So, I made a commitment. Once a month, I would speak to give back to the real estate industry. I did that for two years between '94 and '96. Finally, I was getting overwhelmed. There were so many calls and emails coming in all the time: "We need more. Can you tell us what you do? How do you do it?" There was a demand. Having been exposed to the personal growth and development business, I decided I would start hosting events to offer more coaching and training.

My first seminar, on February 14, 1996, almost 500 people showed up. Almost all of them were people I had done business with. They respected how I treated them. They knew I really strove to take care of the customer. At the end of it, they said, "I want you to teach me how you do what you do." That was the beginning of what started out as Providence Seminars and later became Buffini & Company. In short order, with the seminars, coaching, and training, there was no room for real estate.

I handed my business over to a couple of guys I had mentored. Next thing you know, I was doing a hundred seminars a year. At one point, we had 450 coaches training people all over the world. Now, 25 years later, one out of every eight homes sold in America, and one out of every seven in Canada, is sold through people we coach. If you go to Australia, South Africa, and several other countries, you have to take our training to be a real estate agent. It started out with something small, something simple, something very focused, and the spirit has grown from there.

Compounding Your Relationships

I have a principle. If you want to make your business big, make your focus small. My focus has been on serving the individual customer. When I'm speaking, when I'm doing a podcast, all I want to do is provide value. If people find value in what I share and want to find out what else I can offer them, I'm here to serve.

In today's market, I believe building a business is simpler than it has ever been. Customer service is almost dead. It is easier than ever to stand out from your competition by following through on service better than anyone else on the market.

Albert Einstein said compound interest was the eighth wonder of the world. Those who understand it, receive it and those who don't, pay it. Stocks can compound, real estate can compound, and very importantly, business relationships can compound. The fact of the matter is, when you are transactional, you'll get a transaction, a paycheck. But if you meet the transactional and emotional needs of your customers, you'll make an advocate.

The average real estate agent in America makes $32,000 in gross commissions annually, The average agent we coach makes $358,000. You would think it's a no-brainer. Still, some people come to our events—They talk to people. They see the system works. But they wonder in their heart of hearts if it will work for *them*. They are afraid they will be the one who still manages to fail. It comes down to self-belief. They have to take a step of faith and trust themselves.

It Is the Pursuit

I am in pursuit of impact. I'm in a spot right now where I can retire and not do anything. My kids and grandkids are set up, and still, I may be more driven now than I've ever been. I'm ramping up to build out a Buffini & Company business division to reach more people. I want to broaden the impact I have.

I've been blessed to stand on the shoulders of giants: Og Mandino, Jim Rohn, Zig Ziglar, Brian Tracy, and more. All I want to do is press forward to find more people who I can help and give as much as I can. We're a world that's drowning in information and starving for wisdom. So, I want to broaden my influence and impact more than I ever have.

Going back to the very tenets of what makes America, life, liberty, and the pursuit of happiness—the pursuit of happiness is happiness. The pursuit is the happiness.

When Brett Favre won the Super Bowl, he was standing up on stage holding the trophy, the confetti was falling, and he said, ". . . is that it?" He hadn't, yet, thought beyond the Super Bowl to the next goal. I think having a clear set of goals that you're pursuing for what pursuing will make of you, that is the pursuit of happiness. To achieve that goal, you will develop your character, discipline, and daily habits. That's the magic.

If I had to do it all over again, there's one or two things I might've done differently. I would have trusted more in the gifts God has given me. I didn't need to try as hard as I did. God gives everyone unique gifts. Our job is to give our gifts back to Him. For the first two-thirds of my working life, I was in a life and death struggle to make my God-given gifts go. Today, I say just let the gift be the gift. Trust the gift will produce the rewards it's supposed to.

And then, trust that those same gifts are inside our kids. Create the best environment for them, nurture them, bring them along, and they're going to be just fine. Each child is unique. Each is a chance to appreciate and celebrate different gifts. In my six kids, I see their discipline, their character, their communication. I see they don't have the same hang-ups as their dad. So I became a student, and I let them influence me as much as I've ever influenced them.

And lastly, remember that life does have challenges, along with many ups and downs, but when you have it all in perspective and you strive to do and be your best, it is indeed a good life!

To learn more about Brian Buffini's programs, live events, books, and his *It's a Good Life* podcast, go to https://www.brianbuffini.com/

Tweetable: Building a business is simpler than it has ever been. Stand out from your competition by following through on service better than anyone else on the market.

ANDREW MCWILLIAMS

Bankrupt to Ballin'

Andrew McWilliams is the founder of The McWilliams Group Real Estate and Andrew McWilliams Coaching. Achieving top 1% status among all RE/MAX agents internationally, Andrew has guided many new and seasoned agents to success, sharing philosophy, lessons, and principles from his personal journey.

Ultimate Failure

It was hot and dry, and the brilliant sunlight on that late summer afternoon blinded us as we emerged from the Federal Building in downtown Denver. I remember blinking and thinking the streets seemed deserted and quiet, especially for a weekday.

The process in the courtroom had been brief, mechanical, and anti-climactic. Years of lack and an exhausting fight against a downward spiral had brought us to this ugly eventuality. We were officially bankrupt.

Bankrupt. Financially failed. At age 41. It was surreal and desolate. I never thought I would find myself here, but I also never had a plan to be anywhere else.

How I Learned to Fail

Growing up, money always seemed in short supply. My father was a remodeling contractor for most of my childhood, and we would ride a rollercoaster between short spells of "extra" cash, nice vacations, and a new car and longer periods of counting coins for lunch money, avoiding bill collector's calls, and coming in from playing to find Mom crying at the kitchen table.

As a young adult, I was financially illiterate. No goals. No budget. No plan. To be honest, I was a bit suspicious of financial success and wealthy people. I believed it was somehow immoral. You might even say that to desire wealth and financial success was a tainted aspiration in my mind.

Looking back, I see the messages life sent me said money was in short supply and never lasted. There was never enough, and when it was present it was to be spent.

Sensing (Much) More

In my mid-twenties, I began to sense that there could be more to my life than what I had known. I remember many moonlit drives under the canopy of stars in the Colorado skies and encountering an awesome sense of transcendence. I took bi-weekly solo hikes in the Rocky Mountains, soaking in the quiet and the incredible beauty. Somehow, I knew that there was "more" in this Universe, and I was determined not to miss it.

I began to pray, to journal, and to meditate that God would develop me to my fullest potential, that my mind, talents, and gifts would be maximized, and that I would become all that I was able to become. This prayer and meditation followed me throughout my twenties. Ironically, I had not been introduced to personal development, mindset, or even goal setting by then. It would be fourteen more years before I even put my first written goals on paper.

Everything Begins with a First Step

At age 31, a year after marrying my wife Heather, I got a license to sell real estate. I had always enjoyed seeing beautiful houses and exploring nice parcels of land. At the time, I needed a new career, and a series of bad experiences with real estate agents gave me the idea that I could do a better job myself.

My first nine years in real estate followed the same financial rollercoaster I had learned to expect from my childhood. I was reactionary and passive, responding to random opportunities but never creating opportunities with intention and design. I had no concept of reliable outcomes achieved through daily, consistent action. I believed that I had goals and that I knew what they were. They were in my head, and I could recite them if asked, but I had never written any down. Then, when I was 41, my wife and I declared bankruptcy.

Many of our choices prior to bankruptcy were not necessarily irresponsible. Some decisions are not "bad" but are also not wise and can lead to unintended consequences that are severe. Our fight to avoid bankruptcy was protracted, including credit counseling, debt restructuring, and repayment plans. Then our four-year-old son was injured and admitted to the ICU. Those resulting bills and one missed payment on our repayment plan nullified over a year of progress and led to the end of our resistance.

Amid the emotional fog and financial uncertainty at the conclusion of our bankruptcy, Heather and I were vulnerable about our situation selectively within a close circle of family and friends. More than empathy, I think we were looking for someone to guide us or give us a recipe for a solution. Unfortunately, reactions varied from hurtful words and scornful disapproval to an awkward subject avoidance altogether. We recognized that no one was coming to rescue us.

No one is coming to rescue me. A simple phrase and common-sense concept, and one of the most powerful and freeing understandings that a person can come to accept. I came to rely on this fact. There was no need to wait for a rescue that was not on its way. I could build something great and sustainable on my own.

My journey out of the financial devastation of our bankruptcy began with a very simple first step. I did not know how to create the life I wanted for myself and my family. However, I did understand that it was solely up to me to figure it out. So, I wrote some goals down on a page.

I have learned that there are two elements to success: motivation and knowledge. You need both to succeed, and if you are not currently experiencing the success you desire, you should look at those two elements to find the reason why. Throughout my life, I had maintained a "want to" type of motivation. But that left me in the world of daydreams and fantasy. I was interested in a different life. More accurately, I was interested in a different result in response to my efforts. It was also true that I had no real expectation that I could affect a better outcome.

The first year I wrote down my goals, I saw my business more than double in volume. It was almost magical. I did not understand it. I had no idea about the role the subconscious mind plays in making our thoughts and beliefs become reality. But that result motivated me to become a student and learn more. I observed the results, dug deeper into goal setting, and opened the wide doors that I would come to understand as personal development. Early influences included John Maxwell, Jim Rohn, Brian Buffini, and Bob Proctor. I began to see the same principles and philosophy everywhere I looked. At their core, the principles of success were simple truths repeated among these voices.

A Great Unveiling

My journey toward understanding more about the philosophy of success was a great unveiling. It was like physical scales literally fell from my eyes. Mark Caine says, "The first step toward success is taken when you refuse to be a captive of the environment in which you first find yourself." I now understood that I was solely responsible for my current circumstances, and to change my life, I had to become a different version of myself. All my previous decisions and outcomes, those experiences in my childhood, the well-intentioned voices of family and those in positions of authority, had filled my mind with the baggage of doubt, lack, and limitation. As Zig Ziglar said, "You are what you are because of what has gone into your mind."

Over the next few years, I experimented with different tools for setting goals. Each fourth quarter, I would bring in outside speakers for my real estate offices, and they would lead seminars on goal setting. At every presentation, I would copy the quotes and books referenced. Hungry for more content, looking up these influencers and reading the books brought me to even more understanding. Like trying to drink from a fire hose, the depth and abundance of resources was truly overwhelming.

The Journey to Success

After our bankruptcy and a few years of renting, my wife and I repaired our credit sufficiently to purchase a major renovation project in a good location. It was an absolute eyesore with no curb appeal and had been on the market for months. Our five-year plan was to renovate the home and leverage future equity on resale, and we had begun picking away at several of the most critical projects. Beyond this, our goal was to own an equestrian property where we could keep our horses at our own place. Within seven months of our "ugly home" purchase, we were called to a listing appointment at a property we had admired for years. An architect's own home, the form and structural design was a work of art. Situated on ten acres and bordered on two sides by a conservation easement and public open space, it was a unique offering and the opportunity of a lifetime.

As little as two or three years prior, I would not have believed in the possibility of owning a home like this. But by this time, I understood that abundance is always present and that I am the only limiting factor to success coming my way. My wife and I asked the owners for 90 days to complete the purchase for ourselves. We went home and orchestrated a complete renovation of the exterior and interior of our current home in 60 days. We listed the home on a Saturday morning and had a contract by that afternoon. Thirty days later, we closed on that sale and the purchase of our dream estate on the same afternoon.

My journals show questions that I asked myself along the way. Was I enough? Could I build something great and sustainable? Doubting thoughts and feelings of fear would continue to creep in. In my imagination, I considered those negative voices to be "tapes," and once I became aware of them, I would picture myself pulling them out and replacing them with positive affirmations instead. I have learned that successful people are skilled at capturing negative thoughts and shifting them, even in the moment, to a positive paradigm.

Building Momentum

While driving through one of the higher-priced neighborhoods in my market, it occurred to me that I could increase the price range of the properties we worked simply by changing my thoughts. So, I made it my purpose that day to rebrand myself into higher price ranges focusing on luxury homes, acreage estates, and equestrian properties.

A short time later, an opportunity came up for me to list an amazing estate at $3.45M. It was owned by a past client for whom I had sold an 80-acre farm. In our market, no properties had sold at or above the $3 million price point in the last three or four years. Beyond that, I had not yet successfully marketed a listing over $2 million in my career.

My journal entry reads, "Opportunity to list $3.45M estate…don't believe I can find a buyer for it." Overcoming that negative thought and the perspective of lack over abundance, we implemented an amazing marketing plan, and after a short time on the market, we found a buyer and closed the sale.

For the first ten years of my real estate career, I would characterize my approach to success as wishful, passive, reactive (to opportunity), and dependent on "good luck." Year nine was the year that we filed for bankruptcy. Year ten was the year that I first wrote down goals on paper and doubled my production from the year before.

Year eleven was the year we started giving away the first 10% of our gross income because the principle of "flow" was introduced to us. In year thirteen, we doubled our gross commission income (GCI), increased our giving to 12%, and I hired an executive coach. Two years later, our GCI doubled again.

Now, our income has become predictable, consistent, and sustainable. I am grateful to share that I have achieved top 1% status among RE/MAX agents internationally for the past five years and earned the RE/MAX Hall of Fame and Lifetime Achievement awards along the way. No longer do I hope for a good market or rely on luck, good fortune, hopes and dreams, or any other external source for my success.

First Steps into My Second 50 Years

In the past ten years, I have served as a mentor and guide for two local real estate offices and more than 80 agents. These agents produced more than $2.5B in volume through more than 4,200 transactions. Starting more than forty brand new real estate licensees in their careers, I am now delighted to witness several surpass me in both production and achievement. I have developed proprietary new agent "boot camps," multiple real estate training programs, and created a highly sought-after continuing education designation, Certified Mountain Area Specialist™.

Thirteen years have passed since the parching heat and hopeless emptiness of the stone steps at the Federal Courthouse in Denver. Thirteen years of growth, becoming, practice, questioning, and discovery.

I have learned that the more clearly defined my goal, the more the Universe conspires to attract resources to achieve it. I have learned to avoid the pull of contraction, where I listen to the voices of fear and uncertainty. Contraction makes me small, a self-fulfilling prophecy of sorts that stops flow and builds into a sense of lack where abundance is forgotten.

I observe that when we are pursuing specific goals, our energy and momentum propel us toward those goals in amazing and unexpected ways. On our journey, the larger the goal, the bigger the energy, and the greater the momentum. When I look back at seasons along the journey where we were not pursuing "big things," the energy and adrenaline of success and accomplishment were also missing.

There is something about pursuing goals that requires me to grow, stretch, and become someone I have never been before. In my twenties, I had a sense, a stirring in my spirit, that there was much more to this life than I was conscious of.

The pace on this success journey is swift. My internal passion and drive are unrelenting. It is not a slog of many years of incremental increase. Instead, it's a rocket ride, and I am now only touching the edges of what I will experience three, five, and ten years from today. My compelling need is to maximize my potential, to be developed to my capacity given by God, to not miss my highest outcome.

I know that there are others just like me. Me at 25. Me at 31. Me at 41. Sensing more. Wanting to stretch and expand. Lacking understanding. Feeling destitute. Needing a guide. My vision is to become that guide for as many searchers as I can.

To get in touch with Andrew McWilliams about starting or growing your real estate career or entrepreneurial business, and for a free initial coaching consultation, send an email to andrew@themcwilliamsgroup.net or connect on his website or via social media.

www.themcwilliamsgroup.net
www.linkedin.com/in/andrew-mcwilliams-1707997

Tweetable: I know that there are others just like me. Me at 25. Me at 31. Me at 41. Sensing more. Wanting to stretch and expand. Lacking understanding. Feeling destitute. Needing a guide.

ANGELA PENTEADO

Coaching Conversations Build Authentic Leaders with Influence

Angela Penteado is a leadership and team coach, and change facilitator. She is passionate about helping people navigate life, career, and organizational transitions. Angela teaches leaders how to create successful outcomes, building positivity and influence through coaching conversations and authentic leadership.

"When one door of happiness closes, another opens" – Helen Keller

Carrying My Teacup—A True Servant Leader

In 1994, I met a man who changed my view on the world, global peacemaker Archbishop Desmond Tutu. The late anti-apartheid leader dreamed of a world that was fair and just. I'd just attended the launch of his book *The Rainbow People of God*, which he'd graciously autographed. His persistence and commitment to achieving truth, peace, acceptance, and freedom in leadership made him a world-renowned force for good. At the end of our conversation, when I asked to take away his teacup and saucer, he insisted, "No, it would be an honor if you'd let me take yours." This small gesture left me feeling special—respected and understood. He was the first true servant leader I'd met, and his warmth and humility left me inspired.

The humble "cuppa" is a symbol of connection. We need this warm connection with others at work and in our community. Throughout my career, my workplace friends and I have often shared conversations over a cuppa. These chats raised my confidence and strengthened our long-term connection. We would discuss our respective challenges at work and be there for each other.

Through the challenges of business—the heartbreak of contracts ending early, work/life balance challenges, family illnesses, and other pressures— these warm business and personal connections have been a constant. They have helped me face all that life has thrown at me and reminded me to heed the well-known verse from Romans 8:28, All things work together for good for those that are called according to God's plans and purposes.

Holding the Door Open for Others

My story started back where I grew up in Auckland, New Zealand. I was the eldest of four. My parents were hard-working, supportive, and loving. But they were also hard-pressed with their time and resources to give us extras and spend time with us.

My dad worked for the same electrical contracting company for over 40 years, and Mum served as an elementary school teacher in the same school for over 30 years. They served as parish stewards at the local Methodist Church for over 50 years, serving a series of ministers. Weeknights were full of meetings for them. In her 40s, my mum followed her father into ministry as a part-time Methodist lay preacher.

My parents were servant leaders who served their family, their community, and their local church. My parents were still working in what they'd trained in after school, so as my three brothers left school, they were encouraged to do trades. In contrast, I was encouraged to move out at 19 and get working rather than study.

Both my parents served as role models to me. They encouraged me to find independence and fulfillment and said they would support my dreams. And they did—allowing me to visit the USA for a year as an 18-year-old American Field Service (AFS) student. I had always been a hard worker, having a job since age 15. At age 19, I made a significant decision to venture into journalism. I was soon in a shared apartment and achieving as a writer and editor of business magazines. I got married at 22 and moved to Sydney, Australia. I was ready to get serious about my career. I worked in journalism and editing for consumer and business titles until a door closed, and I was left with a redundancy check.

When One Door Closes, Another Always Opens

I've always believed that instead of focusing on closing doors, we should get excited about the opening ones as part of a plan bigger than we can see. With my redundancy windfall, I decided to travel to the 25-year reunion concert of Woodstock in Saugerties, New York. A fellow journalist, Michelle, who also just lost her editorship with a business magazine, joined me. Putting the disappointment behind, we set off on a new adventure with our Australian Journalism Association (AJA) credentials in tow. Days later, we were interviewing two of the four original Woodstock Festival founders. They had become friends in high school and had remained friends ever since they ran the festival of 1969. Their story of tenacity in business and friendship inspired me.

Soon after that trip, another door opened, an opportunity to do a public relations contract back in New Zealand. I was looking for something I couldn't put my finger on—something that hadn't happened for me over my six-year working holiday in Australia. I felt like a donut with a missing hole.

Purpose-Driven Life—Finding the Missing Piece

After discovering new friends and hobbies back in Auckland, I finally settled down and found my why. I discovered that the sense of purpose I craved was feeling at home in my old community—close to family, friends, and my faith. A new door opened for a long-term job in local government public relations, I fell pregnant, and before long, the first of our four children arrived.

The doors kept opening for us, ushering in new chapters—supporting hubby in a new pizza business while being a full-time working mum, buying our first home near my parents, and helping hubby study social work while I started a new business as a public relations consultant. That was my first consulting business, and over six years, I developed a range of corporate clients from my home-based office. It was a journey of faith, with our bills being paid by answered prayers at times. There were other challenges too, like my three-year-old daughter being very sick in hospital for some months, then making a miraculous recovery after some new supplements and prayer.

To make life easier financially for my family, I returned to work in local government in 2006, closing my consulting business to focus on my new job. The great thing about serving a community is that everything you do is for your ratepayers. As I delivered community engagement surveys, conducted workshops on sustainability, and helped preserve the Waitakere Ranges as a world heritage area, I partnered with a committed core of "eco-city" warriors who believed in sustainable living. We also encouraged behavior change like watching water and electricity usage to help people save money.

New Business and Concepts on Leadership

Change was coming again to my career as seven mayors of the local councils of Auckland were told their organizations would be closed and restructured to become one Auckland Council. The mayor I worked for, a true servant leader, applauded his 800-strong team for their sustainability achievements and played a uniting role in the transformation period for his fellow political leaders.

Over two years of uncertainty, I saw colleagues unsure whether they'd get a job or a redundancy. I moved into human resources, working alongside people on team culture, industry diplomas, and job applications. In 2010, when "Auld Lang Syne" played as the city council flag was lowered, I was planning to open a new change and communications consulting firm. Soon, my second business, Leadership Insights Solutions, was born.

In 2011, I was consulting at Auckland Council, when another door opened—higher education. Colart, a fellow consultant, shared how his outlook had changed after finishing an executive MBA. After a good word from Colart, I was accepted into Massey University's executive MBA program and started the journey to my Master's degree. Four years of working full-time and studying full-time took a toll on my energy, my family, and my stress levels. In 2014, to thank my family for their support in achieving "our MBA," we went on our first and only overseas holiday together to the Gold Coast, in sunny Queensland, Australia. It was unforgettable.

Burnout After a Perfect Storm

In 2015, just after I completed my MBA, one of life's perfect storms hit. I was working full-time, studying part-time, and traveling an hour a day to visit my mother who had terminal cancer. I also had minor surgery, the result of which was nerve pain from a foreign body reaction to surgical mesh. It left me with reduced mobility, ongoing pain, and constant exhaustion. I hid it well, walking for miles around my workplace campus, but eventually, I returned to the hospital to find out why I was struggling so much. On the same day that doctors told me I had developed an autoimmune condition, my mum took a turn for the worse and died in a nearby hospice.

Those were dark days. With my employer unsupportive of my illness, I started talking weekly with a business coach who had written a book about how he'd pivoted and overcome the after-effects of brain cancer. Over the weeks we talked, I began to heal, and my goal-setting and self-confidence improved. By the end of the process, I'd firmly set my sights on becoming a leadership and team coach. I thought it would be a perfect complement to the change facilitator work I was doing. I wanted to make a difference in the cultures of the organizations I'd been consulting for and in the careers of the leaders and workers I'd met. I enrolled in a coaching training program for executive and organizational coaching.

Through the trials of this period, I re-learned that we need friends and allies to support us when we're going through hard times and with their help we can make it through.

Another hero through that storm was my best friend, my Portuguese hubby, who has traveled with me ever since he met me as a 21-year-old on a Pacific cruise. Jose has always had my back and supported our family. He believed in me when I chose to work from home and live by faith when our four children were younger. He listened tirelessly to my work stories, giving wise counsel. Jose supported my goal to get my health back by agreeing to top up our mortgage so I could have mesh removal surgery in the USA in 2019. Flying with me to St. Louis, Missouri, on our 31st wedding anniversary, he was by my side throughout the process. Four friends also traveled hundreds of miles through the snow to see their old AFS friend Angie. With the full support of my friends and family, I was able to reverse my autoimmune condition and resume my work with renewed vigor.

Connecting the Dots

Consulting for large corporations as an organizational and transformational change facilitator, I help on the people side of change—helping leaders lead, ensuring changes are understood, inviting people on the journey, supporting them with training, changing attitudes, and building systems buy-in. By giving a series of new choices, information, and rewards, people are able to choose to get on the change journey with their peers.

Individual coaching was sometimes part of my work, and increasingly, I found a regular trickle of people were self-referring to me. There were ones who'd been wounded by the corporate world or who needed a trusted advisor to talk through their goals. Others needed to build their confidence or needed a listening ear to help them navigate a challenge. It turns out that not everyone has heroes at work they can turn to or people in their networks there for them.

Lending a Helping Hand

My purpose was becoming clearer. I was passionate about helping others succeed. I wanted to share the wisdom I'd gained by overcoming the highs and lows of the business game. I started virtual and face-to-face meetings with people referred to me.

I wanted to share the values of authentic and servant-hearted leadership. I wanted to help shape and support a new generation of authentic leaders, who took the time to let their staff bring their whole person and situation to the table in meetings and regular catch ups over coffees.

Coaching and mentoring are a calling, and I enjoyed making a difference as I listened in confidence to many stories of colleagues and friends, building my 500 hours towards my professional coaching certification with the International Coaching Federation (ICF). During the lockdowns of 2020, I loved facilitating six virtual masterclasses for leaders from around the world, helping them pivot and discover the value of holding the door open for others.

2020s—A Decade of Change

The first two years of the 2020s have seen enormous change. With workplace culture being an agreed set of common behaviors and values—backed by the underlying mindsets that shape how we work and connect—we need to radically rethink the future of work. Our workplace and team culture norms need to be reframed if we are to get the most from the new model of remote and hybrid work.

As a result of the pandemic, between 2020 and 2022, we have seen a rise in a flexible leadership style—where team members' interests are put first. Those pre-COVID leaders who wanted their workers under their watchful eye are on their way out. While power and control culture is still alive and well, a new breed of authentic, enlightened leaders is developing.

These new leaders are more empathetic and take the time to ask after family members, pets, and work/life balance. Some call this servant leadership; I think of it as authentic, flexible leadership where team members are encouraged and supported through regular coaching conversations.

This shift away from control and condescension to a culture with more humanity is a must. Achieving this shift in corporate culture takes a completely different mindset. It takes a sustained push to help those leading teams stop commanding and controlling and replace those neural pathways with a new mindset. Before the pandemic, many organizations were focused only on getting the work done.

On her podcast, *Unlocking Us*, Brené Brown quoted author, artist, and activist Sonya Renee Taylor,

We will not go back to normal. . . . We are being given the opportunity to stitch a new garment. One that fits all of humanity and nature. Normal never was. Our pre-Corona corporate existence was not normal—other than we normalized greed, inequity, exhaustion, depletion, extraction, disconnection, confusion, rage, hoarding, hate, and lack. We should not long to return, my friends.

In this new world, authentic leaders are rising. They are building a sense of positivity and belonging in teams—and a more authentic, collaborative culture. By cultivating calmness, belonging, fun, and connection, leaders can grow high-performing teams that are innovative and driven.

Leadership Styles for the New Era

You will want to be remembered for who you are. For your personality and your authentic reality. For your loyalty to your team members. And for whether you walked the talk of your vision, values, and faith. For the type of leader that you are, someone known for your empathy and integrity. I love the empathy quote by St. Louis-born author and civil rights activist Maya Angelou, "I've learned that people will forget what you said, people will forget what you did, but people will never forget how you made them feel."

I tell my four adult children as they study, explore, and grow, don't let yourself be stifled, controlled, or put in a box. Ask questions, stand up for your views, and don't follow directives without doing your research. Dare to be vulnerable and share your opinions. Open new doors. Take new opportunities and adventures. Hold the door open for others and stand up for your team and for free speech. Work in fields you are passionate about, never stop innovating, and work to make your environment better than you found it. I guess we all want to make a difference and change our corner of the world. As Archbishop Tutu ("Arch") said, "Do your little bit of good where you are, it's those bits of good put together that overwhelm the world... It is through weakness and vulnerability that most of us learn empathy and compassion and discover our soul."

If you need to talk through your career and business goals, personal brand, and transitions, get free "future of work" tips from Leadership Insights' authenticity blog, or join an authentic leadership mastermind group, email angela@leadershipinsights.co or visit her website www.leadershipinsights.co

Tweetable: In this new world, authentic leaders are rising. By cultivating calmness, belonging, fun, and connection, leaders can grow high-performing teams that are innovative and driven.

MARK LIVINGSTON

Keep Climbing the Dream Ladder

Mark Livingston is an executive who has built successful teams in multiple industries. Currently, he leads finance teams in three countries. He also uses his extensive experience to design financial strategies that help people preserve wealth, minimize taxes, and generate passive cash flow.

Time for a New Life

In 2011, my marriage of 25 years ended. Once we were fully separated, I took inventory of my life. I had two kids entering high school and expecting to go to college, a good stable job, a house, and friends. These are all assets in life. Especially my two children who I love so much.

There was a lot missing on the financial side. Especially for a man in his late 40s. No college fund. Almost no retirement savings. We had followed the life of keeping up with the Joneses and enjoyed life, but did little to prepare financially for the future.

The only way I was going to be able to send my kids to college and prepare for the life I wanted in my later years was to really start thinking bigger. Luckily, I already had some experience doing just that.

Big Corporate Dreams: Director of Internal Audit

Early in my professional career as an accountant, I migrated into the field of internal auditing. Once I was in that field, I knew I wanted to be the internal audit director, the one in charge and directing all the work of the department. That was my dream. I just needed a plan to get there.

I knew it could be done, but it would not be guaranteed or a short climb. All you have to do is look at the numbers to tell that this climb to the top is not completed by everyone. If a typical director has nine people they lead, then the director is one of ten in the company. Not everyone can be the director.

As I started my climb, I learned that the director determines the audit plan for the company. To be successful, the director needs to understand the business and all the risks the company faces. This meant just performing the audits was not going to get me where I wanted to be. I needed to invest the time to learn the business and its risks.

And so, as I performed audits, I spent time getting to know my colleagues, how they measure success in their departments and what risks endangered that success. With every audit, I put in extra effort to learn something new about the business and develop relationships in that area of the company.

Over the years, this paid off. Within a few years, I was promoted to manager of the department. Less than five years after that, I had my first opportunity to be the internal audit director. The sad part was that I was going to have to move to another company to fulfill that opportunity, leaving the people I had enjoyed working with for over eight years.

I would be responsible for creating a completely new internal audit function and department where none had existed. I made the move. The new position was a fantastic learning experience. And, over twenty years later, I am still friends with my colleagues at that previous company.

That internal audit director opportunity led to others. At three more companies, I either built new internal audit functions or significantly enhanced the scope of responsibility of the internal audit department. I had completely achieved my dream.

But then, after my divorce in 2011, I had to reassess my life, especially my career. And now I had a new dream.

The Next, Bigger Dream: Public Company Chief Accounting Officer

Now in my 40s and starting a new life, I dreamed of doing something else. I was confident I could use my experience and talents within the corporate world to get the resources I needed to design the life I dreamed. Being in charge of all accounting for a public company seemed like a logical step for me. This position is most commonly known as the chief accounting officer. The challenge was figuring out how I could make the transition to leading a company-wide accounting function when I'd never held any of the accounting positions below that.

I started talking to CFOs of companies to get input. Internal audit directors and chief accounting officers both reported to CFOs, so it made sense to talk to them about what they were looking for and potential ways to make that jump. I was never afraid to be upfront with what I was hoping to do, and my forward-thinking positivity seemed welcome in each conversation I had.

Within a year, those conversations led me to an opportunity directly under the CFO in my current company—director of SEC reporting. My primary responsibility was to write the company 10-Qs and 10-Ks and file them with the Securities Exchange Commission quarterly and annually.

Additionally, I was responsible for keeping all accounting policies up to date, keeping the company in compliance with generally accepted accounting principles, and being the main liaison with the external auditors. These other responsibilities were an easy transition because I had audited against those policies as an internal auditor and worked with the external auditors.

Writing the 10-Qs and 10-Ks allowed me to understand from the top down how all the information from the accounting functions flowed. I couldn't help being grateful for how perfect this was for getting me ready to be a chief accounting officer.

After three years, I accepted the chief accounting officer position at another public company. And, to my great satisfaction, my dream had been achieved again. I kept that role until three years later when our company was taken over by a larger company and my role was downsized.

After a few months of searching, I found an opportunity to be chief accounting officer again. I have been in this role for over three years and am now grooming someone to replace me to ensure a smooth transition as I move toward pursuing my next big dream.

Pivot into Private Investment Opportunities

While I pursued my dreams within the corporate world, I started a private investment business: Match Real Asset Partners. It started as a way for me to invest in "real assets" rather than the paper assets offered by Wall Street firms. My colleagues and I call this investing in Main Street rather than Wall Street.

As I did more of this type of investing and networking with like-minded investors, and as we learned from each other, I realized that I wanted to "go bigger and go faster." Investing was always a way to secure my future, and as I worked to design my new life, I realized investing could play a much larger role in creating that. Going bigger, faster meant I needed more money. That meant syndicating investments and attracting money from third parties. This was the biggest dream I'd had yet.

I found other people who had achieved this dream for themselves and were willing to share ideas. They realized, and I did too, that you can always learn from other people, that better ideas come from collaboration and that this isn't a competition. Through collaboration, we can develop better strategies and achieve even bigger things.

The more I have worked with this collaborative investment community, the more I've learned and the more I've accomplished. In 2021, I completed my first true syndicated investment with other people's money. I raised $1.4 million of equity. In total, those investors received $2.8 million of tax depreciation to reduce their income tax burden and will receive over $3.9 million cash in return. Those numbers proved to me that I could do this.

My next step, or next dream, is to make this a bigger business and do more. We will find ways to attract tens of millions of dollars per year to investments in real assets because I can give my investors better returns than Wall Street, preserve their wealth, and give them tax benefits. To do this, I am building a team so that I can focus my time on developing financial strategies with the investments I offer and communicate with existing and potential investors to learn more about what they need and want in their investments.

When You Think You're Stuck, Think Big

When I think of thinking big, I think of the future. I think of change. I think of making something much better. Sometimes we daydream about doing something completely different or being able to do more.

But society constantly bombards us with negative messages: *One person can't change that. You'll never be able to do that. What makes you think you can do that?*

When I was struggling with my career, always dreaming big helped me move forward and achieve my dreams. This is the process I have followed for years. First think big and then turn those big dreams into action and results. I know that you can do that too.

Mark Livingston's purpose at Match Real Asset Partners is to match busy professionals with high-performing real assets to preserve wealth, minimize taxes, and generate passive cash flow. If this is important to you, send an email to ThinkBig@MatchRealAssetPartners.com to get more information and start a dialogue on how you can think bigger.

Tweetable: When you think you're stuck, think bigger!

CHERI PERRY

Go BIG & Go HOME!
Powerful Lessons from My Father

Cheri Perry is the owner of a national credit card processing company, an author, trainer, speaker, and business coach. She grew up in a family business and, over the years, has built her legacy by applying massive action, success principles, and BIG thinking. She will inspire you to push the envelope and think bigger!

Big Thinking Evolves Over Time

The funny thing about BIG thinking is that it changes over time! What we think we can do at the beginning of any endeavor versus what we think we can do at the end is often VASTLY different.

Developing our ability to think and do BIG things takes time, energy, and effort. It's like working a muscle really; the more we work it, the bigger it gets. Our seasons of life impact our thinking. How we define BIG thinking, if we are lucky, also matures over time.

When we started our business in the late '90s, our "thinking big" revolved around big, simple goals like making our house payment, managing bills, and not losing our car to the bank! In those early days, it was about survival. Can you relate? We did not take the time to think of things like impact, legacy, or making a difference. It is fair to say that thinking big back then was not the same as the BIG thinking we do today. And how could it be?

"Go as far as you can see: when you get there, you'll be able to see further." – Thomas Carlyle

Learning how to see further and think bigger requires action, and in my case, that action was inspired in large part by my father. I had the distinct advantage of being raised by a BIG thinker! My father was the epitome of a go-getter. He whispered into the fertile ears of his children until his very last day: you can do anything, achieve anything, accomplish anything, and overcome anything if you just keep going. Here are some of the BIG lessons I was fortunate enough to learn from my dad.

Keep Going: Everything ALWAYS Works Out!

During the early years of our business, times were tough. Often, it seemed like a never-ending struggle. We were in the MESSY MIDDLE. When we were in a valley, I would get so irritated when my dad would tell me that everything always works out. "ALWAYS?" I would say. Because, in the hardest of moments, it often feels like the exact opposite. It can feel as if NOTHING ever works out and as if EVERYTHING is stacked against you.

Many people give up at this stage. They change direction, change jobs, and even change people. Look around, and you will see the results of giving up. Lost momentum, lost opportunities, and broken families. It is seriously heart-BREAKING if you think about it. There's nothing worse than looking into the eyes of someone who has lost their spark. The emptiness is soul-crushing.

During those difficult times in our business, we did as my father said—we kept on going. We focused on growing the business and finding a way to make it BIGGER. As it turns out, my dad was right. Everything really does have a way of working out! We soon worked our way through the survival struggle and to the next hurdle in expanding our thinking. We made it to the comfort zone.

If you ever find yourself in a tough situation, will you allow me to pass those wonderful words of wisdom on to you? Keep on going because everything always has a way of working out! Yes, ALWAYS.

Visit BUT DON'T LIVE in the Comfort Zone

Once we got past survival mode in our business, we entered into a dangerous phase called the comfort zone, and to be honest, we overstayed our welcome! It felt VERY GOOD at the time. Bills were being paid—we could actually answer the phone without wondering if it was a bill collector—and we were able to get pretty much whatever we wanted. Things were decent. From the outside looking in, we were making it! But the comfort zone is a fickle place, a place where things are just comfortable enough to keep you feeling pretty good and calm enough to keep you STUCK in an eerie kind of neutral position. Some people never manage to shift out of that gear and they build an existence living inside of their comfort zones. They end up settling for pretty good, okay, and in more cases than not, they settle for mediocre and a weak legacy. It is easy to see how it happens.

When the pressure is relieved, it is normal to let the foot off the proverbial gas pedal. After all, many times when we are seemingly "reaching for the sky," we get tired and actually need a rest. The trick is visiting the comfort zone when necessary but choosing not to reside there. If we linger too long, we run the enormous risk of losing the drive needed to find our best self!

That reminds me of a time when my parents had gone through a series of very deep personal hits including the loss of their business and my grandfather's passing. They had moved to a new city, and my father did something I NEVER saw him do during my growing up years—he took a job working for another man.

One evening, I visited my father and asked him a question that, I would later find out, pierced his soul. I asked him if he had given up. His answer will never leave me. He said, "Sweetheart, there is a difference between taking a rest and giving up. I'll be back shortly." And he was! Taking a rest for my dad was working 12 hours a day for another man. He was visiting a comfort zone, taking a breather before the next big push.

Now that my father is gone, I often reflect back on that conversation and realize that if he would have overstayed the comfort zone moments on his life's journey, many of the life lessons he shared as well as the enormous feats he accomplished afterwards would never have occurred. I might not have seen the example I needed to see in order to keep moving forward in my life. Our actions matter. What we do and what we do not do sends a message to everyone around us, and we have no idea what the long-term impact will be.

When my father let me know it was okay to take a step back or take a break, he also showed me that staying inside the comfort zone was not where my future advancements would be found. Thank you, Dad. I'll rest when it is needed, but I will ALWAYS look for the next mountain to climb!

Are there areas in your life where you have settled for a comfort zone existence? Are there things left on your IMPACT list that will remain UNDONE if you don't step across that line? Are there people watching you who may miss out on an incredible life lesson if you choose to stay in neutral?

Make Room for Growth

We were feeling comfortable when my dad challenged my husband and I to get out of the comfort zone by moving the business out of our home.

Our first response was WHY? Things were going well. The commute was SUPER EASY and we had developed a rhythm. It was pretty good!

Moving into an office would mean more debt, the need to add employees, and so many expenses we had no idea about as newer business owners. It meant jumping out of the comfort zone and making room for our company to grow.

Researchers are divided on whether the size of a fishbowl impacts the size of the fish, but one thing was very clear to us as we made the decision to expand our fishbowl. We had to think differently. We had to think BIGGER!

When we moved the business from our home to the first office, our lives changed in many ways. But one of the most important changes was the FEELING that we REGAINED. We went from neutral, satisfied, and good to eager, excited, and hungry. As we expanded our fishbowl, we had to expand our thinking.

If we would have stayed in our home, we would have hindered our growth, and we might have become satisfied with the size and the limited impact of our business. There are lots of successful home-based businesses out there, but the impact we wanted to make required a move. It required risk, and it required us to make room for growth.

As you look at your business, or any area in your life for that matter, can you say that you have made room for growth? There is absolutely nothing wrong with being satisfied with your business or life circumstances, but if you are not living the life you want to live or making the impact you want to make, it may be time to consider this question: Is it possible that you need a bigger "fishbowl" in order to make bigger or possibly even better decisions?

REMEMBER Your Why

Let's get real. When we are in the struggle and focused on the growth and development of our company, it becomes very easy to lose track of what we have accomplished and who we are doing it for. This is why so many business owners wrestle with balancing their personal and professional lives. They are working so hard to provide for their families, but somewhere along the way, they get lost.

"No worldly success can compensate for failure in the home."
– David O. McKay

My father passed away before we ended up purchasing our own building and increasing the size and impact of our company. He would have LOVED sharing the success of the journey. But before he graduated to heaven, he had a final lesson to share, and it's one that definitely requires BIGGER thinking.

For 30+ years, I watched my hero work through every possible business situation you can imagine.

- Starting businesses from scratch
- Shoestring budgets
- The good, the bad, and the ugly of staffing
- Overcoming tragedy
- Near financial ruin
- Surpassing all expectations
- Achieving impossible tasks

My father was a mountain of a man who saved his most important lesson for last.

We were on one of our last visits when we decided to go to Home Depot. On the way over, he was uncharacteristically quiet. I asked my dad what he was thinking about, and he said that he wondered if he had spent too much of his life building businesses and perhaps not enough time enjoying the fruits of his labor with his family.

His comments made an indelible impression on my soul. The patriarch of our family was staring his mortality in the face and sharing a vulnerable moment to teach me what a lifetime of hard work and big thinking had taught him. He was not one to have regrets and not one to be overly emotional, so this moment was rare.

We always had a great lifestyle, but we did not get to spend as much time with my father as we would have liked. My big thinking hero was taking some of his last few precious moments to make sure I knew that my family needed to be in the priority position in my life. I will always treasure those heartfelt moments with my father.

Building a business or crafting a life takes lots of energy, and it is very easy to lose sight of why we are working so hard. Pushing the pause button and being intentional with carving out the necessary time to revisit why we are doing the things we do requires us to think BIGGER.

- Bigger than the stack of bills
- Bigger than the next business goal
- Bigger than the next obstacle we will face

"The main thing is to keep the main thing the main thing."
– Stephen Covey

During the early years of our business, we learned that things ALWAYS work out but that we have to KEEP ON GOING in order to make that happen.

We learned that in order to make bigger and better decisions, we have to MAKE ROOM FOR GROWTH and keep a fresh perspective so we can keep growing.

Over time, we found that we really did need to take a break on occasion, and we learned that it was wise to VISIT THE COMFORT ZONE as long as we did not overstay our welcome.

As we got older and experienced some of the most painful losses life has to offer, we learned that REMEMBERING YOUR WHY and taking great care to cherish and pour into your family needs to be the real focus.

Thinking BIGGER can help you live the life you imagine. Let me close with this—

That last trip to Home Depot rocked my world. I always knew my dad loved us. He spent all of his years not only working hard but also living a life that taught invaluable lessons to anyone he came into contact with. With the clock ticking down, I believe my father did what we will all do—he looked back and measured the moments of his life. He wasn't counting money, comparing balance sheets, or regretting the things he did not purchase.

He was thinking BIGGER and helping me to understand the POWER of focusing on my family and my WHY.

As you go after your dreams and knock down the obstacles that stand in the way, please remember to keep the first thing first. GO BIG and GO HOME!

Connect with author, trainer, speaker, and business coach Cheri Perry for business development and leadership training or inspirational keynote presentations. Her authentic, uplifting delivery inspires teams and their leadership to develop rich and productive cultures that deliver results. Training@CheriPerry.com, 360-980-0392

Tweetable: Building the life and business we desire takes lots of focus. Thinking BIG and keeping our priorities straight will help us get the results we desire.

BOB BEAUDINE

Challenges You to Think . . . Differently!

Bob Beaudine, CEO of Eastman & Beaudine, is a nationally recognized search executive, author, entrepreneur. **Sports Illustrated** *named him "The Most Influential Man in Sports You've Never Heard Of!" Bob is the bestselling author of* **The Power of WHO!** *and* **2 Chairs**, *which provides a definitive roadmap to personal transformation.*

Early Lessons

I thought growing up with a mom and dad that loved, hugged, and encouraged you every day, was the norm. Unfortunately, for far too many, that's not the case. Looking back, I think God gave me great parents, so I could write books and speak to remind people that each of us has an assignment, purpose and dream all our own that we need to discover or rediscover.

I'll never forget my dad taking me backstage to see Frank Sinatra. I was about 13 at the time and it made an *indelible imprint* on my approach to business and life. Frank Sinatra was the greatest singer of the day, so going backstage and meeting him was not only improbable but was something most normal people would find intimidating. But not my dad! He wanted to show me something; **"That the greatest limitations in life are not external, but internal."** When we got to the backstage door, there was a large man guarding the entrance. My dad announced that "the Beaudines are here to see Frank Sinatra." The guard snickered and said: "Mr. Sinatra is not available." My dad then said; "Tell him Frank Beaudine and his son Bobby are here." He said: "Mr. Sinatra is not seeing anyone!" It's then, that my dad forcefully and confidently leaned in and said: "Tell him Frank Beaudine from Chicago is here!" The guard's face changed when he heard that! You could see him think to himself: "I wonder if I didn't tell Mr. Sinatra, I might lose my job?" Now, we didn't know Frank Sinatra, we never said we did. But the guard didn't know that. What happened next is AMAZING! The doors (BAM) opened, and Frank Sinatra walked toward us and said: "Frank, Bobby! How are you? How's Chicago?" And we marched in! "Where's the wife," Frank asked? My dad said: "Martha arrives tomorrow!" Mr. Sinatra then told Joey to make sure there are 3 tickets/VIP—out-front tomorrow on me!" I was stunned! We sat for 20 minutes talking with Frank Sinatra! What's my takeaway? "Every dream you and I have has an obstacle at the door saying; "No Entry!" But We're Going In! How? You have to know "WHO you are," just like my dad. You have to look at them and say: "Frank Beaudine from Chicago!" **Life is made up of moments and choices—Don't miss yours!**

The Disruptive Power of Three Simple Questions: 2 Chairs

When I was just about to graduate from SMU, I had a lot of questions surrounding life goals, dreams, finding a mate and what to do in times of unexpected trouble!

Normally, I'd go to my dad on subjects like these, but not this time. I had this feeling… I needed "something more." Something, I knew my mom could provide me—a unique spiritual insight! When I asked her these questions, she said, "Oh, Bob, those are really good questions. Of course, I don't have the answers. But I know WHO does! I'm going to teach you a *"Secret"* that was passed on to me, a *"Secret,"* that I'm not sure, you even know is a possibility." She said: "If you set this up and do it every day, it'll change your life!" I have to tell you; that was very intriguing to me, and I hope it is to you too. She then said: "Let me ask you three questions. I believe, they will lead you in the right direction. Now, these questions are simple. Simple, in the fact that you can't believe you actually haven't asked them, but they're also disruptive."

These three questions became the premise of my book *2 Chairs: The Secret That Changes Everything.* When you apply this *"Secret"*—I believe you'll find God's plan for your life. What I love about these questions is that they bring us all to the same conclusion.

1. **Does God know your situation? Yes!**
2. **Is this too hard for Him to handle? No!**
3. **Does God have a good plan for you? Yes!**

So, take a deep breath and think about the magnitude of the opportunity. God is *calling you* to an intimate conversation at 2 Chairs! He's not mad at you, He made you, and He makes no mistakes! In fact, the complete opposite is true. What He desires is a deep and intimate relationship; He calls you "friend!" Once you meet with Him, you'll discover something amazing! He has a fantastic plan for you! But to know these plans, you have to stop and listen.

A good friend told me that he'd been doing 22 years of quiet time with God; he just never knew that he was the one who was supposed to be quiet! We laughed, but unfortunately, it was so true! We're always talking, aren't we? The better question would be: "What did God say?" What if for every one minute we talked, God got four? Or, if we wanted two minutes—He got eight! God has plans for each of us—*every day*! And we need to hear them! Because this world of ours—is filled with trouble! Five minutes in the presence of God, changes all our best laid plans.

So, how do you get started? Simple! All you need is 2 Chairs. One's for you, one's for God. You sit and have a conversation, first thing in the morning. I always start out and say: "Good Morning! Thank you for coming! I'm a mess!" Tell Him all that hurts, all that's bugging you! He knows! Then, make the exchange! You give Him the problems, and He then gives you; peace, joy, insight, wisdom, power, and favor for the day! It's a good trade!

Now, for some of you, this concept of 2 Chairs is exciting and couldn't come at a better time. But, for others, this might sound crazy. Do it anyway! You'll be amazed. At some point, we all come to a realization that there's a limit to what we can do on our own. Believe me when I tell you, 2 Chairs is what you've needed all along! My mom knew if she could just get me to try 2 Chairs, the enormity of what would occur would be life-changing! I'm confident you'll come to discover what I've been reminded of every day for over 40 years!—Mom was right!

I am excited to say that this book has gone big! I have people all over the world sending me pictures of their 2 Chairs. Someone the other day bought 265,000 copies of *2 Chairs* to go to prisons, active military personnel, first responders and social servants. The letters I get are so heartwarming and encouraging! We're in tough times and people have gotten isolated and settled into the status quo. You were never created for the status quo. You were created for greatness!

Pursuing Your Highest Value

My dad was one of the pioneers of the executive search industry having started back in 1967 out of McKinsey & Company. He and I worked together for 20 years. My dad had a simple mission statement for our firm, and we still live to this statement some 50-plus years later. Here it is: **"Make friends. Help your friends in every way possible. Don't be surprised that you do a lot of business with your friends!"** I'm proud to say: "My dad was my best friend, he was my dad, and my business partner!"

Are you doing what you love? With people you love? In a place you love? Where your family loves it? And are you doing it for all the right reasons? I was in my late 20s when I first joined my dad's executive search firm, Eastman & Beaudine. I never really thought about this being "the job." I was just seeking a field where I felt I could excel and where I loved the people I worked with, and they loved me. After several years of doing the same thing, I began a growing uneasiness and a longing for "something more." I liked executive search, but I loved sports. I often wondered if there was a way to involve my passion for sports with my career as an executive recruiter. One day, I approached my dad with the frustrations I was feeling. He asked me two very simple, yet direct, questions. "What do you want to do? What do you love?" Those questions awakened my dream, and in a flash, I began to speak with clarity about how I would love to develop a division in our firm that would accommodate the worlds of sports and entertainment. His response: "Go get it!" The rest is history. All it takes is—One thought, one idea, or one friend and you can change the entire trajectory of your life, if "love" is the operative word.

Bestselling author Max Lucado wrote an endorsement for my book *The Power of WHO!* He said: "People matter most. God teaches us. Our heart teaches us, but we forget." Do you know that you have friends right now, that are out of work or in trouble, that will never call you or tell you they need help? Why? Unexpected change can be overwhelming! When a crisis comes, people do the craziest things. They go bonkers and begin to bunker. There's something inside us that just hates to "ask for help!" That's so interesting, because, if you and I were best friends and I asked you for help, would you help me? The answer's always yes! So, why would you deny me the same joy of helping you? It never works in reverse! That's why we have to stay in better touch with our friends! If you're pursuing your highest value, you must remember—that the core of "true success" is love!

A Dream Not a Job

When I was young, my dad was out of work for eight long months. Each day, he'd get dressed in a suit and head to the office. At least that was what we thought he did. When we finally went off to school, he'd circle back home to look for a job. He just couldn't bear for us to be worried; it was a different generation. Years later, when I worked for my dad in executive recruiting, if people came to our office looking for a job without an appointment, we'd always treat them as though they had one. We'd welcome them to the office, get them a cup of coffee and sit and talk. Dad taught us how vulnerable it felt to be out of work. My dad always told me, "There's something great in everyone, Bob, it's your job to find it!"

From time to time, I have friends ask me, to meet with one of their family members or friends because they were fired, downsized, or their company was acquired. They're hoping I would encourage them and possibly point them in the right direction for their next job. When they come to my office and tell me about their trouble, they're usually shocked when I tell them: "Congratulations! This is the greatest day of your life!" They say: "What are you talking about?" I remind them: "You never liked that company; it was just a job! Isn't it about time to do something you love? Wouldn't it be great to come home with joy on your face and happiness in your heart when you finish work? What if, you could do something that is not just a job, but a dream? Of course, they all say YES! But then ask: "What does that look like? Is there something great people look for in a dream job?"

There are Five things leaders look for in a Dream Job, and you should too!

1. **People** – Go where you're Celebrated, not where you're Tolerated.
2. **Tools** – They want to be able to do the job they're hired to do. This involves factors like staff, budget, and being empowered to make a difference.
3. **Family** – Success is geographical. No leader can maximize their potential if their family isn't excited and on board with the opportunity.
4. **Legacy** – The importance of feeling a sense of significance as it relates to job and life satisfaction. The opportunity to do something

that hasn't been done before and leaving it better than when you found it.

5. **Money** – Being paid commensurate with the role and then being rewarded financially for great results.

The Power of Who! It's Not About Selling, But Alignment

In *The Power of WHO!*, I challenged many widely held, preconceived notions. One of which, is the popular concept of Networking which is Not-Working! Why? Because the concept is filled with cold calls, mass emails, and 15 second elevator speeches instead of with people WHO know and love you! Add to that, it's faceless, it's handing out business cards to strangers like they are mints! I get thousands of resumes sent to me: Dear Sir, To Whom It May Concern, and Dear recruiter. Dear recruiter is an oxymoron. In 40 plus years of executive recruiting, I've never placed anyone from a resume.

But what if I told you that you didn't have to go any further than the people you already know! Hear me on this: it's all about your inner circle of friends! Did you know that over 80% of all real jobs come from "one" phone call from a friend? You know that's true, because references, endorsements and testimonials are your greatest allies. My purpose in writing *The Power of WHO!* was to introduce you to a revolutionary concept that would get you moving toward your goals and dreams in ways you never imagined possible. This strategy has been time tested and has worked successfully for over 50 years. This idea of the WHO is really important! These are the people that know you, know what you really want, and in fact; they may know WHO you are and what you want… even better than you might remember!

My greatest honor is to be there for my friends on their worst days. They have been there for me, and I am always looking for ways I can be there for them. Friends are treasures! When you start to understand the Power of WHO and the magnitude of 2 Chairs, everything changes! Step out of the box and into your WHO. And then take a seat across from God, WHO always has something helpful to say, if you listen!

Find *The Power of Who!* and *2 Chairs* at all major book retailers. Learn more about Bob Beaudine as a speaker, author, and search executive online and through social media:

bobbeaudine.com, eastman-beaudine.com
IG: thebobbeaudine | YouTube: Bob Beaudine
Facebook: BobBeaudine.WHO | LinkedIn: Bobwho

Tweetable: There is greatness in everyone. You are drawn like a homing signal to do something you were created to do, something you do better than anyone in the world. Step out of the box and into your WHO.

BABETTE BRIGITTE TENO

Oprah Winfrey to Reality TV
to Sisters on Stages

Babette Brigitte Teno is an entrepreneur, celebrity nutritionist, wellness expert, speaker, philanthropist, and wish granter. She is the founder of BabetteTeno.com and SistersonStages.com.

You Were Made for More

For years, people have asked, "How were you chosen to be on *The Oprah Winfrey Show* and then invited back 23 years later?"

People also ask, "How were you chosen to be the consulting nutritionist for a reality TV show?"

I was at the gym running the row of ellipticals. The show *The Biggest Loser* came on the multiple televisions above us. As I watched, I saw an ambulance pull up and paramedics tend to one of the contestants. I thought to myself, *Most people cannot sustain exercising multiple hours a day. And they need nutritional guidance, as body composition is 70-80% diet.* I was sad and disturbed by what I saw.

When I got home, I wrote a letter to a few of the directors offering my nutritional consulting services pro bono and sent it the next day via Federal Express. I received a call the following day from the executive producer who said, "I do not want your services for *The Biggest Loser*. However, I am the executive producer for several other reality shows, and I would like you to consider being a consultant on another show. If you're interested, can you meet with my team and me this Thursday?" I agreed to meet, and the rest is history! It was fun and interesting, to say the least. And, I made connections that allowed me to serve more people.

People have also asked, "How did you get into the inner circle to work for a top talent agency? And an entertainment public relations firm? And to connect and collaborate with top CEOs, entrepreneurs, doctors, celebrities, producers, directors, athletes, authors, and speakers for the past 30+ years?" The answer is God, mindset, work ethic, perseverance, suiting up, showing up, serving, and the commitment I made to my dad as he lay on his deathbed to continue my education and help as many people as possible throughout my lifetime.

I was born and raised in a small town, Simi Valley, CA. I was a shy, overweight child who was teased endlessly and who was always last to be chosen on the team. I aspired to be a good student, athlete, and team member, so I worked extra hard to get good grades, continue to learn and grow, be better, and do better. It was a bit challenging for me to sit still, focus, and remember things in the midst of a loud and dysfunctional household, so I did what was necessary for the outcome I desired. I spent a lot of time thinking and dreaming. I closed myself in my room and immersed myself in studying for countless hours to escape reality. I often prayed about how I could help my family. There was so much confusion and conflict in my head and in our home.

We all have a story! It's important we learn the lessons from our stories in order to heal and move on.

By the time I was in junior high, I had experienced multiple traumatic events that added layers of adversity to my life. I used many things to help me get through, including participating in sports and attending classes, workshops, and seminars. When I faced challenging times, it would've been easy to give up, have a negative attitude, and live life as a victim. I knew God had a plan for my life. Through struggles and surgeries, trauma, and betrayal, I drew closer to the Lord.

REVIVED! The 19-Hour Surgery

In junior high school, they did scoliosis screenings in physical education class. My parents received a letter that I had scoliosis and to schedule an appointment with an orthopedic doctor. At age thirteen, my first set of X-Rays showed a 26-degree curve in my spine. Regular appointments, X-Rays, and verification tests were recommended to monitor the curve and look for growth plate closure which would allow us to schedule surgery.

At age seventeen, tests confirmed that I was finished growing. The doctor recommended a femur shortening surgery on my longer leg to "fix" the curve. The four-hour surgery at Children's Hospital Los Angeles turned into nineteen! Eventually, my parents received an update. A fairly routine surgery in those years turned into much more. I lost too much blood while in surgery, died on the operating room table, and had to have emergency blood transfusions to be revived.

Over my week in the hospital, I witnessed young children in the oncology unit as they had IV pole races down the halls. I'm grateful I was there just so I could see the pure joy and laughter. By watching, I learned to appreciate every moment I am given, to leave people better off than I found them, and to treat every single person I meet with dignity and respect . . . like they matter . . . because they do!

Timing Is Everything

As an overweight child, I made unhealthy choices which lead to an eating disorder from ages 12-19. While in a nutrition class in college, the instructor assigned each student a topic to write about. It was no coincidence that the topic I was assigned was eating disorders!

I waited until every student left the class that night and asked the teacher where I could get information about eating disorders. She asked where I lived and shared that an eating disorder unit just opened in the town hospital. When I arrived at the hospital, the nursing supervisor asked if I was there to check in. "Check in? I just need information to write a paper. Do you have any printed materials?" She handed me two brochures. I read the first brochure in my car in the parking lot: "If you answer 'yes' to more than three questions, you may require medical or professional help." I answered "yes" to 9 out of 10 questions. That was definitely a God moment! I realized I had a problem and I needed help. Nothing got my attention prior to that moment, including getting down to 83 pounds.

I finished the semester in school and checked into the six-week inpatient eating disorder program. I would like to give a special thanks to my professor Dr. Judy Alexander for allowing God to work in and through her to assign me the exact topic I needed to save my life!

From watching my mom struggle with her weight throughout her lifetime, healing from an eating disorder, and the commitment I made to my father to continue my education and help as many people as possible throughout my lifetime, I was inspired to help people achieve and maintain optimal health throughout their lives.

I began taking and continue to take health, wellness, nutrition, functional medicine, mind/body/spirit classes, seminars, and workshops. As my knowledge developed, I began to coordinate continuing education seminars while serving in numerous positions in nutraceutical, homeopathic, and pharmaceutical companies. I've served as a director at a health sciences university and have been mentored by some of the best and brightest doctors and scientists in the world.

For years, I've specialized in eating disorders, invisible illnesses and autoimmune conditions, and cancer in honor of many family members and friends who have passed away from the aforementioned. I have served in integrative health centers and private clinics and made house calls. I'm honored to have had the opportunity to help many people. I enjoy continuing my education and staying current with research to provide the best possible recommendations, connections, and referrals.

It Takes a Village

I'm grateful for the mentors, coaches, family, and friends who have taught me many things while supporting me through every chapter of my life.

Though it was 32 years ago, I remember the day like it was yesterday. After my dad passed away from cancer, my mom and I were at the mortuary planning his funeral. We picked out the casket and were going over burial details when I asked where the money was that would cover the costs.

Mom showed me a check. It wasn't enough. I remember vowing I would never allow myself or a loved one to be in a situation where they did not have enough money to cover final expenses for their loved one. I remember thinking how important consistent and complete communication is in marriage so both people know details of household income, budget, expenses, savings, spending, insurance, and investments. One can never be too prepared. Unforeseen circumstances can happen anytime. My mom never thought that her husband would pass at age 49 or that she would be a widow at age 46.

My mom remarried. My stepfather was one of the top aerospace engineers in the country. They led full, active lives and loved to travel until my stepfather was diagnosed with Parkinson's disease then dementia.

The medical maze and confusion started—treatment options to levels of care, specialists, insurance policies, inclusions and exclusions, and more.

In June 2021, after 20 years of suffering and struggling, my stepfather lost his battle with Parkinson's and dementia. I flew to Oklahoma to help my mom with funeral arrangements and paperwork and support her while she grieved.

Through helping my mom, female family members, and hundreds of friends and clients throughout the years, a seed that was planted over 30 years ago is coming to fruition today—a training and coaching company for women, Sisters on Stages!

Dream Big! Think Big!

When I was in my twenties, I worked for a talent agency and an entertainment public relations agency. I met, worked with, and became friends with many cool and amazing people. So many fun memories!

I will never forget the day that Dudley Moore came into the agency without a scheduled appointment. He introduced himself and waited for a response. I didn't know who he was. He thought it was funny and appreciated that I didn't treat him differently. Then there was the time I went to a tennis party at Merv Griffin's house with the "who's who" of Hollywood. From those interactions, I learned that everybody is a human being and deserves to be treated as if they matter, because they do, regardless of position, title, fame, or fortune.

I started taking time to learn people's stories and to ask more and better questions. I learned the importance of edifying people and a proper introduction and how to write press releases that got attention and secured bookings. People knew I genuinely cared and had their best interests at heart. I became affectionately referred to as "everybody's friend" and the "world's best connector." It's been said that if I don't know people where I'm going, within minutes, I will.

I love meeting people, learning their stories, and connecting them with others. For many years, I've been introducing and referring people for talent representation, speaking gigs, reality shows, collaboration, strategic partnerships, and much more. I've had opportunities to work with and refer Oprah Winfrey and her team, Les Brown, Ed Mylett, Shemane Nugent, Garrett Gunderson, Eric and Marina Worre, Ray and Jessica Higdon, as well as other celebrities and experts.

These associations and my experience put me in a unique position to give back to my community and people in need. Enter Sisters on Stages!

The idea was initially born 36 years ago in response to the need I saw for support for women in our society. Too often I have seen family members, friends, and clients suffering. Over the years, I have done what I could to help, and now I would like to help on a larger scale through training and coaching.

At Sisters on Stages, we train and coach women in different chapters in their lives—from single women to moms, widows, empty nesters, and those seeking a different career—in healthy family dynamics, leadership, work ethic, communication, speaking and stage presence, media interviews, emotional and financial wellness, and civic duties and responsibilities. We book speaking engagements, media and podcast interviews, and guest appearances. We host retreats and mastermind events.

Similar to functional medicine, which I've practiced for years as a healthcare professional, we focus on long-term strategies to get to the root causes and real problems versus quick Band-Aid fixes.

We give women what they need to succeed in life. We foster independence by teaching women so they can provide for themselves and contribute to their communities.

My personal mission is to meet women where they are and lead them to where they want to go by empowering them with information and opportunities to continue to learn, grow, and thrive throughout their lifetime.

God has a plan for everyone, and once you've discovered that plan, no one except you can stop it from coming to fruition. This has certainly been true in my life. I have personally experienced what it means to be victorious through Him who loves us. All of the things I've experienced have given me platforms to inspire others and share the love of God. By His grace, adversities made me stronger and helped me become the person I am today.

Contact Babette Brigitte Teno, Founder of Sisters on Stages, for individual and group coaching or to book speaking engagements and media interviews. Babette specializes in women's leadership development, creating strategic partnerships, speaker bookings, and media interviews. bteno@sistersonstages.com, sistersonstages.com, 818-577-5552.

Tweetable: My personal mission is to meet women where they are and lead them to where they want to go by empowering them with information and opportunities to continue to learn, grow, and thrive throughout their lifetime.

RASHEED LOUIS

Your Purpose Never Changes, It Only Evolves

Rasheed Louis is an award-winning entrepreneur, community philanthropist, and host of local mentorship-focused events. He has founded three different businesses in the marketing, media rental studios, and legal and tech staffing industries. Rasheed is passionate about helping people find their next level.

A Happy Life

As a kid, I had a great home and upbringing with both parents who had strong beliefs about culture and life. My father was my hero, an entrepreneur, and as my mother used to say, "a straight get-it-done hustler." My mother is a woman of faith and a nurse with a heart for downtrodden women. They were my pillars, and I believed I would always have that.

My life hit a reset point at nine years old. One night, I had a dream that would soon begin to manifest. In the dream, I was in a limo approaching a red carpet with my future wife. As we exited the car, a reporter asked, "How did you become successful with your father passing away at such a young age?" My reply was uncertain. My father was still alive. Within two weeks, my father passed away in a tragic car accident, leaving my mother and four children behind.

I believe a son should never live in his father's shadow for too long, for he should learn to shine his own light and cast his own shadow. In the years that followed my father's passing, I would often wish to have been in his shadow longer. I no longer had my muse, my archetype of what a man was supposed to be.

Welcome to the Dino

Soon after my father's passing, my mother moved us to San Bernardino where she had gotten a job at the local hospital. She would work 12-hour shifts five to six days a week. You can only imagine the free time I had to get into trouble.

Growing up in San Bernardino helped make me become more and continues to be a part of my driving force. My friends were the gangsters and drug dealers you hear about on the news. They also were the creatives and athletes you seldom hear about. The city was a melting pot of culture, experience, and hope.

I still remember my first introduction to the city and its dangers. I was about 12 years old. While standing in front of the school bus stop, a young boy approached me, pulled a gun, and pointed it at me. At that moment, I felt fear, pain, and anxiety. My life didn't flash before my eyes. My only thought in that moment of frozen time was, *How did I get here?* The next thought was that he couldn't have been more than a year older than me.

When I came out of my head, I heard the guy with him say, "That's not him." I found out later I had been mistaken for someone else and it was about a girl. I never told my mother. I was in shock, and I guess, I didn't want to shake up our world anymore than it already had been.

That would not be the last time I would be in a life-threatening situation or at the wrong end of a gun.

The Teacher Appears When the Student Is Ready

Five years later, I was in high school. I had become a bit of a troublemaker. A French teacher, Madame Brannon, started me on a better path. Madame Brannon was young, bold, and cool. She let it be known, she was there to teach and make sure everyone was held accountable for their own success. Well, I was failing. One day, I was acting my normal class clown self, so she asked me to stay after class. There was an awkward silence at first as she looked at me. Then she shook her head and said these exact words, "Rasheed, get your shit together."

I knew what she was talking about. I was way behind in school, and I was having issues at home and had court appearances to make. She spoke to me with concern, not pity. There are blessings all around us. In a place of desperation and stillness, I could finally hear this one.

Madame Brannon also gave me advice. She told me to seek out stories of people who were in a hard place in life and then figured out a way to level up. That was easy enough. She also suggested I become friends with this student at school who I just did not like. This would certainly be a challenge.

After she suggested I befriend this enemy, he and I had an altercation, and he challenged me to a fight in the wrestling room. I accepted. When I arrived, I saw young men working out, leveling up, and challenging each other physically and mentally. It was different from what I had seen on the streets. The aggression was there, and I was intrigued by the idea of winning by outworking your opponent by first building yourself.

The coach of the wrestling team allowed us to battle it out. I got my butt handed to me. After I picked my face up from the floor, the coach talked to me. He said I didn't do as bad as he thought I would and that I should join the team. So, I did. For the first time in my life, I was working on myself. I saw myself for the first time, and I knew if I worked hard, I could build something. I was ready to think of myself as more.

By the time I finished high school, I had won league titles for wrestling, a job at McDonald's, and an appetite for more in my life. Seeds planted by individuals saying "I see you" had helped me see myself.

Questioning Uncertainty

Shortly after graduating high school, I started to realize limitations in my basic life skills such as communication, finances, and self-knowledge. I quit McDonald's and tried college, then dropped out and started my first business, a marketing agency, at 19 years old. At this point in my life, I understood very little of the world.

I began to seek out every resource I could find on leadership, manhood, business, and communication. I found books, YouTube videos, conferences, and people that I could learn from. At first, my drive was about not being broke and hearing family say, "Just go to nursing school." The more I focused on what others thought about me and what I should be doing, the more I struggled. I didn't want their vision. I wanted to fulfill my own vision. I just didn't know what that was yet.

In my first year of business, I had only made a few hundred dollars. I was seeing friends start college or go off to begin new lives. I was starting to feel as if I made wrong decisions and maybe I should just give up. I even re-enrolled in college. In this uncertainty, I decided to seek advice. I met with a San Bernardino newspaper publisher who was well-connected in the business community. His advice was to ask local business owners why they get up in the morning and choose to build their businesses.

I met with restaurant owners, PR executives, entrepreneurs, and many other leaders. The reasons they built and operated their businesses were all different, but they were all connected to their purpose.

I learned from all of them and found the answers I was looking for. Finding your purpose is a game of risk. Protecting it is a game of commitment. I was not committed to my purpose. I didn't even know what it was. I began to realize that the creation of anything starts with purpose; anything that is built cannot be designed without purpose and intention. I was building to prove others wrong rather than prove myself right. My intentions and my purpose were misaligned. If I was to become more, I needed to know my true reason for being an entrepreneur.

At this point, my marketing agency only provided services for flyers, business cards, and websites. I wasn't exactly raking in the money. I wanted to get into major branding projects. I could help companies tell amazing stories and create impact, but I wasn't sure how to make that jump. I needed and wanted to level up.

The Shift

A good friend of mine, a business coach, helped me see that just because you have the vision doesn't mean you know what's next. Sitting down to our weekly talk, she asked me, "What type of projects would get you jumping out of bed every single morning?"

I told her I wanted to create brands for companies and help people create impact. Her next question was, "What would a deal like that cost and who would you need to execute it?" At that moment, I realized I had never thought it through. I was waiting for an opportunity that I was not prepared for.

Up to this point, the law of attraction made no sense to me. I always thought it was missing the law of action and principles. That evening, I went home and began to create my first full-scale marketing campaign priced at $10,000.

After pulling two all-nighters because I was excited about this new vision, I received a call from a client. They were looking to go in a new direction, and they wanted me to help. The following Monday, I went to my client's office and began creating the campaign to launch their new brand. The final price tag for the campaign was $12,000. If I had not prepared, I never would've gotten this opportunity or been prepared to articulate it.

After that deal, I focused on brand creation for companies by crafting campaigns that reflected their core vision. I had found my purpose, helping people get to the core of who they are and sharing those stories.

The Demand to Grow

It wasn't long before I would have to make another imperfect move and truly believe in the "why not attitude."

I was heading out of a meeting when I received a call from an unknown number. I answered and said, "Hello, this is Rasheed."

A woman said, "Hello, one moment, please. His Majesty would like to talk to you." I believe that strange and wonderful things happen, but I never thought they would happen to me. Soon, I was speaking to a Ghanaian king. Yes, a real-life king. Decades before His Majesty was crowned king, my grandfather had mentored him. His Majesty had recently reconnected with my mother, and she told him that I had started my own business. He decided to take an interest in me, and a new journey began. I would go on to be mentored by the king in life, spirituality, and leadership.

He invited me to Ghana for three months. When I first arrived, he asked a series of questions. He asked me about mentors, what I had learned about life, and what I knew about being a son. These were questions I had never asked myself, and I would need to truly think about them. Time would reveal that this was his leadership and teaching style. He was a true teacher, a confident man who only expected excellence. In Ghana, I sat in on meetings, discussions, and decisions on many different topics as people came to him for guidance. Watching him taught me how a leader should communicate, delegate, and move.

I was still rough around the edges, and that became evident during a meeting one night. There was a problem being discussed. I was supposed to just be watching and learning, but I decided I was going to solve the problem for everybody. My input was not well received. This was my first lesson on knowledge versus understanding. You may have knowledge, but you must understand a situation before you give your input because, without understanding, what you think is a solution may just lead to more confusion. I wanted to add value and solve a problem but had no understanding of what was actually needed. I was excused from the meeting, and later the king asked me, "Where were you when we were we?" This was a Ghanaian phrase that meant: What you know about the past is learned, not lived. Experience cannot be taught, only lived first hand.

Back in the States, I was on a high and low of life because of what I had seen and learned. I remember praying and asking God, *What's next? This can't be it for me, right?* I began to ask myself questions of growth. What does what I'm doing look like on the next level? How can I help people, deliver more value, and create an impact?

Those questions led to hosting an annual gala-style event called Night of Mentorship, with three speakers talking about mentorship, belief, and image. From that work, I was recognized by the American Advertising Federation for my marketing and community work. I had begun to hit my stride of impact and purpose, so I was ready to add another piece to my growing vision. I was given the opportunity to take over a multi-use space in downtown Pomona, CA. There, I created an event space for creatives and a space for the community to gather. That space has grown into two locations. A few years later, I asked myself those questions again and launched a staffing firm where we hire and help place people in great careers.

In my life, I've had recurring themes and moments of people saying "I see you." These moments were possible because I wanted to be seen. I was able to move ahead because I made moves, identified my purpose, asked myself what the next level would look like, and put a demand on it.

I've come to realize *your purpose never changes, it only evolves.*

Connect with Rasheed Louis online or on social media through reachingepiphany.com. To learn more about marketing and branding services or staffing needs, email him at rlouis@variablm.com.

Tweetable: Finding your purpose is a game of risk. Protecting it is a game of commitment. I realize the creation of anything starts with purpose; anything that is built cannot be designed without purpose and intention.

ERIC ZUZACK

Powerless to Powerful

Eric Zuzack, host of the five-star rated podcast Porn Talk, *is a porn and sex addiction recovery coach. He helps addicted salesmen worldwide not only break the habit but also transform their sexual energy to repair relationships, increase sales, and vigorously pursue a great life.*

Success Mastery Academy

It was 1997. I was giving a presentation for a large group of salesmen at a San Jose, California, auto dealership while working for Kyle Wilson to promote Brian Tracy's new Success Mastery Academy event. But I got tongue-tied because, in the midst of the presentation, I remembered the pornography I'd watched the night before.

This was my big break. I always wanted to give presentations on personal development. I was getting to do that for Kyle and Brian Tracy. And I was blowing it!

We lived on the road, going city to city, promoting Brian Tracy's Success Mastery Academy. It was exciting. Between cities, I would go back to St. Louis to rest. While there, I made a lunch date with my friend Heather. She had breast cancer. The day we were supposed to meet for lunch, I was watching porn and lost track of time. So I called Heather and rescheduled. Days after, I ran into a mutual friend who told me Heather had died! I was devastated. I chose to watch porn over having lunch with my friend. *I'm never going to see her again. I am such an idiot.*

I realized that I had a problem and sought help from professionals. I was told to go to 12-step meetings like Alcoholics Anonymous (AA) but for sex and porn. Being a good student, I followed doctors' orders. I went to Sexual Compulsives Anonymous (SCA) for several years.

Car Repo

Kyle and Jim Rohn International had changed gears and would no longer need a road team. So, I became a stockbroker for Morgan Stanley. I worked hard and passed the test on my second try. I trained in the Twin Towers in New York City. I was emotionally high as a kite when flying back from New York City to St. Louis. I was going to put on financial seminars to build my business.

When I got back from training, I discovered my Dodge Intrepid had been repossessed. I thought, *You can't do it. You're just a porn addict. How will you help people with their money when you don't have any of your own?* I wanted to build my business with financial seminars, but a new boss wanted me to make cold calls on bonds instead. After that, I never quite got that spark for the work back. I was miserable.

Down in the Dumps

My brother said I could drive a delivery truck for the telecommunications company he worked for. Eager to escape the pain of cold calling on bonds, I accepted the position. Scott, the president, was a great guy who I knew from grade school. He said, "You say you're going to stay for a couple of months. But I'm warning you, this place has a way of sucking people in." He was right.

I floated along until September 11, 2001. I was disposing of boxes in a dumpster at work when my brother Dave ran out to tell me what had happened. I went inside, and there, live on the screen, we saw the second plane hit. The telecom buildings we worked for all went into lockdown, so we had no choice but to go home. John Pertzborn, a local TV personality, relayed a message from a St. Louis man who had escaped the towers. The man was my old boss from Morgan Stanley. I about fell off my chair.

It scared me. I had trained in the towers just a year before. We had even talked about how scary it would be to be in the buildings if they were attacked. Did it inspire me? No. I sunk further into my addiction. I went to more twelve-step meetings. I said, "I am powerless over porn. I am powerless over porn." That is NOT what is taught in self-development. However, the professionals told me to do this, so I did.

I wanted to be a speaker and trainer. But how could I? *Who wants to hear what a broke porn addict has to say?* I was filled with self-pity, anger, and anxiety. I felt like I couldn't reach my goals and dreams. So I took my mammoth collection of self-development books, cassette tapes, and CDs and trashed them in a church's dumpster. As I dumped them in, I thought, *This shit doesn't work!*

Not knowing what to do with myself, I sunk further into the addiction. Speaker Les Brown says not pursuing your goals and dreams is like committing spiritual suicide. I agree. It often seems like the world is full of people who are just settling—walking zombies. Now, I was one of them.

Having abandoned my hopes and dreams, I tried Sex and Love Addicts Anonymous (SLAA).

Paranormal World Series

One single event changed me forever. I understand that I may lose credibility by sharing this paranormal story. However, I need to give the facts, and you can choose to believe it or not. After the St. Louis Cardinals won the 2006 World Series against the Detroit Tigers, I started the car to leave my girlfriend's house, and the radio popped on. I listened to the celebrations of the Cards' win on The Big 550 AM KTRS, then a paranormal show, *Coast to Coast AM*, came on. That is not usually something I would listen to, but it was Halloween. The program's real-life ghost hunters said they used a simple method to capture spirit or ghost voices called electronic voice phenomenon (EVP). They said anyone could capture EVP with a cheap digital recorder. I was a skeptic at the time, but something came over me to try it.

The first several times I tried it at a cemetery, it did not work. Having given up on this silliness, I returned to my apartment and sat on the couch. Not expecting anything and really kind of playing, I tried it again. To my shock, when I played it back, there was a response. It was so faint that had I not been listening for something, I would have missed it. I cranked the volume. There was no question. There was a response. How could this be?

Padded Room

I knew what I was hearing was real because I could play back the audio. The challenge was that without the audio cranked up or special software, other people could not hear it. Then, other bizarre things started to occur like things moving and me hearing things without using the recorder. Apparently, paranormal and porn don't mix.

I was so frightened that my parents and good friend John spent the entire night in a church adoration chapel with me. After that night, my dad suggested I check myself into a hospital. I was too scared to go back to my place alone, so I did.

Let me tell 'ya, waking up in a padded room will get you to question your life choices. I thought, *How did I get here?* On top of that, I had just been told I would be on strong antipsychotic medication for the rest of my life. I felt like I was in a bad episode of *The Twilight Zone*.

Broken Engagement to Married

After that horrific experience, I started wanting answers. My girlfriend and I went out to eat and wandered into a metaphysical bookstore next door. After some time, I accepted a job in sales there. That's where I received an education in metaphysics. I took many classes and read countless books. Eventually, I even gave my own paid classes at the bookstore about my paranormal experience. I've got to hand it to my girlfriend at the time. Despite the scary events, she still wanted to marry me. However, I felt deep in my heart that she was not the one, and I broke off the engagement.

Things in my life began to settle down. I was happy in general, but I did feel in the back of my mind I was not doing what I was put on this earth to do, and I wasn't making very much money. Then, one fateful day, a pretty woman named Amy came into the bookstore. Within thirteen months, we were married.

Solar Power Challenges

After working at the metaphysical bookstore and getting married, I finally was able to pull myself back up and found an excellent job in solar power sales. I wholeheartedly believed in solar power. The trouble was, our local power company did not. I was so excited to pursue my goals and dreams using solar power.

The first day on the job, my mother-in-law called to tell me that my unborn baby girl, seven months along, had a deformation of her brain and would die soon. I was so devastated that I could not put it into words.

Unfortunately, we'd had other miscarriages—none this far into pregnancy. At 42, I thought I would never have a child or reach my goals and would most likely be addicted to porn forever.

Despite my despair, I plowed ahead in solar power. I got a couple of big deals and was optimistic. I was doing okay and had a new mentor, Wayne. Wayne was very successful in solar sales and was showing me the ropes. But he was also an alcoholic.

Wayne and I were working on a large commercial sale. I was at the potential client's office when my good friend and colleague John called and said very plainly, "Wayne is dead." Wayne had committed suicide in his hotel room. I was the last person to see him. I was devastated once again.

I wanted to build my solar business by giving public presentations about solar. But I never quite got my swag back after Wayne's death. Then, the power company pulled a stunt to slow down solar, and our office closed. Was I ever going to reach my goal of speaking and training? It just seemed impossible.

I knew I was on the wrong path when my wife said, "You're not a very motivated person." I thought, *What!? I AM one of the most motivated people I know.* But she was right. I was settling. I was jaded. Broken and despondent, I knew SLAA wasn't cutting it, so I started going to Sexaholics Anonymous (SA).

Coach Powerful Eric

At this point, I had tried countless 12-step programs. SCA, SLAA, SA, DA, AA, CODA, etc. The running theme was that you're powerless. At every meeting, I said, "Hi, my name is Eric. I'm a sexaholic and powerless over porn." Then I described some of my worst behaviors. After many years of saying that I was powerless, I realized it wasn't going to work.

After countless relapses, I thought, *There has to be another way.* The powerless mindset was the opposite of what I was learning in self-development. On a desperate search, I stumbled onto a little app that used the science of mindfulness to break porn addiction. Unfortunately, that app no longer exists, but I met my friend and mentor, Craig Perra, through it. When I was creating my screen login and password, on a whim, I put my login as "Powerful Eric." At that moment, Powerless Eric died, and Powerful Eric was born!

I reinvented myself. I stopped labeling myself and I changed my habits. I stopped counting how many days I did not do the thing and instead counted the positive behaviors I was adding to my life. Every day I strive to be Powerful Eric.

I am now a certified porn and sex addiction recovery coach who uses mindfulness as one of my primary tools to help salesmen worldwide break addictions. Between my successful podcast *Porn Talk*, speaking engagements, and private clients, I aim to help one million porn and sex addicts stop committing spiritual or mortal suicide and reach their goals and dreams.

By the way, my wife and I went on to have two healthy boys, Alexander and Isaiah.

Golden Buddha

If you are addicted to porn, sex, or something else . . . if you feel jaded or hopeless . . . I know how you feel. I've been there.

This reminds me of a story about a golden Buddha.

> *A monastery knew an invading army was coming in a few days. They had a giant, solid gold Buddha. There was no way to move it. The monks knew that the invading army would melt it down. So, they buried it to look like a large hill. The monks' idea worked. The invading army did not find the golden Buddha.*
>
> *The Buddha remained buried for hundreds of years and was forgotten. One day, a monk was sitting, meditating, and he noticed a glimmer of light coming from the hill. He investigated and found gold, unearthing the massive golden Buddha.*

The golden Buddha is us. Maybe you are like me—buried in tons of shame, guilt, sorrow, addiction, and anguish. But once you get out from underneath all of the dirt, you can find your beautiful golden Buddha . . . your true self, your higher self, your best self.

If you are buried now or know someone who is, let me help you uncover and discover the beautiful golden Buddha, the beautiful soul, you are.

You can do it because I know you are powerful!

Eric Zuzack offers powerful programs for helping addicted salesmen, professionals, and their spouses. To get a free copy of his audiobook, *Everything You Know About Porn & Sex Addiction Is Wrong,* or to book him as a speaker, go to www.PowerfulEric.com or call 314-717-0377.

Tweetable: I reinvented myself. I found my powerful, true, higher self. I stopped counting the days I didn't do the thing and instead counted the positive behaviors I was adding to my life.

BRIAN TRACY

You Can Change Your Life

Brian Tracy is the top-selling author of over 70 books, has written and produced more than 300 audio and video learning programs, and has spoken, trained, and traveled in over 107 countries on six continents. Brian speaks four languages and is happily married with four children.

Early Years and Learning to Be an Entrepreneur

I grew up in Edmonton, Canada. It's not the North Pole, but they say you can see it from up there. It's really cold, 35 degrees Fahrenheit below zero in the wintertime.

I began my entrepreneur journey early at the age of 10. Because of my family situation, I had to earn my own money, so I went out and did jobs in the neighborhood to buy my clothes and school supplies.

So, for me, to go out and work, to start something and make it work, is as natural as breathing. I've started and built 22 businesses in different enterprises including hiring, recruiting, training, producing, selling, and marketing.

When I was 32, I saw an ad in the paper for an executive MBA at the University of Alberta. So, I applied, got in, and spent two years and $4,000 to get an MBA.

Getting Paid to Speak

After university, I put together the content to what eventually became The Psychology of Achievement. Early on, when people went through the course, the feedback was fantastic. They basically said, "Oh my God, this is great," and they began to tell their friends.

The first seminar I gave, I had seven people, and six of them were family members. The seventh was a paid customer for $295. My next seminar was 12 people, and my next was 15 people in Canada. I then hired a guy for three months to sell for me full-time. Business grew and grew. Soon I was speaking to 100, then 200 and 500. And then, people started to invite me to speak to their entire audience.

The Power of Our Thoughts

In my seminars, I talk about the superconscious mind and understanding how you can activate the incredible mental power that you already have. You can turn on this switch and start to attract into your life everything that you want: opportunities, ideas, people, resources, and more, just simply by using the power that you already have within your brain.

Every single great accomplishment in history has been an accomplishment of superconscious thinking where people have learned how to turn on this switch.

Imagine that you live in a nice home and there is a garage, but you've never been into the garage. You're making an average living, as most people are. Then, one day, you go into the garage and turn on the light. And to your great surprise, there's this massive supercomputer there that is capable of answering any question you come up with. You just turn on this supercomputer, and suddenly you're producing 5, 10, 20, 50, 100 times more.

Perhaps you say, "I want to be wealthy, successful, and highly-respected. Maybe I don't have a university degree, and I don't have any money right now, but I do have my brain and my ability to **work**. And that's what I'm going to do," If you actually do the work, you set up a force field of energy in the universe that conspires to get you what you want.

The Power of Goal Setting

The most common occurrence when I travel and speak is audience members coming up and saying, "You changed my life. You made me rich. Thank you!" They grab my hand with both of their hands. "Thank you, Mr. Tracy. You changed my life." Because I speak on so many subjects, I then ask what about my material was so helpful to them. And almost always, they beam and say, "It was the goals. I'd never heard about goals before. I never understood how central they are to success."

You build your whole life around your goals. There is a wonderful quote from a dear friend of mine, Vic Conant: "Success is goals, and all else commentary." Wherever I've been able to persuade a person of that, their life changes.

I now have thousands of self-made millionaires and three self-made billionaires who have told me personally, "You made me rich. I was struggling. I was going nowhere. And after I learned about goals, here I am."

The Story Behind *Eat That Frog*

I was asked by a publisher to write a book on time management. I came up with twenty-one great ways to double your income and double your time off. The publisher loved the title of chapter 21, "Eat That Frog." It was from a story by Mark Twain where he said, if the first thing you do in the morning is eat a live frog, you'll have the pleasure of going through the day knowing that was the worst thing that could possibly happen to you.

Then I added the two corollaries of eating a frog. If you have two frogs, eat the ugliest one first. And if you have to eat a frog, it doesn't pay to sit and look at it for too long.

I followed the publisher's advice and included in all 21 chapters aspects of eating that frog, which means doing the worst and most important task immediately when you get up and start your day. They were a great publisher. *Eat That Frog* went on to sell 10 million copies and is still one of my bestsellers.

Take Action

One idea can change your life—if you take action on it. One of the most important things I teach over and over again is action. Action! It's not enough to have good ideas or the best information. There are a lot of average people who are self-made millionaires. I have a really great hour-long program called *The 21 Success Secrets of Self-Made Millionaires.* I spent two months preparing before recording it. I buried myself in research on self-made millionaires. What I found is that they had characteristics and qualities that made it inevitable that they'd be successful. And if you simply practice the same things they practice, you become the same people they are. And action is one of the main traits of self-made millionaires.

Zero-Based Thinking

Every time I do a strategic planning program worldwide, we start off with an exercise called zero-based thinking. In zero-based thinking, wherever you are in life, you draw a line under your life to this date. You imagine that you're starting over and ask yourself:

Is there anything that you are doing that, knowing what you now know, you would not start up again today?

Is there any investment that you have that you would not make again today? If you had to do it over, is there any relationship that you would not get into? Is there any person that you would not hire?

You keep going through each area of your life, and you keep asking.

And if the answer is "No, I would not get into this again." Then the next question is, how do I get out? And how fast can I get out? Because once you've reached the point where you have that intuitive feeling that you would not get into this again, you cannot save it.

I often say to my friends to ask themselves that question. Is there anything you're doing in your life that, knowing what you now know, you wouldn't get into?

If the answer is yes, get out and get out now.

We Make Our Living by Contributing Value to Other People

Today, we have this big thing in politics about inequality. It's not inequality of money. It's inequality of contribution. We make our living in a free country. We make our living by contributing value to other people. Sometimes I ask my audience how many people work on straight commission, and maybe 10% will raise their hands.

I then say, "Well, that's interesting. Maybe I didn't phrase the question properly. Let me ask it again. How many people here work on straight commission?" And then there's a pause, and it's wonderful, the light goes off! Absolutely everybody works on commission.

Everybody works for themselves. And each person creates value. You get a piece of the value that you create. So if you want to earn more money, create more value. Make a greater contribution. Do more.

The great line from Napoleon Hill that brings tears to my eyes still decades later is, "Always do more than you're paid for. Always go the extra mile. There is never a traffic jam on the extra mile." The one thing nobody can stop you from doing is doing more than you're paid for.

Earl Nightingale said, if you want to earn more than you're earning, contribute more than you're contributing, and an increase in earnings is automatic.

If you're not happy with your income, go to the nearest mirror and negotiate with your boss, because you are your own boss. You make your own contribution. You make your own decision. If you don't like your income, earn more.

Closing Thoughts

The happiest people in the world are those who feel absolutely terrific about themselves, and this is the natural outgrowth of accepting total responsibility for every part of their life. They make a habit of manufacturing their own positive expectations in advance of each event.

Never complain, never explain. Resist the temptation to defend yourself or make excuses.

Develop an attitude of gratitude and give thanks for everything that happens to you, knowing that every step forward is a step toward achieving something bigger and better than your current situation.

To learn more about Brian Tracy's book and audio programs, go to BrianTracy.com.

Tweetable: Develop an attitude of gratitude and give thanks for everything that happens to you, knowing that every step forward is a step toward achieving something bigger and better than your current situation.

BOOK EDITOR AND WRITING COACH

Takara Sights is the editor of *Think Big!* She has been publishing inspirational and motivational books with Kyle Wilson since 2015. Takara is all about developing clear and impactful language that connects readers with age-old wisdom from new voices, and she revels in working one-on-one with authors as they develop and share their stories. She currently lives with her partner and their fantastic dog in Los Angeles, California.

BOOK PUBLISHER

Kyle Wilson is the founder of Jim Rohn International and KyleWilson.com. Kyle has filled huge seminar rooms, launched and published multiple personal development publications, and produced/published over 100+ hours of programs. Kyle has published and sold over 1,000,000 books including titles by Jim Rohn and Denis Waitley as well

as his own books including *Success Habits of Super Achievers* with Brian Tracy, Les Brown, Darren Hardy, Denis Waitley, Mark Victor Hansen, *Persistence, Pivots and Game Changers*, and *Bringing Value, Solving Problems and Leaving a Legacy*. Kyle is the host of the *Success Habits of Super Achievers* podcast and the Kyle Wilson Inner Circle Mastermind.

ADDITIONAL RESOURCES

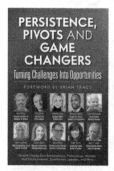   

Order in Quantity and SAVE
Mix and Match
Order online KyleWilson.com/books

Made in the USA
Monee, IL
02 June 2022